THE MAN FROM
ENTERPRISE

THE MAN FROM ENTERPRISE

The Story of John B. Amos, Founder of AFLAC

By
Seymour Shubin

Mercer University Press
Macon, Georgia

©The John Beverly Amos and Elena Diaz-Verson Amos
Foundation Inc.
1998

Published by
Mercer University Press
6316 Peake Road
Macon, Georgia 31210

The paper used in this publication meets the minimum requirements of
American National Standard for Permanence of Paper for Printed Library
Materials ANSI Z39.48–1984.

Library of Congress Cataloging-in-Publication Data

Shubin, Seymour.
The man from enterprise: the story of John B. Amos, founder of AFLAC /
Seymour Shubin
p. cm.
ISBN 0-86554-615-0 (alk. paper)
1. Amos, John Beverly, 1924-1977. 2. Insurance, Life—United States
History—History. 3. Executives—United States—Biography. 4. American
Family Life Insurance Company—History. I. Title.
HG8952.A45S48 1998
368.32'0092—dc21
[B] 98-35590
CIP

TABLE OF CONTENTS

ACKNOWLEDGMENTS

I want to express my gratitude to the many people who have shared with me their recollections of John Beverly Amos. Without their help this book could never have been written.

They are, alphabetically: Daniel P. Amos, Jacob O. Amos, John Shelby Amos, John W. Amos, Olivia Amos, Paul S. Amos, William L. Amos, Walter F. Barton, Bea Beck, Donald Beck, Sachiko "Chiko" Beck, Father J. Kevin Boland, Linda Bowick, Ignacio Carrera-Justiz, Lennie Davis, Earle Denson, Ana Maria de Rojas, Salvador Diaz-Verson, Jr., Silvia Diaz-Verson, Julie Ellis, Ron Feinberg, George Ford, Luis C. Garcia, Miguel A. Garcia, Nina Garcia, Beverly Greer, George Othell Hand, Ph.D., Senator Orrin Hatch, Katherine Hazouri Hess, Malcolm A. Hoffmann, Terry Hurley, George Jeter, John B. Land, Maria Teresa Amos Land, William D. Land, Jr., Duke Liberatore, Jan Liberatore, M.D., Frances King Lolley, Mayor Frank Martin, Orestes Martin, Brooks Massey, Sue Mathews, Lourdes Diaz-Verson Jones, Pedro Menocal, Matthew S. Metcalfe, Esther Meyers, Ira Meyers, Sam Meyers, Frank Morast, Senator Sam Nunn, Pat O'Connor, Leroy Paul, Carol Royer, R. Richard Schweitzer, Robyn Smith, Judith Snyder, Anita Stone, Kay Stover, Charlton W. Tebeau, Ph.D., Judge Albert W. Thompson, Glenn Vaughn Jr., Nancy Vaughn, Jr., and Clinton Wardlaw.

I want to convey my special thanks and deepest appreciation to Elena Diaz-Verson Amos, who extended to me her justly famed hospitality, and whose love for her husband—and as his love for her—are the very heart of this biography.

PREFACE

Dear Reader,

I am delighted that the story of John B. Amos can be told, for it is a story worth telling. There are many character traits that outstanding persons have in common, most have to be dreamers, but to be a truly successful person takes someone who has the energy and tenaciousness to make his dreams come true.

John Amos was such a visionary. He was also a man with abounding energy and tenaciousness, never taking no for an answer, whether it be from a young girl from a different country he had only met, but whom he decided he should marry, or from the skeptics who said he was crazy in thinking that he could build a world-wide insurance company from Columbus, Georgia.

Living with John Amos was like living in the eye of a hurricane, calm in the center with massive bursts of energy in all other directions. Even asleep, I do not believe that John ever stopped thinking or dreaming. He involved everyone, from family to friends, in whatever activity he was pursuing. There was no separation of his private and business life. Family, friends, associates, and acquaintances were all interwoven in a never ending cavalcade of projects, visits, dinners, parties, and business and social gatherings. It was a whirlwind life for a whirlwind individual, and it is a testament to his character, as well as to his love for and loyalty to family and friends, that those whom he left behind will never be able to forget him. He made an indelible impression on all with whom he came in contact.

The many lessons that all of us can learn from John Amos' well and fully lived life are still being absorbed by his family and friends. The readers of this book will also be able to heed those lessons so evident in his life and which made him so successful, but even more importantly, beloved by so many individuals, great and small. Who should know better about those lessons than I, his first, and hopefully, his best student.

In conclusion, I would like to thank Jacob Beil, Matt Metcalfe, Dick Schweitzer, Salvador Diaz-Verson, Jr., Ana Lopez, Gladys

Zamora, Orestes Martin, Ana Brubaker, Bob Behar, the Mercer University Press, and the *Columbus Ledger-Enquirer*, without whose efforts this book would never have been published. If I have omitted someone, it is unintentional and I ask for their forgiveness.

This book not only tells the story of John Amos' life, but also the history of AFLAC, and it recalls to mind many moments lived in making AFLAC what it is today. I will always be grateful to everyone who gave so much of themselves to John and to the Company, and in doing so, to me. It is their story as much as ours.

Elena D. Amos
Summer, 1998

FOREWORD

The following pages set out an anecdotal biography which because of the essential diversity of its subject, can convey only the "snapshots" and sketches made by others of the passage among his fellow beings of a man of formidable accomplishments that took place during a period of epic change in the American South. No matter how intense the images, how exact the words and memories, it is almost impossible to capture the essence of this man.

Philosophers have said that an unexamined life is not worth living. The life of John Beverly Amos cries out to be examined to yield us some concept of his accomplishments, the manner of their achievement, the obstacles overcome and circumvented, and the results from which so many, many people, in diverse parts of the world, have gained so much. His was a life worthy of being lived. As these pages tell, it was lived to the full, in a way that made, and still makes, his life significant to all he touched, and significant to many coming after his life has ended; for what he did has not gone and he has not gone from the lives of others.

The life of John Amos is much more than just another story of another successful businessman. In poetic terms, he not only achieved, but was, success. The scope and human impact of that success is exemplified in the great international institution he created, structured, restructured, and nurtured. No true history of that institution, today called AFLAC, could be written without writing the life of John Amos. There are few men of his time, or in our times, of whom that can be said.

And what of that time? All of us are fated to be shaped in part by our environment and, some more than others, to be shapers of the environment in which we live. This biography gives the reader a sense of where John Amos came from, and intimations of what he brought with him in his rise. For he did rise, and in rising raised others. He more than others has shaped the environment in which those following after him now live.

For many, it may seem adequate to say he "founded," under its original name as American Family Life Insurance Company, an institution that grew, with name changes, to become by his genius today's AFLAC. It is a company that today serves over forty million policyholders worldwide with benefits that would otherwise have been unobtainable, has over twenty-seven billion dollars in assets, annual revenues of over a seven billion dollars, over 4,000 employees, tens of thousands of agents and agencies, but, most importantly to him, millions of beneficiaries, confirming his concept of their needs. Indeed, those are extraordinary markers for any man's achievements. Still, "founded" is not adequate for what John Amos has done; nor does it convey any sense of what was involved in his work or his doing of it.

When, at age thirty-one, John Amos determined to create "his" insurance company, the South of the mid 1950s was rife with "promoters." Many, if not most, sought funds from the public simply as a means of existence, with no real conviction in a particular objective, seldom with any sense of obligation to the investors. Capital was most often raised by "door to door" salesmen usually exclusively within a single state. Dozens of small, minimally funded life insurance companies were set up in Georgia and surrounding states.

Though efforts were made to taint his work with that era of "promoters," John was not of that ilk. His objective was a conviction. He always felt deeply an obligation to even the smallest providers of capital, and he was not engaged in self-advancement. Perhaps in part for those reasons, few other than John's creation survive to this day. While it is beyond the purpose of these words to describe the lack of crucial capital resources and the economic atmosphere of the South in those formative years from 1954 through 1970, they must be noted to understand what John achieved at a time when mere survival was a major accomplishment. He did much, much more.

At that time, a great bulk of individual life and health insurance was bought on the basis of small weekly premiums, sold and collected by direct-contact house-call sales people. John quickly realized that his small company could not compete with the older, larger companies offering the same kind of "product" and offering more to the usual type of insurance sales people.

It was a mark of his genius to look for a need, even a need others might not be aware they had, to conceive of a way to fill that need, and then to develop a unique way of distributing the "product" that filled the need. He began by studying the forms of insurance offered by other companies to provide benefits to victims of polio, which had been rampant in the South in the summers. It was truly a dread disease.

But John did not copy or follow others. He made an intense study of the incidence and impact of cancer and of how little the populace knew or understood of its incidence. All of this was the individual work of John Amos, his own work, not that of actuaries, statisticians or technicians. It was done by his "hands on—mind on" voracious reading and thinking. He conceived of and created a unique form of insurance to help people meet the extraord-inary expenses caused by the occurrence of cancer. John Amos did this.

Almost simultaneously he focused on how to create awareness of the need for this form of economic protection—how to make people aware of a need they did not realize they might have. His principal thrust came from official data showing that at that time one person in every four would incur cancer, a ratio that was to increase tragically. He was roundly castigated for promulgating such "scare tactics."

Today we recognize that his program was a major step in generating public awareness of the spreading impact of cancer incidence. Many who later worked in that field came to realize his accomplishments in increasing public awareness of cancer incidence, particularly in the eleven southern states into which his company initially expanded. John Amos did this.

Concurrently with his development of this form of insurance, John came to grips with the problem of how to acquire public acceptance. This meant devising schedules and benefits balanced by an affordable price, as well as a simplicity of explanation, and absolute, unquestioned benefit entitlement upon a pathology determination of cancer in the insured. For distribution and sales people, John moved away from competition with the larger life and health insurers.

In the early years he moved toward people who sold only his form of insurance. They were trained and licensed by the company for this single specialized "product." In effect, he became a "niche" marketer, long before the value of that approach was widely recognized by the investment community. He had his associates seek out those who would work only part time, as little as one or two nights a week. But the additional supplemental income almost always became important to them and led to greater efforts, more sales calls. Many left their former work as teachers, bank clerks, and other "steady" jobs, often to become more economically successful than they had ever dreamt of being. New livelihoods were created. John Amos did all this.

John recognized the overwhelming importance of the individual salesperson. "Conventions" were held every year during his tenure. As the sales and income of the company grew, John's attention to those responsible never waned. Unlike many closely surrounding him, who upon the success of the company and its forms of insurance adopted a "merchant's mentality," John preserved a salesman's mentality. He knew instinctively that his company's "market" was not the general public who bought policies, the "market" was the sales force which required "something they could sell." For many years, the producers of sales were compensated far beyond John's personal level, as he elevated many to managerial responsibilities and rewarded results, making many of them millionaires with sincere gratitude, not resentment. John Amos did this.

Today, from the perspective of John's astounding success, it would be difficult for those who did not experience it with him to understand the enormous strain under which he labored in dealing with bureaucrats and of government regulators, and a critical need for capital, yet was able to move his company forward.

In addition to the need for capital raised from the public, the successful nature of John's sales activities drained the company's resources, requiring other backing to bear part of the risks of claims while the company bore all the costs of selling and issuing policies. John obtained that backing through Lloyds of London.

For "political" reasons, with practically no notice, one insurance regulator arbitrarily denied John credit for the essential backing from Lloyds. Lack of insurance backup would have stopped sales after only three years of growth and placed the future in extreme jeopardy. Because of his friendships with other regulators and his innate ability to explain his business clearly and simply, John found other insurance backing that could not be challenged. In time, he raised the company's capacity to the point that no further insurance backing was needed. John Amos did this.

John's efforts to provide a market and some degree of liquidity for his investors in the early days raised the ire of the then Regional S.E.C Administrator in Atlanta, who had his own prejudicial views of John's activities. The even more prejudiced local press used the wording of the regulatory charges to imply that "fraud" and "manipulation" had occurred.

The local calumny almost caused John to move the company to Albany, Georgia. But he hung on, finally compromising his personal pride for the sake of his shareholders, agreeing, for their benefit, to a settlement without hearing, in which the S.E.C. staff did not keep its word to him. John's drive to meet what he saw as his obligation to those who provided the capital cost him great effort and concern, and as noted, disagreeable publicity for a man justifiably proud of the name he was making for himself. Still, he never backed away from that obligation, ultimately achieving the listing of his company's shares on the New York Stock Exchange and exchanges in other nations, where today more than $1.5 million worth of those shares trade on an average day today benefiting close to 90,000 shareholders. All of this came from John Amos.

In a crushingly short period of time after the crisis for insurance backing, the company desperately needed further capital to maintain its sales, which, from the expanding sales forces John was creating were increasing exponentially. In fact, sales, and the related pre-paid costs, which would be recovered from future collections, had consumed all the company's resources that the laws required it to have. At that point of time, there was still no market for, or trading in, the company's shares, there was no time to mount a new stock sales program like those that provided the original capital. Under extreme pressure, John brought together with him two of his close friends to find a solution. He then structured a merger by which his company absorbed another small company that had no significant activity. He personally guaranteed the shareholders of the absorbed company that they would at least double their money by holding shares in his company. If not, he would buy the shares from them, if buyers at the desired prices could not be found within the periods specified.

It was a daring gambit which turned out to be touch-and-go throughout the periods of his commitment, and caused him severe personal stress. The foresight to use a trust mechanism to hold and transfer the shares, and crucial help from his two friends enabled him to meet every commitment, much to the surprise of many skeptics. Those funds provided the company with a cushion for all further growth until John decided a few years later to expand nationwide. He always maintained his company had help in this vital effort at a crucial time, but the fact is, as acknowledged by those who worked with him then, all the contributions they and any others may have made "to the company" were really contributions to John's work. It was John Amos who got the job done.

As if the crisis for additional funding, and meeting his commitments made to implement the merger, were not enough, it was in this same time-frame that John had to face the attacks, described earlier, from the Regional S.E.C. Administrator in Atlanta. He had to deal with the hostility of the local press, and with deprecations from financial writers in the Atlanta press; while none paid attention to what he was achieving in the fundamentals of his company. Those kinds of burdens and attacks crushed many others. John overcame all this.

And that was only the beginning. As his form of insurance gained more and more acceptance by the public, John realized that he could face regional competitors elsewhere in the nation. Obtaining licenses in additional states was a slow and tedious process. To give his company a national market, he personally worked out an arrangement with a larger non-competing health insurer to issue his form of insurance, to be sold by his selected agents, for which his company would, by separate contract, assume all the risks and costs, in all the states to which John wanted to expand. As John obtained licenses in more territories, the arrangement shrank. In a sweep, John had taken his regional, specialized insurance company nationwide. John Amos did it.

Going nationwide created a need for more capital resources, his company was going to need a lot of money. John's diverse abilities showed their strength when he made a private placement of a large bloc of stock for the company with a huge California mutual fund together with a large bloc of warrants entitling the fund to buy company shares in the future at an advantageous price; especially if the share price continued to rise steadily in the still thinly-traded broker-dealer markets. John had no teams of MBAs, or investment advisors. Again, it was a gambit that had its risks, but the resources provided were crucial to his planned expansion. John Amos did it, and John Amos made it work.

John's genius was evident again when the fund wanted to sell the shares it would get with the warrants. John had his company comply fully with its contract with the fund, registering the shares with the S.E.C., but the fund could not find a way to offer them to the general public. John did not want them "dumped" into the market driving down the values for his investors. After two years of fruitless efforts by the fund, John came up with a unique solution that created a pool of shares to be used as part of the incentive compensation to his sales forces, giving them an almost unheard of chance to become shareholders in the company that gave them a livelihood, on unusually advantageous terms. This generated even more very rich people from John's insights and efforts. He solved the problem of the fund that had helped his company and made his people richer. John Amos did this.

The company came under attack by the IRS. John's response was again singularly analytical and beneficial to the future of his company as well as to the nation's knowledge of cancer incidence. The IRS asserted that John's company was not a "Life" insurance company by the tax definitions. They claimed he did not set aside assets to meet the obligations to renew policies for people who incurred cancer. John had them proved wrong, from facts he knew to be certain, by having a new actuarial table created, known now as The American Family Table of Cancer Morbidity. That table showed that the assets set aside for obligations on policies did indeed cover the liability to renew. That table, as John had it maintained and developed, has proven invaluable in the field of cancer research for information available nowhere else. John knew when to call in the right experts, and what to ask of them.

The tax liability asserted, in the millions, would have sunk his company; he didn't let it happen. Once again, John got it done.

After that, John was audited personally, regularly!

John always intended that his form of insurance should be a supplement to, not a replacement for, general health or hospitalization coverage, whether under group or individual policies. He was certainly a leader in, if not the originator of, what is well-known today as supplemental insurance. That was the whole point of his company and its form of insurance.

As his company grew, John calculated that it needed to expand from just sales to individuals and families by moving into some form of "mass" marketing, dealing with large numbers of people at a time, but giving them individual policies they could own and control, not subject to group insurance or employer problems. John had sales forces developed that began to sign up people through payroll deduction plans that lowered costs and provided individual protections to employees and others in groups, ranging from small to very large. The results were astounding. So much so that John soon found his form of insurance challenged by the giants who sold group health insurance. They began refusing benefits to someone who incurred cancer if they had a policy covering only cancer incidence with John's company. It appeared that all the big companies planned to do this, so John engaged in a long struggle to stop that practice, showing that regular group insurance often limited benefits needed in the event of cancer, or perhaps excluded cancer, and that no one "caught" cancer to get insurance payments. Years of effort, direct lobbying of legislatures, anti-trust actions, and work with policy-holders and beneficiaries, finally resulted in laws and regulations against that practice by the big group insurers, and then gradually, the dropping of the practice with respect to John's form of insurance. While John took comfort from the final results, he was never fully satisfied that he had truly, totally won. John Amos did win for the beneficiaries of supplemental insurance.

In the pages that follow is something of the distinct flavor of how John Amos went about doing all this and in getting things done. John was always a human moving among humans, with an awareness of motivations and inclinations that could affect his company and his family, which were closely intertwined. The cliché, "He never lost the human touch," is applied to a lot of people who never had much of it to lose in the first place. John's every touch was human, in both its strength and its vulnerability. He was vulnerable. He seldom tried to do intentional harm. Never a betrayer, he was sometimes easily betrayed, because it was not in his concepts. He often faced consistent resentment, which he just as often refused to acknowledge because he was not resentful of the success and honors of others. He kept commitments that others failed to keep to him. But for his own reasons, he cloaked his compassion, perhaps to shield his vulnerability. However he reacted, he was an inordinately effective executive, whose style, techniques, and most of all character, can not be replicated, if even replaced. John Amos was that singular human.

John surrounded himself with associates whose sole functions were essentially administrative; decision making power, and "execution" was only as he delegated. He could forgive or even rationalize errors of judgment, lack of diligence and other defects in performance as partly his error in the assignments, but he was adamant about breach of trust or intentional harm to others. John Amos did not assign blame.

As his company grew, the human interactions within it, and of the people inside it with those outside it, increased dynamically. Still, they never got beyond his grasp and direct involvement where needed. During his tenure, corporate bureaucracies were thwarted before they could take root. He could disrupt incipient cabals by making would be "conspirators" competitors with one another, possibly part of his political talents that are spoken of in the pages that follow. He would "cure" matters by subtly shifting people about, whenever that was humanly possible, but by absolute expulsion when inescapable, but always with generous parting benefits, so much so that some were heard to say: "I wish Mr. John would fire me."

John Amos was never ruthless. John Amos was always human.

As corporate affairs became more and more complex, John never had a General Counsel for legal and regulatory matters. He was the General Counsel, and lawyers working for him were always made to feel they were working with him. It would quickly become clear to them that where he had knowledge of the law, it was penetrating and full; that where he did not, his capacity to absorb, master, and then use legal knowledge, was supreme. In all this John served his company, its shareholders, and its policyholders well.

Much has been written already about John's company and what has transpired in Japan. Missing from much of what has been written is what John did, his insights, and how he got things done. Chiefly, he was more calmly persistent than patient, a characteristic that came to win him deep respect from Japanese officials and executives. His respect for their ways, rather than some foisting of "American know-how," was rewarded with a special relationship between him and all those who became part of his enterprise in Japan.

To take his company into Japan, establishing an autonomous branch, selecting from among Japanese perhaps the most loyal and devoted associates he had ever known, John literally had to drag, and sometimes browbeat, nag, cajole and ridicule others in his company, and those close to him, into accepting his perceptions and determinations—often so reluctantly it must have been heart-rending; for it was always his strength to convince, not threaten, to enthuse, not force. John Amos did this his way.

A major factor in John's success in Japan was again his willingness to let others profit, and gain economic advantage from the beginning, without resentment and without stint. Tens of thousands of agencies and agents were created, retired persons found continued employment, huge Japanese corporations and other institutions quickly saw the benefits to them and their employees of what John was bringing to Japan that had never been available there before. The honors he was accorded there, during and after his life, were well deserved. From his own direct efforts and thought, John Amos earned all this.

One of the greatest injustices John encountered came as his company was achieving phenomenal growth in Japan and had established its specialized forms of insurance in the United States. The collusion of the staff of a Congressional Sub-Committee with a network television news program wrongly, if not falsely, entangled his company in an investigation of sales abuses foisted by others on the elderly. While his company did not discriminate against the elderly, it was not a desirable segment of insureds because of the higher incidence of cancer as age increases. Despite John's testimony before Congress (which is illuminating reading) the network, by devious altering using splicing and editing of a sales interview obtained by work of the Congressional staff, and by combining it with other materials, imputed serious misconduct to John's company.

The results of the specious television presentation were extremely damaging. Many in the sales forces were being demoralized, sales declined in some areas, his company's share prices were adversely impacted over a long period, causing losses to his investors. While John immediately went to the defense of his company, his sales forces and his shareholders, the legal actions he took encountered delays he could not control. One of his chief trial lawyers died, and his own health was becoming impaired. A major accomplishment was finding people who recovered for him the portions of the televised interview that had been wrongly altered to achieve sensationalism. But, in this one instance, time and the delays worked against him, and as his company's basic soundness and growth overcame false perceptions, John ended the legal proceedings without the satisfaction of a judgment he wanted so fiercely. John did suffer injustice and disappointments. Still John Amos never quit defending and pushing his company forward.

Difficult as it is to describe, without many more words than should be used here, John Amos nurtured his company. That may sound an odd term for a relationship of a man to the institution he created. But, no other word seems apt. It was not just the nurturing of individuals. It went further, into ideas, tests, searching, constant study that never ended. It was defending. It was shaping people as his own physical strength waned. It was being aggressive, in the admirable sense of that word. And it was so much more that eludes comprehension through mere words. But, it was there, and its effects remain. John Amos was nurturing.

Through it all, the creating, the structuring, the tortuous restructurings and the nurturing, John Amos had his own personal agonies and his disappointments; had some truly glorious moments; had his love repaid with resentment and envy; had his humanness repaid with undying loyalty; gave unmatched friendship, for John Amos sought always to be a friend and to extend friendship to all. John Amos is not gone, only a little of what could be touched is gone. Much remains physically and in minds and hearts, as you can read. Friends may die, but friendships live. So it is, John Amos is here. Find him.

Dick Schweitzer
June 1998

INTRODUCTION

John Beverly Amos didn't want his biography written during his lifetime. He once made an attempt to write his life story, jotting down some notes and working with a writer. But then he called it off. He just had too many things to do yet in his life, he explained in that soft-spoken, gently-smiling, down-home way of his.

He was right. He had accomplished more in his life than most people even dream of, but there was so much more to do—to *contribute*, a word he probably would never have used in regard to himself, but which so many people whose lives he touched use to help define him. Even on a night soon after he had undergone surgery for cancer, as he stood on a dais, drained and slightly bent, to receive one of the many, many honors that had come to him (this one in 1986, as Georgian of the Year, from the Association of Georgia Broadcasters), he said in a determined voice, "God must have something awful special for me to do. And if He will give me the slightest hint of what this is, I'll get about the business of doing it."

After talking to people who knew John Beverly Amos, I was struck by some common threads that ran through their reminiscences of him. One was that he was the epitome of the American dream. Born in a small Alabama town, he started a weekly newspaper when he was thirteen, became a country lawyer, and eventually became primary founder of the billion-dollar American Family Corporation, whose chief subsidiary is an international life insurance company—American Family Life Assurance Company—which he founded when he was in his early thirties. He was a friend and advisor to presidents, legislators, and international leaders. But that doesn't begin to say it all. The rest is encompassed in something else I kept hearing from person after person:

There will never be another John Amos.

A deep love of family...philanthropist...active in community and national affairs...a wide-open door to people in need of money or counsel...friendships that encompassed the poor and the rich, the left and the right of the political spectrum...an innovator and constant fount of ideas...with it all, an absolutely wild sense of humor—and that's still only part of the complex man that was John Beverly Amos.

In his notes, he mentioned that in his father's day, while spinsters, were objects of pity, "old bachelors were privately the subject of scorn by male and female alike. They were considered men who for a lack of character, refused to take upon themselves the responsibilities of a wife and children."

John Amos then added, "I have never scorned old bachelors. In fact, to me they are objects of pity, for they will never know what it is like to spend this life with a wife you truly love and who truly loves you, let alone the twilight years when you have children and grand-children to share your joys and sorrows and fortunes—good or bad. What a waste of the only life they will ever have on this earth."

Thus, with a beautiful wife, two children, and six grandchildren, life would hardly have been a "waste" even had he not accomplished all the things he did.

How often he referred to his wife as his main support! And so in a very real sense, this is the story not only of John Amos, but of his wife, Elena Diaz-Verson. In her case, it begins in Cuba. In his, it begins in a town called—and how appropriately!—Enterprise.

1

THE FRIEND

The waiter in the restaurant at the posh St. Moritz hotel in Manhattan appeared somewhat astonished at his customer's request.

Grits?

"I'm sorry," he said. "We don't serve grits."

The man at the table, distinguished-looking, white-haired John Beverly Amos, was a familiar figure at the St. Moritz, since he generally stayed there during his frequent trips to New York. So when he came back a month later, the waiter—a different one from before—recognized him. Again John Amos asked for grits.

"Mr. Amos," the waiter said, shaking his head, "you know we don't have grits."

John opened his briefcase and took out a box of grits he'd brought from home.

The waiter looked a little bewildered. "But I don't know if the kitchen knows how to fix it."

"That's all right. Never mind," he said. And he stood up and walked into the kitchen and prepared the grits himself.

From that day on, his son John Shelby, 11, recalled, the St. Moritz kept grits for him.

John Amos—"Mr. John" to his employees and acquaintances—never forgot where he *came* from; his roots were always a part of him, even in "high places." There was the time, for instance, when he had lunch at the White House with President Jimmy Carter, Senator Edward Kennedy, and the industrialist Armand Hammer. Toward the end of the meal, finger bowls were brought in.

"I was sitting directly across from President Carter," he recalled. "Both of us put our fingers in and rinsed them, when we both looked up and caught each other's eye and started laughing at how ridiculous a couple of boys from South Georgia and Southeast Alabama could get."

John Amos was born at home on June 5, 1924, in a white, frame house his father built across the street—College Street—from Enterprise's grammar school. It was, he wrote in his notes years later, "the first house in town to have the kitchen on the front." Indeed, since the family was to live in several houses over the years, "It was always referred to by my mother as the 'house with the kitchen on the front.'"

He was delivered by a Dr. Stanley at four in the afternoon, an event intently made obvious to his older brother and a friend, who were playing in the yard when they "heard a loud cry through the open window—and I had suddenly arrived on earth well and sound."

That same afternoon, his father marked the event "by planting a pecan tree outside that window."

John was the second of three children, all boys. The oldest, William (Bill) Lafayette Amos was born on February 8, 1920; the youngest, Paul Shelby Amos, on April 24, 1926.

Their father, John Shelby Amos, was born in the crossroads community of Jack, in Pike County, Alabama. He was born in a log cabin, the youngest of six children—two boys and four girls.

Their mother, Helen Mullins, was born on October 31, 1898, in Ozark, Alabama. She was the oldest of four children, two boys and two girls.

John Amos knew many details of the Amos and Mullins family history "'despite,'" as he said, "little or no written records." The answer, he explained, was that from the time he was about four he would sit up with his mother and father, much of the time sitting on his father's lap and plying them with questions long after his brothers had gone to sleep.

"I can hear him now," he recalled, "saying, 'Son, please, just one more question and then we'll all go to bed.'"

The Amos and Mullins families were of Scotch-Irish—primarily, Irish—descent, with roots in the South that go back to pre-Revolutionary times. This is reflected in some of their names—the surname Lee, for instance, on Helen Mullins's side, while on his father's side there was a George Washington Amos and an Isaac Lafayette Amos (whose middle name, of course, became Bill Amos's). And there is an American Indian heritage, too. George Washington Amos—John Amos's great-grandfather—married a "Cherokee maiden," John wrote, "whose tintype picture, showing a young woman with coal black hair parted in the middle and combed straight back, is ample evidence of my claim to descent from the original Americans."

The Amos family up to his father's generation, John Amos noted, "were Hardshell Baptists. The Hardshell Baptists were a cross between the Quakers and the Presbyterians. They believed in predestination, were opposed to Prohibition—even though few imbibed—had no paid ministry, had all day services during which the Lord would call one Brother after the other to take the pulpit, and when he finished they would sit in silence until the Lord called another Brother to the pulpit. They permitted no musical instrument in the church."

Another distinguishing feature about the Hardshell Baptists, he continued, "was their sacrament. Rather than partaking of the symbolic eating of the body and drinking of the blood of Christ... they had a foot washing ceremony where each washed and dried the feet of the others as Christ had done to his disciples. My dad said there were never any cleaner feet on earth than the feet of Hardshells when they entered the church door for the footwashing ceremony."

John Amos's grandfather was a farmer and a skilled carpenter: "He followed carpentry when the crops were laid by in the Spring and after the harvest in the Fall." He was a hardworking, mild man who "was not given to argue, but John's grandmother "was a true Irish woman with all the fight and fury that went into her heritage." Indeed, when "Grandma's Irish got up—he just walked out."

The only story John ever heard about "Grandpa Amos" getting mad was when someone kicked his dog. "He calmly went home for his shotgun" and went hunting for the culprit. "I'm certain that both were very lucky that the offender saw fit to take to the tall timbers until Grandpa had time to cool off and be receptive of an apology, for there were three things you just didn't do anywhere in the rural South in those days and live to tell about it, and that was to mistreat a man's wife, his children, or his dog—in no particular order."

Grandma Amos was the "boss" of the family, a stern disciplinarian, a tireless worker, a good cook, seamstress, and homemaker—and at the same time "could plow a mule along with the rest of them. Dad told me one time of Grandma plowing and killing a rattlesnake with a hoe at the end of a row. He claimed that the poison thrown off by the dead snake into the air as Grandma continued to plow back and forth around the snake made her deathly nauseous. I don't know anything about dead rattlesnakes throwing off poison into the air," John added. "She might have also eaten a green apple, but his story was enough for me to know that she took her place behind the plow when necessary."

But though Grandma Amos might have been the boss, there was at least one thing she could not stop her husband from doing.

"A God-fearing man who was happy with his farm, mule, and family and thanked God for all his blessings," John Amos recounted, "he was also a generous man and a gracious host." On Sundays after church, and "in spite of Grandma's advance threats to murder him, he would stand up on the back of his mule-drawn wagon and holler out, 'All who ain't got someplace to go, come to my house for dinner.' As churches were few and far between and the congregation came from near and far, he always had plenty of takers." And then John Amos added something that everyone who knew John and Elena Amos would agree with: "My wife and I are like my Grandpa Amos in that everybody who 'ain't got no place to go' are certainly welcome at our house and there is always room for one more at our table."

Grandma Amos saw to it that her children went to school. They walked two miles to a one-room school, where classes were held only when there was no farm work to be done. She also had dreams of her family being able to move from the "piney woods" into a town.

With this in mind, she sent John Amos's Uncle Beverly to a business school. Afterwards John's Uncle Beverly went to work in a general store in the town of Elba, Alabama (which was to be the start of a successful business career), and not long after this, "Grandma got busy about the business of getting the family into a town—namely, Elba."

Grandpa Amos sold the farm and built a house in Elba and also bought a farm outside the town. He continued to do carpentry in addition to farming. John Amos's father worked alongside of him on the farm and with carpentry. Meanwhile, two of the Amos sisters became expert seamstresses and started a successful shop. Elba proved to be "too small" for their business, and they moved to Enterprise, twelve miles away. The rest of the family, except for Uncle Beverly, moved there, too.

According to John Amos, his father had been underweight and sickly until, at the age of sixteen, his problem was diagnosed as hookworm. He was cured "with one course of medicine," and in the year that followed he grew to be six feet in height, never again weighing less than 220 pounds "and strong as an ox. He hauled lumber on his back. He delivered ice in 50-pound chunks."

He went to work in a general store, and later on "somewhere learned the craft of shoe repair." He opened a shoe repair shop, but an incident that John Amos recalled with special pride in his father took place in the general store, a store that carried just about everything, including caskets.

One night his father, who had the keys to the store, was awakened "by the only Jewish farmer in the county, who lived alone with his wife on their farm some miles from town. His wife had died that night and he had come to buy a casket. He also bought a new shovel that caused Dad to find by inquiry that he and his wife had developed no close friends and that it was his intent to dig her grave and bury her himself. As a result Dad took a shovel out of stock, hitched up a mule and wagon from the livery stable, and followed Mr. Solomon's wagon home. Together he and Mr. Solomon dug the grave, said the prayers, eased the coffin into the grave, and covered it up.

"Such a man was my father."

As for his mother, Helen Mullins, little is known of the history of the Mullins side of her family, John Amos reported. But one of the things that comes across strong in his notes was his love for *her* mother, whom he affectionately called "Big Mama" and who in her later years lived with John's mother and father until her death in 1965. Her maiden name was Ora Clyde (?) Byrd, and she was born on a farm in Dale County, Alabama. Big Mama's grandparents had come to Alabama from North Carolina, and Big Mama would regale young John Amos with stories about how, when they first came to the wilderness-like valley where they were to settle, they had to sleep in hammocks swung high enough in the trees to be safe from wolves.

"Several years work lay ahead," John Amos recorded, "that had to be approached on a communal basis. The men and women worked in teams to build the cabins first to house the families, then to clear the land, and then to clear the land for planting. The log clearings were called 'log rolling.' The men cut the trees, dug out the stumps and roots, and smoothed the surface for plowing while the women conversed, tended the children and livestock, and prepared a feast."

The Mullins, Byrds, and Darlings "from whom my mother descended," he continued, "were either Hardshell Baptist or Pioneer Methodist—which wasn't far from the Holly Roller of today."

Big Mama attended "any church that was open—as did Mother and Dad and we children—but she lived, died, and was buried a Hardshell. This in spite of the fact that Grandpa Byrd had been thrown out of the Hardshell Baptist Church after a full and fair trial on the charge of attending a church with an organ in it. His defense was that the organ was broken and didn't play."

Grandpa Mullins married Big Mama when she was fifteen or sixteen, "rather advanced in years for a bride in those days." He had been twenty-five. Big Mama was seventeen when John's mother was born.

Grandpa Mullins became postmaster at Elba. There, John noted, he was a "joiner. He joined every lodge from the Masons to the Knights of Pythias to the Odd Fellows to the Woodmen of the World to the Red Men...Grandpa Mullins was something of a ladies' man and I believe that might have had something to do with his joining so many lodges; the only excuse for leaving the house at night was to go to a lodge meeting, and he had one almost every night. Mother loved Big Mama dearly and I am sure that this had something to do with her lack of affection for her father."

In some ways, John Amos wrote, his mother and her father were alike in the sense that "both of them were high-strung, and in money matters even when she was a small child he had met his match. He never conquered my mother and he never broke her spirit."

She became his clerk in the post office at the age of fourteen, and "he paid Mother as he would have paid any other. No pay, no work. Thus Mother was able to afford the best clothes and her own horse and surrey as a teenager."

At some point, probably after Grandpa Mullins's death, Big Mama moved her family to the same town the Amoses lived in—Enterprise— where she started a boarding house. John Amos did not know exactly how his mother and father met, but "I do know that after she set her cap for Dad he was a gone goose. She was his only sweetheart, he her only beau." They were married in 1917.

2

BEFORE THE BEGINNING

In those years, Enterprise was a town of about 2,000 people. It depended strictly on farming. It had a wide Main Street and, as John's older brother Bill recalled, at each end was a cotton gin. But since there wasn't enough room in the gins to hold all the cotton, they would also store cotton bales along the middle of Main Street. But then along came boll weevil to decimate the cotton, forcing the farmers to plant peanuts instead. But what seemed like a disaster at the time ended up with the townsfolk erecting a little monument to boll weevil, since peanuts turned out to be more lucrative.

One of John's Amos's memories of his childhood in the early twenties was that there were about as many mules and wagons in town on Saturdays as there were cars— Model T and Model A Fords.

"The Twenties were good to Mother and Dad," John recorded. His father was appointed postmaster of the town and also sold insurance on weekends and during vacations for a fraternal organization, the Praetorians. "In addition, at Mother's instigation, Daddy borrowed all he could in the late Twenties and built houses for rent." They were very cheap houses to build (carpenters, for instance, got about a dollar a day, and he himself did a lot of the work). Sometimes the Amos family would move into a house he built, and then he would sell it and buy another with the profit. One day, when John was about twelve, he talked his father into running for the state legislature and even ran his campaign and helped write his speeches. His father lost, but ran again at the next election and won. However, he was less than enthralled with political life and didn't run for re-election.

John Amos described his father's family as being loving and close. And John was raised in a family that was no less so.

"We had a mother and dad who always went along with us," Bill Amos said. "Anything we wanted to do, they were willing to do all they could to help."

Said Paul Amos, "They were gamblers—particularly my mother—when it came to making moves which might better our way of living. And we did move a number of times. She was the dreamer, she was the 'air castle' builder."

Their father, John wrote, had completed the tenth grade before going to work full time. In those ten years he had "mastered Latin, English, and mathematics, and continued his education throughout his life, as did my mother." While their father was a big man at about six feet—"handsome, not fat, but big," as Bill Amos described him—their mother was petite. "When we were young," Bill Amos continued, "she did her best to reach ninety pounds. She took vitamins and raw eggs and everything to gain some weight, but she did not gain any until late in life."

Petite as she was, however, she was always a driving force behind her husband. "She was very ambitious for Dad," John said. Indeed, though John Amos didn't know exactly how his father came to be appointed postmaster, he could "see my mother's 'fine hand' behind it."

His father had a "healthy respect" for both his mother's and his wife's feelings, which sometimes required that he "walk a tight rope between the two. Often he would get a call from his mother asking him to stop by her house for a special lunch she had prepared for him. He would go early and finish a hearty meal, only to have another lunch with my mother—without her ever knowing the difference."

The first "crisis" in the family, he continued, occurred the year he was born, when his brother Bill had what appeared to be a fatal case of pneumonia.

"He knew or thought he would die," recalled John, "and he begged Dad and Mother in his feeble voice to bury him in the front yard so he could be near them and not alone out in the cemetery." Pneumonia always reached a "crisis" stage in those days, during which the patient either died or began to get well. "On the night Bill's crisis came, Dad had been awake for three days and nights, never leaving his baby son's bedside. Dad fell asleep praying on the floor at the side of Bill's little bed. Dad's mother or sisters eased a pillow under his head and covered him with a quilt. When he awoke, the sun was beaming on his face through a window, and even without looking he knew that his baby boy had survived. Otherwise, he would have been awakened for the bad news."

At six weeks of age, John was the next to throw a scare into his family when he developed a very serious case of whooping cough. "Dad, Mother, and my aunts took turns patting my back to keep my breathing going. During that year the first-ever chiropractor in Enterprise had moved to town and rented a house Dad had built next door. I was going down, down in spite of the twice daily calls by our family doctor and all the cough medicine the doctor could prescribe." Then, from the chiropractor's wife, Mrs. Delaney, came "a message of hope." Her husband had said that if all hope were gone he believed he could bring "the baby" through.

Since all hope *was* gone, "Dad and Mother—knowing nothing about this form of treatment—invited the chiropractor in. He placed me stomach down on the top of his thigh and manipulated my spine with two fingers for a few minutes. He ordered no more cough syrup and left. By the time he returned for another manipulation, my cough had begun to subside and within twenty-four hours I was weak, but almost well. Of course we will never know if Dr. Delaney's treatment was that effective or if the time had just come for an abrupt change for the better, but for decades to come, if Dr. Delaney was within driving distance, he was the family doctor. That is not to say that he was the only family doctor. Dad and especially Mother believed in a good mix of the healing arts...and a lot of earnest prayer."

According to John, his younger brother Paul "had no mishaps." John, however, had another crisis at the age of four, when he accidentally stuck a knife in his right eye, piercing the pupil.

"It wasn't painful," he recalled. "The first thing, it started watering. And I started seeing colors. So I went to Mother and I said, 'Mama, I'm seeing colors.' She took her skirt and wiped my eyes. In a few minutes I came back to her. She called to my father, and the minute Daddy looked at it he could see what happened. By terrifying coincidence, his own father had lost his vision in both eyes as a result of a splinter." They rushed the boy to an eye specialist in Dothan, about twenty-five miles away.

12

"In those days the most horrible thing we kids would talk about was having a tonsillectomy and ether. And I was as scared of ether as I was of a rattlesnake."

John's Uncle Beverly, who lived in Dothan, met them at the hospital. John sat on his lap in the waiting room while they were getting the operating room ready.

"They finally said okay, and then I heard the word 'ether.' Daddy said it took six nurses, him, the doctor, and my Uncle Bev to hold me down long enough to get that cup on me and get me to sleep. It wasn't that complicated an operation, even though they had to put some stitches in it. Afterwards we went to Uncle Bev's house to spend the night. I slept with Dad, and he said I screamed all night, 'Don't give me that ether! Don't give me that ether!'"

When they brought him back to the hospital a week or two later, the doctor "took the bandage off, took me to the window, and asked me what I could see. I said, 'Well, I can see the sun.' He said, 'What else can you see?' I said, 'I can see shadows.'" He eventually regained some of the sight in that eye, but then "lost a lot of it through lack of practice. When you have one strong eye and one weak eye, your strong eye tends to do all the work." Describing the vision in that eye, he said he could see "shadows, outlines. I can see something coming toward me. I may not know what it is, but you hit at me and I'll jerk."

But "vision," as his life was to prove, was the very last thing he lacked.

John, said his brother Paul thinking back with a smile, was an entrepreneur all his life. "He and I were very close There was only an eighteen months difference in our ages, and we were little boys together, played together, and had mutual friends until he reached around age thirteen. That's when John left the world of adolescence and went into the world of the man. His closest friends were—well, they seemed like old men at the time. Mature men, wiser men, might be a better description."

Actually, although John entered the "working world" about this time, he had been an entrepreneur long before that.

"He must have been in the fourth grade," Paul recalled, "when he founded an 'insurance company.' He sold me a 'rather limited' accident policy that paid twenty-five cents if you stepped on a cigarette and twenty-five cents if you stepped on a nail. I think the premium was five cents a week. I don't know how many he sold, but he got my nickel."

Added Bill Amos, "When he was a little boy, he and our dad used to talk about starting an insurance company. John was one who never went to bed until my mother and dad went to bed, and John would tell him he ought to go into that business."

But John's was also a childhood of play and Saturday afternoon movies.

"We'd go to a movie," John Amos recalled, "and come back and reenact the whole thing—the shoot-out, for instance, with chinaberry limbs under us for horses. Then we'd switch. We'd play with play money, wheel and deal, then put that away and build towns and whatnot."

One of John's fondest memories was of going fishing with his father: "Mother was never asked or allowed to pack a lunch for us," since a big part of the fun was to stop at the general for food and soda pop to take along. "Dad's pocketknife could open any can ever made."

Early on, too, he developed a sense of humor and a lifelong love of sometimes-outrageous practical jokes.

One that Bill Amos remembered in particular was when their father was sick in bed with the flu.

"My dad was just as scared of snakes as he could be. John found an old rope that had tar all over it, and he walked into Dad's bedroom and said, 'Look what I killed,' and he dropped it on the bed. And my dad—you would have thought he hadn't been sick.

"John went under the house and stayed till Dad promised not to whip him."

Although John Amos did not know exactly how his father became postmaster of Enterprise, he knew of one thing that paved the way for his appointment. In addition to passing the examination for postmaster, his father had become a Republican in a section of the South that was particularly Democrat-free; he did this during a Republican administration. In fact, it was such a disgrace to be a Democrat that, according to John, "Grandma Amos was not told of the appointment until Dad had been sworn in. After he did tell her, he left her at home crying, but her son being one of the highest paid men in town"— making two hundred dollars a month—"helped soften her shame and grief at having a Republican in the family."

With the election of Franklin D. Roosevelt in 1932, he resigned rather than "wait for the ax to fall." He sold his properties for the value of the mortgages, and moved his family to Mobile, Alabama, where he worked as a full-time salesman for the insurance company. They stayed there about eight months, then moved very briefly to Pensacola, Florida, in the hope that sales would be better, then came back to Enterprise.

"My Dad was just about broke," explained Bill Amos. "There weren't any sales of life insurance; it was the heart of the Depression. He was able to scrape together, I believe, $500, and he had a cousin who had $500, so they went into the five and dime store business in Enterprise. Mother helped out in the store and so did I." As for John—he would have been about eight, and Bill twelve—"It was a little bit too early for him to do much work at that time."

Their father decided that there was too much competition in the area in and around Enterprise, and he started looking to open a similar store at another site. He finally settled on the town of Milton, in Santa Rosa County, Florida, which at the time had a population of about 1,500. They packed the fixtures and merchandise on a truck and started off.

"The day we got to Milton, you never saw such a rain in your life— several inches of rain an hour," Bill Amos recalled. "The townspeople pitched in to help unload the truck. My dad had his change from the store—about twenty-five dollars in change—and everybody who helped unload the truck stood in line, and he'd give them fifty cents until he ran out of money—kids and men, too, because money was hard to get. Paul and I both worked at the store, but John didn't like dime store work, and he worked at a newspaper and a theater."

"Times were hard," Bill Amos said, "But we never suffered. We always had everything we needed—not everything we *wanted*, but everything we *needed*. We had plenty to eat, and always had a maid;

we were paying her, I think, about two dollars a week. Mother had to work at the store." They also had a clerk in the store, who was paid a dollar a day, working from eight to six on week days and until midnight on Saturdays, because the workers in the nearby sawmill didn't get paid until eight o'clock on Saturday night and would come to Milton to do their shopping.

John described Milton at the time as having one cafe and several places that were called confectioneries; they sold such things as hot dogs, hamburgers, ice cream, and 3.2 beer. There were four major merchants. Next door to his father's store was a store owned by a man named Jacob Cohen.

"Dad and Jake had a long-standing—I wouldn't call it a rift, it was more of a—practical joke. There was plenty of room for both of them to park in the back alley, but Jake would park his car in front of Daddy's store so there'd be a parking space in front of his. And Daddy would watch until there was a vacancy in front of Jake's store, and he'd run around and park in front of Jake's store."

The first job John—who used to be called "Bev"—ever held was during that first summer, at the *Milton Gazette* where "I cleaned up the presses, distributed type. I spent weeks washing off ink that had been caked for years."

He worked for "a very busy, conservative gentleman, who put me to work at a dollar a week. But he forgot to pay me the first week, and the second week he gave me a dollar, saying, 'I'm just paying you fifty cents a week for the first two weeks because you are learning.' And I told him," John remembered, laughing, "'Well, if I learn that much the rest of the summer, I'll own the newspaper.'"

That Christmas, he bought a small, cast-iron press he saw advertised that would print three-by-five cards. "It cost twelve dollars-and-something, which was a lot of money when you made only a dollar a week. I remember going to an old gentleman who worked two days a week at the newspaper, and he helped me put my press together and showed me how to use it. I had fun with it, but I didn't try to sell anything. Then the next summer, or sometime thereafter—I'm not sure—I went to work for the local theater as usher and popcorn boy. I was paid three dollars a week."

One of the incidents he was to recall of his experiences as an usher involved the fact that the theater had no toilet.

16

"I was traipsing around one matinee afternoon with my flashlight when I saw this little streak of water coming down to the stage." He started trying to trace where it was coming from, when suddenly a boy sprang from the darkness and ran out to the street. "I didn't even see who it was. But it turned out his daddy had a grocery store and was a real tough hombre."

The following day when John came to work, the father was sitting outside the theater in his car. The father opened the door and asked him to get in.

"I got in and he closed the door and drove me out to the back end of the cemetery. I wasn't scared. I knew the family. I respected him. I always respected my elders, period. And he wasn't a criminal or anything."

What had happened was that the boy, who was about nine, had run all the way home, "just scared to death when he saw me with that flashlight. He told his daddy that I had hit him or slapped him or something. He didn't know if I was going to report it, and he was covering himself up. And of course his daddy was also incensed that we didn't have a toilet in the theater, and he should have been.

"When we got into the cemetery, he says, 'I'm going to give you a whipping.' It was in the days when you had fenders on automobiles, and he pulled off his belt—he was a man of 250 pounds—and he told me to lean over the fender. And I say, 'All right, I'm certainly not going to oppose you and I'm not even going to try to run. But I think in all fairness that I ought to tell you that you'd better kill me while you're at it and leave no traces, because if I get back home and tell my daddy, he's going to take his .38 and he's going to find you. And one of you is going to be a dead man.' He thought about that and then he says, 'I think that you've been scared enough.'

"Well, I never had been scared. I could take a whipping, and I knew he had better sense than to do anything. My daddy would have killed him. You didn't touch my daddy's dog or his 'young-uns'," John Amos recalled with a laugh. "You could come to him and report it and he'd take the appropriate action. But you didn't do it to us yourself unless you were the school principal."

The incident concluded with the man driving John back to the theater and letting him out. Later when John got home, he told his father what happened.

"Daddy's reaction," John continued, still laughing, was, "'Thank God.' So he didn't have to kill anyone."

But another similar incident was to follow. Amos senior believed in letting his boys fight their own battles, but nothing angered him more than bullies, particularly bullies his boys didn't have a chance against. While John was still working at the theater, he took another job in a dry-cleaning and pressing shop that was owned by the manager of the theater. One Saturday afternoon a tall, redheaded, freckled-faced "stud of the community," as John described him, came into the shop "about half full of beer," apparently looking for nothing more than trouble. He had about twenty-five years to John's twelve and was well over six feet.

For no reason other than he was drunk, he began cursing John. The shop owner, who was standing by, was too frightened to intervene. While "Red," as the other fellow was called, kept bellowing at John, gesturing menacingly, John swung at him, grazing a boil—a "rising," as John described it—on the fellow's neck. Red let out a roar, grabbed him up by the ankles and almost drowned him in a tub of bluing water. John managed to get away and ran, soaked, to his father's store.

"Daddy asked me what happened and I told him. Meanwhile, the theater manager used enough judgment to tell the guy, he said, 'Now, Red, if I were you, I would go to Sheriff Allen and ask him to lock me up until Mr. Amos cools down, because he'll shoot you like a dog wherever he can find you this afternoon.' And sure enough, Daddy had gone about a block when one of the deputy sheriffs stops him and says, 'Mr. Amos, we've got Red locked up now and you can go on about your business and there won't be any trouble.' Well, before the weekend was over, Red had written Daddy a note apologizing, and Daddy had called the county judge and asked him to turn him loose."

As someone asked John, in what had to be one of the greater understatements after hearing this story, "So everybody knew how your daddy felt about his boys?"

"Yes, sir," he responded laughing, "especially me, because I was the only one who ever got into trouble."

John, meanwhile, was interested in buying an old seven-by-eleven printing press, one of the presses he had been called on to clean at the *Milton Gazette*. He had wanted it almost from the time he had seen it. He couldn't see it costing much, but almost *anything* was more than he had. One day he was walking by the publisher's house when he saw him out in the yard. He approached him and asked him what he wanted for it.

"He said, 'Well, I'll take fifty dollars.' And I said, 'Could I buy it five dollars down and five dollars a month?' And he said, 'Yes, that sounds reasonable.'"

It took a couple of weeks, John recalled in his notes, to save the five dollars, and with the help of some friends he hauled away the press. Then with fifty dollars he borrowed from his brother Paul, he bought several cases of type and other supplies.

The first job he got was to print a circular for the theater where he worked. The publisher became upset when he saw it, because he was doing commercial printing as well. He contacted City Hall and demanded that John get a license, which was twenty-five dollars.

"Dad put up the money for the license and for a year or so I printed letterheads and envelopes for ministers—any little job I could get. I worked by myself with a little boy named Snooky.

"All this time I continued to work at the theater. And school work came very easy to me. For one thing, I was not a perfectionist. I wasn't working for straight A's and I could work at the theater until eleven at night and had no problems with school work."

The theater was part of a chain owned by a man named Fred T. McClendon. John Amos approached him about printing circulars for all of his fifteen theaters.

"He let me have the job, instructed all his managers to order from me instead of anyone else. Bill came in with me then. We went to the bank and borrowed three hundred dollars—of course, Daddy had to sign for us—and we bought an old twelve-by-eighteen press." With that they started a weekly newspaper.

Bill was seventeen and was just graduating from high school.

John was all of thirteen.

3

ENTERPRISE—THE BEGINNING

After hand-setting the type, they published the tabloid-sized paper in the basement of their father's store. John sold most of the advertising, while Bill did most of the printing.

"I covered the courthouse," John related, "and we got news from people who came into the store—everyone in the county came in at least once a month. And people would send us items about things going on in their communities and churches. I couldn't touch-type on a typewriter, so I would just compose my stories with the type itself—get a type case and start setting."

However, since Milton already had a flourishing paper, the two brothers decided they would do better to publish one for Jay, Florida, a town some thirty miles away that didn't have a paper. Though Jay had only about four hundred people, it was the center of a large farming community and had a consolidated school that was one of the largest in the county.

They began publishing the weekly *Jay Tribune* from Milton, but then decided that if they were going to have a paper in Jay they had better publish it there. Not only did they move to Jay, but they were so close a family that their parents did, too. Their father, who in the meantime had opened a second five and dime in Milton, opened another one in Jay. The brothers published the paper in back of the store.

At first they continued to hand-set the paper, hiring an old, former printer at ten dollars a week to help them. But the *Jay Tribune* was a larger operation than the one in Milton, and hand-setting it became too much of a chore. They decided to buy an old linotype machine, and Bill became a proficient linotypist.

John Amos recalled how he borrowed $750 from a multi-millionaire in Pensacola to purchase it. "I just went in and told him who I was and what I was doing. He was always gruff. 'How you ever gonna make any money out of a newspaper? How you ever going to pay me back?'—that kind of thing. But he always came through."

Later, as their business prospered, John went to him for a loan of $2,500 to buy a new linotype. "I'll never forget when I went to pay him back. I wrote him a check on our account in our local bank. And he looked at it and threw it back across the desk and said he wanted a check from a New York Exchange bank. I didn't know what a New York Exchange bank was, but I knew that the check I'd gotten from him had been on a local bank." And, in no way cowed, John told him exactly that, and the man took the check.

Furthermore, when his high school needed $500 to purchase uniforms for the band, John went to him—something no one else would have had the nerve to do—and got the money.

Unlike Bill, who had graduated by now, John still had the problem of how to fit in his life as a busy publisher, editor, reporter, and advertising salesman around his schoolwork. Somehow he arranged to have all his classes in the morning and to have two study hall periods in the afternoon and most—if not all—of the time, he simply left after the last class. But his mind and energies were more on the newspaper than on school. He dropped out in mid-term of his junior year.

Said Bill Amos, "He was so intense, so busy, he didn't have time for school."

John Amos was a full-time entrepreneur now. But one day he was to be a student again.

Donald Beck was a grade higher than John, and a neighbor of his in Jay. "They were very industrious people," he said of the Amoses. He and John became lifelong friends. Beck would eventually marry Bill Amos's wife's sister, Bea, and John would be the best man. And one day Beck would be an executive in John Amos's insurance company.

Beck, who worked as a pressman at the *Jay Tribune* for three dollars a week while going to school, told of another side of John as a teenager. Beck, whose father was a rural mail carrier, said that "John's dad and my daddy probably had the only two cars in town. We used to drive so fast, we're lucky we weren't killed. We drove like maniacs, and if we'd been *drinking* teenagers, we would never have lived through it. And the roads were horrible—just dirt and sand roads."

One night, John took the family car—a large, brand-new, yellow Oldsmobile—to go out on a date. When he came home he found his father waiting up for him. Paul Amos, recalling the incident, said that his father asked John, "Where's the car?"

"John said," Paul recounted, "'Well, Dad, I had a flat tire and I got someone else to bring me home.' And Dad said, 'Well, all right, we'll take care of it in the morning.' The next morning, Dad said, "'Bev, how flat is that tire on the car?' John answered, 'Well, it's pretty flat, Dad.' And Dad responded, 'Do you think it's flat enough that we need a wrecker?' John—who actually had run into a tree stump— said, 'Well, I think so, Dad.'"

His father had instinctively known it was a lot more than a flat tire.

John eventually got his own car—a small, old clunker—in exchange for some ads in the paper.

Recalled Donald Beck, "It wouldn't do but about 40 or 45 miles an hour, but we went to Mobile and Pensacola in it a lot of times. And when he'd ride it around in Jay on those sandy roads, one wheel would be in a rut, the other would be up, and a lot times the muffler would drag. So we'd pull the muffler off."

One night they were double-dating, with Beck driving, when they came to a steep embankment, Beck recalled. "John said, 'I dare you to drive off the road!' I'd have probably done it, too. He'd probably have done the same thing; we were just that foolish. But he no more had gotten it out of his mouth when all four wheels just bogged down in the sand, up to the axles. We were stuck. We couldn't get out, no way.

"By that time, we'd no more than pulled off the road when the sheriff came by and he asked what happened. And John just immediately spoke up. He told him, 'Oh, some guy came by with bright lights on and blinded us.' The sheriff said, 'What kind of car?' and John said, 'It was a black one.'

"The sheriff took off, trying to catch it. In a few minutes he came back and he said, 'Well, I couldn't find no car, but I'll help you all get out.'"

They used to have a lot of fun together, double-dating on many occasions. "But," Beck added, "John was usually too busy to have a good time. I never saw him ride a bicycle in my life. I rode a bicycle but I never saw him ride one. Never saw him skate or play ball, any of that. He talked business a lot of the time. He had an uncle who was a druggist and sold a cough syrup that everybody liked, and John wanted us to manufacture it out of my garage and sell it—go on the radio and advertise it. Another time he wanted me to get in the shoe business with him. He was always thinking."

After about a year and a half, John and Bill decided that the paper wasn't profitable enough in Jay. They began looking around for a larger town that didn't have a paper. They moved to Jacksonville, Florida, where they did typesetting for small papers while they continued looking for a town where they could publish their own paper. They settled on Auburndale, Florida. Bill had gotten married in the meantime, and John moved in with him and his wife, Olivia, a teacher.

"We were really doing well," John noted. In addition to putting out the paper, "We were doing a tremendous amount of printing for the packing houses—the orange packing houses, the grapefruit houses." The two brothers, with the help of their father, bought a bigger, more sophisticated press. But then came Pearl Harbor. Said John, "Bill volunteered within the first ten days or so and went into the Coast Guard, and I was left with it all. I managed to get a linotype operator and struggled through until the next summer when I became of military age. I leased the plant out and went home."

He tried to volunteer but found that he was ineligible because of his bad eye. "I went by bus to Washington to see a congressman who was a family friend. He got me examined by the Surgeon General of the Navy in the hope he could get me a waiver. But they would not waive it. So I caught a bus back home."

But then several months later, though he'd been unable to enlist, he was drafted into the army. He reported to Camp Blanding, where he was put on "limited service," which meant that he couldn't be sent into combat.

"They swore me in and sent me home for a week. When I reported back they really didn't have enough work for all of us to do. It was a case of getting your clothes and shots, things like that."

One afternoon he went to the office and asked if there was anything for him to do because, otherwise, he wanted to walk around the camp, just to see it.

"They said they didn't have anything for me that day. So I went straight to camp headquarters and made a call on the public relations officer, told him I wanted a job. My feeling," he recalled with a laugh years later, "was that if I was on limited service, I could 'limit' my service in Florida as easily as in Alaska or the Great Lakes or wherever. So he asked me to sit down and write a story. I wrote it and he said 'Okay.' He sent me to Personnel, and the next day I was transferred to public relations." John Amos then went on to tell a story of himself as a prankster.

While he was working in public relations, an order came through that everyone on limited service who hadn't had basic training had to have a week of it. "We had a captain who was very tolerant of the 'sad sacks,' which we really were. I remember one day we were on a hike to join a bivouac about five or ten miles away. It was hot in that Florida sun—*hot*—and I wasn't used to walking. I was used to riding or sitting. I saw an army carrier coming down the road, and I said to two boys alongside me, 'Now look, if I faint, you all can put me in that carrier— stop that carrier. So I fainted and they stopped the carrier. They were giving me water when the captain came up and said, 'Put him in that carrier.' So they put me in and got in with me. They drove us out to where we were going to camp for the night, and we put up our pup tents and waited for the rest of them to get there."

Not long afterwards, he was selected to be a guard in a nearby German prisoner of war camp. And there some of his prisoners were to get an example of his bent for "practical jokes." The prisoners kept making fun of him because he was short—about five-nine—and very thin; they would say things like, "If something happens you cannot do anything about it." One day he finally had enough—decided to show them what he could do if necessary—lined them up against a fence, raised his rifle, and shot in the air.

They did, as he was to relate, acquire respect for him.

But his service in the army wasn't to last the duration of the war.

"Word came through," he said, "that all who weren't fit for combat duty should be discharged unless they were in an acute position."

Before he was discharged, he had the good fortune to have an officer who liked him sit down with him and tell him that he ought to get on with his education.

That captain, John Amos acknowledged, had as much influence on his becoming a lawyer as did anyone else.

Determined to go to college, one of the first things he did after his discharge in 1943 was to make an appointment with the superintendent of the school district where he had dropped out of high school. Chances are the superintendent never met a better salesman in his life. The essence of what John Amos "sold" to the superintendent was that "I am much better off if you give me a diploma and I am able to go to college than if I just stay like this." The superintendent gave him an oral exam, and John got his equivalency diploma.

He went to a Methodist college first—Birmingham Southern—but after a semester, transferred to the University of Florida in Gainesville. After two semesters he transferred again, this time to the University of Miami, where he could get more credits to enter law school sooner.

Early one morning in 1945, soon after the start of summer school, he walked into his American History class and saw a girl with jet black hair sitting toward the back of the class. For some reason he hadn't noticed her before. He started to head to his regular seat when he saw that there was an empty chair right behind her. He took it, then kept staring at the back of her head. After a while he saw her head sag to the side; she'd fallen asleep.

He stretched out his leg and tapped his foot under her chair. Her head immediately snapped up. He saw her look all around in confusion, but then, suddenly aware of what happened, she turned and stared back at him.

He smiled. But she glared, then quickly turned away.

John Amos did not know it then, but he had just met Elena Diaz-Verson.

4

EARLY VENTURE

Elena Diaz-Verson had come to the University of Miami the year before, in 1944, as an exchange student from Cuba, the first exchange student at the University. Her father, Salvador Diaz-Verson, was a distinguished journalist and author who, several years earlier had also served for a time as Chief of the National Police; her mother, Teresa Baña Cancela, was manager of Columbia Pictures in Havana. Elena once described her family as "very idealistic." If anything, it was an understatement.

Her father's father was a journalist as well as a court clerk, his mother a poet. One of the bonds his parents shared, Salvador wrote in his book *One Man, One Battle*—he was the author of fifteen books— was a childhood "when Cuba was casting off its long Spanish tyranny to create a new Republic. Small wonder that they were born with Independence as their banner and Revolution as their beacon torch." His father, Salvador Diaz Rodriguez, "wrote exultantly of freedom in the newspaper *El Imparcial* where he worked." His mother, Lucila Verson Echemendia, though a daughter of ultra-aristocrats, "used to remind us all that one's name in a social register meant nothing unless it was earned by outstanding achievements She often impressed it upon us that the 'real' Cuban families had given their jewels and gold to buy arms for the revolution." Indeed, as a little girl she had won a poetry contest on the theme *If You Had Not Been Born in Cuba, In Which Country Would You Choose to Have been Born?* The title of her poem was HAD I NOT BEEN BORN IN CUBA, I WISH I HAD.

Elena, her first granddaughter, spent more time with her than did the other grandchildren, a lot of it, said Elena, "listening to stories about her brothers going to the war and fighting and eating rats because there was no food. She also taught me how to crochet and embroider. And most important, she taught me values."

For instance, recounted Elena, "There was a count who wanted to date me. He had been in Cuba for ages but he was still called a count. I was really excited that a count wanted to date me, but my grandmother said, 'That is ridiculous. Anybody who has a title of nobility all those years, you shouldn't even talk to him.' And she brought him down to earth, and I finally saw it and said, "Yes, that's ridiculous."

On the other hand, Elena's mother's father, José Baña Pose, had come from Spain to fight *against* the Cubans—"the last pearl in the crown of Spain." Afterwards he remained in Cuba and married Elena's maternal grandmother, who died when Elena's mother was only fourteen. Jose Baña Pose went off to became a school teacher in a poor rural area, inexplicably abandoning his two young daughters.

It was a tragedy that was to result in Elena's mother and father eventually meeting.

Elena's mother was placed in a home for girls that had been established by an American, Mrs. Janette Ryder, the wife of a San Francisco physician. She had started the home after a visit to Cuba, during which she had been appalled by the plight of abandoned children. In addition to the home, she started an animal humane society.

Elena's mother became Mrs. Ryder's favorite, and the two of them would get up at four in the morning to go to the various food distribution markets and distribute coffee and cake to the draymen in the hope they would treat their horses better.

Salvador Diaz-Verson met his wife-to-be, Teresa Baña Cancela, when he heard of what she and Mrs. Ryder were doing and he went to interview them for a story. They were married on October 9, 1923.

"My father," Elena said with a laugh, "was a very, very handsome man—and he knew it. Handsome and charming. When I was a little girl he would come to school to see me, and all the other little girls would be flirting with him, and it used to make me very mad that they would go for this 'old man.'"

Her mother became "good in business, while my father was a crusader and dreamer." And even though he was a successful, well-known investigative reporter, "my mother was always wishing he would just settle down to business. And she wouldn't go with him to some public functions."

As a result, since there was much they didn't have in common—the marriage would one day end in divorce—and since Elena was their only child, she became her mother and father's confidante. Even when she was a young girl, her father would often read to her what he had written and ask for her opinion.

"We were very, very close. He taught me how to write before I went to kindergarten. When I got to be a teenager and started reading love stories, he said, "That's not for you,' and he made me read the classics."

At one point when she was a child, her father had to flee Cuba for Spain because he was part of a plot against the dictator Batista, for whom he had served for a while as chief of police. It was a hard time for Elena and her mother, both financially and, of course, emotionally. For instance, as her father was to write years later, Elena couldn't even attend a school picnic she had had her heart set on because she didn't have the fifteen cents that it cost. And there was the time when she was on a school bus trip and "a spiteful child who knew that Elena's shoes were battered insisted that all the little girls show off their new footwear. Sick with shame, Elena hid her ill-shod feet under the bus seat. Joined by others as vicious as only small children can be, her tormentor pulled her feet forcibly into view to mock her worn slippers."

When her father was permitted to return to Cuba nine months later, the family's way of life improved dramatically.

Anita Stone, a lifelong friend of Elena's since the second grade—though Elena never let on to her or any of her other good friends the emotional torture she went through during those months her father was in exile—recalled her as "a dear, a very intelligent girl. I was always impressed with her intellectual ways since we were very little, and of course she was very much a part of her father's life and was very influenced by her father's relationship with the world. I found her very worldly since we were little, and so I looked up to her and learned a lot about channeling my own interests."

Elena was also fun-loving and daring, said Anita Stone. There was the time when they were both youngsters and were in downtown

Havana and Elena wanted to buy a certain candy, even though it meant they wouldn't have enough carfare home. And she couldn't be dissuaded. "Oh, it will work out," she said cheerfully. And sure enough, after she bought the candy, she told the conductor they had "lost" their money, and a man stepped forward and dug into his pocket for the rest of their fare.

Although the Diaz-Versons were Catholics, they had taken Elena out of Catholic school and placed her in a Methodist missionary school because she had come to them one day and told them she wanted to be a nun. They didn't want this for their only child. Then when she was old enough to go to high school, her father—a fervent anti-Communist who one day would flee Cuba when Castro came to power—made her go to an American-run school in Cuba, because he felt that Cuban high schools were hotbeds of radicalism. And since he felt that this was even more true of Cuban colleges—though he hated to see her leave Cuba—he encouraged her to go to an American college.

"I was very outspoken," she explained, "and he didn't want me getting in trouble with these people, didn't want me involved in politics."

Coming to the States was to be quite a change for her. Customs, of course, were so different. Whenever she had gone on a date in Cuba, for instance, she had always been chaperoned by her mother. And, also, she had never really been on her own before.

Though her eventual goal was to be a lawyer, she majored in journalism and languages at the University of Miami, where she also became a member of the debating team and worked on the school paper and joined a sorority. She lived in the dormitory and would ride her bike to and from her classes.

American History, which she took one semester in summer school, turned out to be a particular problem for her. Since she had had little—if any—grounding in it back in Cuba—for instance, she wasn't clear about who the Pilgrims were and if they had come over with Columbus—she was having a difficult time with it right from the beginning. Furthermore, the class was at seven in the morning, and since she would be up late studying, sometimes it was hard for her to stay awake.

And now, the one time she actually dozed off, here was this rude, *rude* fellow in back of her, actually kicking under her chair!

After a quick glare at him, she tried to concentrate on what the professor was saying. But it was hard to; she was angry, angry at herself for falling asleep, but mostly at whoever that person was behind her. Boys were so different in Cuba!

The next day she made sure to change her seat. But then to her astonishment she saw him enter the room just as class was about to begin, walk up the aisle, and take the seat right behind her!

She made up her mind not to give him the satisfaction of even a look. But the couple of times her glance went by him, he smiled pleasantly. Still, he wasn't "forward" in the sense of trying to catch up to her in an attempt to talk to her when she was leaving class. In his own way he seemed a little shy. All she knew of him was his name from the professor's having called on him a couple of times.

A few days later, as class was breaking up, the professor, Dr. Charlton Tebeau, called to her and asked her to wait.

"He told me he was afraid I wouldn't be able to pass, that I needed special tutoring. I said that sounded good, that I knew I needed it badly."

But then, to her dismay, he called John over and introduced him to her as a possible tutor.

"Oh, I was so mad," she remembered. "I said, 'Do I have to take the lessons?' Dr. Tebeau said, 'He's the best history student I have; he'll be able to help you.' And so I finally said to John, 'Okay, when do we start?' And he said, 'Tonight, I have made arrangements for such and such a time and at such an such a place in the school.'"

(Dr. Tebeau, however, was to remember this quite differently. "They say," he claimed, "I introduced them. I didn't introduce them, but I did say to John, 'John, there's a little Cuban girl over there who needs some help. Do her a big favor. Go cheer her up.'")

In any event, when they met that evening John's first word was such a friendly "hi" that she felt herself becoming at ease. He had come precisely on time. Indeed, if he had followed the pattern that he was to follow all his life, he had probably gotten to the building early and walked around until the exact minute. It was the first good look at him that she had permitted herself. A very thin young man, he probably weighed no more than 120 pounds, with a sensitive face and an easy smile. He was already showing strands of gray hair.

"Hi," he said again. He reached out his hand.

"Hello." She reached out hers.

They took chairs at a table, and he with his soft, Southern drawl, and she with her Cuban accent, began discussing the problems she was having.

"Well," he said, "let's first clear up this matter of the Pilgrims. "They did *not* come over with Columbus."

"*No?*"

"No. Now let's start from the beginning."

After a few evenings he asked if she would like to go to a nearby drugstore for a soda. One of the privileges her history professor had been able to obtain for her was that as long as she had a tutor she did not have to be in the dorm at the regular hour. And so going to the drugstore for sodas was a part of her "studying."

John Amos was hardly her first date since she had come to the college, but that first evening she saw something quite different in him from the other young American men she had met. As they sat there at the counter, barely touching his soda and occasionally lighting a cigarette (he was, she noticed for the first time, left-handed), he talked of things her other dates rarely if ever did.

"He was a young man," she said, "but he was not a young man like the others were, talking about movies and dances, things like that. He was not like the 'sophisticated' boys I'd been used to. And I loved that. He would talk about his family and about such things as social justice and what he would like to do to help people."

In the days that followed, one of the things they would talk about was their careers; he was going to practice law in Florida, and she was going to practice in Havana, and they would refer clients to each other, perhaps as partners.

"I don't know," he said once, very slowly, as if something deeply disturbing was on his mind. "I don't think my wife would like me being in practice with a beautiful young woman."

She stared at him, her heart sinking.

Married? He'd never said anything about being *married!*

But now, seeing the look on her face, he was smiling.

"Just kidding," he said. "Just kidding."

Though a part of her wanted to strangle him for teasing her, she was also suddenly aware of how very much she liked him. Not only did they begin to date, but he would write her letters, signing them "John Amos, M.C." The letters stood for "Member of Congress"; it was, he had told her, what he wanted to be.

Still, her upbringing and background were such that something that happened soon afterwards came as a surprise.

He had a car, and she asked him to teach her how to drive. Specifically, since he had said he wasn't a good dancer, Elena—who loved to dance—had put it this way: If he would teach her to drive, she would teach him how to dance.

On her first driving lesson, after having her watch him carefully, he let her take the wheel. She was doing very well when he told her to pull to the side of the street. She was just stepping on the clutch to change gear and to put on the brake, when he suddenly reached over and kissed her for the first time.

"It got me real angry. I didn't believe in kissing on dates unless you were engaged. I told him I was never going to see him again," she recalled. Then, smiling, "But I didn't tell him that I actually liked it. And that I *would* see him."

The University was so small at the time that soon afterwards it became obvious to just about everyone there that these were two young people in love. The school authorities felt so protective and responsible for this exchange student from Cuba that the Dean of Women called each of them in separately to ask if they were thinking of getting married.

"It was very awkward," Elena said. "John had told her he would like to marry me. I told her I thought so, but I had to talk to my mother and father. They were divorced by then.'

Before they could marry, John followed Cuban custom, where his father had to contact her father on his son's behalf. Her father came to Miami to meet John. Before Elena and John went to see him, said Elena, "Johnny asked me, 'Do I have to wear a necktie?' In Miami, nobody wore a necktie. I said, 'Yes, you have to wear a necktie and jacket.' And he had to borrow them because he didn't own any."

John and her father first had a private meeting, in which John—with another Cuban writer serving as translator—asked formally for

Elena's hand. Afterwards, with Elena serving as the translator now, they took a walk, talking about various subjects, and stopping once for waffles. Later, said Elena, "Daddy told us that water seeks its own level, that in spite of us having different religions, and Johnny being from a small town and I from a big city, we had a lot in common. He said he really thought that Johnny was more grown up than anybody I had dated. And he gave us his blessing. He and Johnny were to become very good friends."

John then spoke to her mother, who was still in Cuba, by phone.

Even Dr. Tebeau, their history professor, came through in a caring way. Hearing that they were going to be married, and realizing they would need time to work on the arrangements, he gave Elena her examination before the wedding. And she passed.

Although Elena wanted to be married in a Catholic church, her priest would not preside over it since she was marrying a Protestant. Since John was a Methodist, she and John were married in the First Methodist Church of Coral Gables. They were such a popular couple that all of the faculty at the University, and just about all of the students, attended.

"Her father spoke Spanish and his father spoke English," Dr. Tebeau recalled. "They communicated with each other without saying a word. They were both ecstatic."

The wedding was on September 23, 1945. This was just six weeks after they had met.

5

ELENA

Before the fall semester started, John and Elena went on a honeymoon to Lookout Mountain in Chattanooga, Tennessee. When they came back they "inherited" an apartment that his brother Bill, who was in the Coast Guard, and Olivia Amos had in Miami.

"It was an efficiency apartment with a Murphy bed," Elena recalled happily. "I had never seen a bed that came out of the wall. It was like something from the Funny Papers. I loved that apartment; it was my little doll house. But at first I didn't know anything about house-keeping. And cooking especially scared me to death. Just about all I knew how to make was salads and Cuban desserts."

The first meal she cooked, she would always remember, came from a recipe she found for barbecued chicken, which she served with rice and "beans I got from a can." John helped teach her how to cook and bake, as did Mrs. Tebeau, their history professor's wife. The Tebeaus, with whom they were always to be friends, were their first dinner guests; they ate on a card table. "We had pork chops, mashed potatoes, peas, and applesauce," Elena recalled. Soon that little apartment was to see many parties, many gatherings, as their friends from school came to look on it as almost a second home. At the same time, John and Elena made up their minds that being married wasn't going to interfere with their studies and school activities, such as Elena's sorority, or John's fraternity. If anything, their grades improved.

Elena's father paid for her tuition and books, and John was going to school on the GI-Bill and receiving some help from his father, but they had to supplement their income. This was partly a result of their own joy of life together. They often wouldn't think of money until they *had* to think of it. On at least one occasion, a friend recalled, John would find himself with just five cents, enough only to pay for one bus fare to school, and so after he and Elena boarded the bus he would pretend—without letting Elena know the truth—that he had forgotten a book at home, and he would get off and then run to school. Once, with a week to go before their next check, they had to eat rice pudding for a week. "I haven't been able to eat rice pudding since," Elena said.

"John," reflected his younger brother Paul in later years, "was an individual who never worried about money. He had such confidence in his ability to make money that he felt there was no need for him to worry about spending money. He always told me, 'You're never going to save yourself out of debt. You're going to have to work hard enough to earn enough so that you can live the style of life you want to live.'"

Before they had gotten married, John had come up with an idea for bringing in some money. He had learned from Elena and other girls in her dormitory that they were often hungry in the evening but were not allowed to leave the dorm after eight o'clock. He began selling hamburgers under the windows, either tossing the wrapped, hot hamburgers up to them or sending them up on baskets they lowered on string. Now that he was married to Elena, he got permission from the housemother to come into the dormitory itself and sell sandwiches which he and Elena made.

John ran for president of the student body, but lost. But he had the wonderful ability of not lingering over negatives. His mind kept working on possible projects. He was always trying to think of a publication he might start—his father, with John and Bill's permission, had sold their last newspaper—and he kept trying out his ideas on Elena.

One day he told her that he would like to publish a book of the late Franklin D. Roosevelt's "Fireside Chats"—the weekly radio talks the president would give to the nation.

"Let me tell you why I'm thinking of it now," he went on excitedly. He had learned that Roosevelt's vice president, Henry Wallace, was visiting in Miami, and John thought that Wallace would be the perfect person to write the Introduction. "I know which hotel he's staying at, and I'm thinking of sending him a letter. What do you think?"

As usual, Elena encouraged him, though it was almost impossible to believe that the busy, former vice president of the United States would bother with a project by a twenty-year-old college student.

John immediately sat down and began composing the letter. He wrote several drafts, reading each one to her until he finally had one that satisfied them both.

"I'll be right back," he said. He was going off and leaving it at the desk of Wallace's hotel.

A few days later, early on a Sunday morning, they were still in bed when a knock came on their door. John got out in his pajamas and went to the door just to peer out and see who it was. In bed, Elena could hear voices, but she couldn't recognize the other person's voice.

John was back in about five minutes. His eyes were wide.

"You'll never believe who that was," he said, his voice filled with awe.

"Tell me."

"*Wallace*. Vice President *Wallace*."

"Johnny," she said chidingly. She always called him Johnny, but now it was with a "please don't try to fool me" tone He always joked and teased so much that you just never knew.

"I'm *telling* you," he said. He sat down on the side of the bed, his eyes still wide, shaking his head. She immediately sat up straighter. There was no mistaking that look now.

"He told me he can't do it," John went on, but it was as though *that* really didn't matter anymore, that the important thing was that the vice president had actually come to their door. "He said he was sorry and appreciated my thinking of him, and he just wanted to return my letter."

And Vice President Wallace had said one other thing to him. It was something John Amos seemed to have learned on his own when he was only a boy.

"Keep thinking big," Vice President Wallace had said.

John didn't pursue the book of Fireside Chats any further, but it was an early example of something he was to have phenomenal success with later, an example of the accessibility of people in high government places to someone with ideas and drive.

Years later John Amos was to write of a family "clan" reunion—of family members he himself had not seen in years—that took place about this same time. It was held at Claybank Church, in Alabama, a log church on whose grounds the various family groups set the contents of their picnic baskets on "table cloths lying on the pine straw covered ground." He remembered "as if it were yesterday," he continued, "the large crowds, the hugs and kisses, the 'my, hasn't this child growns,' the children frolicking, the young blades 'courting' an older cousin...."

It was a reunion, too, where two far different cultures met.

"I came," John Amos wrote, "to show off my beautiful Cuban bride to the clan."

The following summer, deciding to vacation in Havana, John and Elena sublet their apartment to a woman for the time they would be away. John fell in love with Cuba. When they came back, however, the woman they had rented to would not move. Because of housing laws resulting from the war, it was hard to evict tenants, and it would have taken John and Elena months and far more money than they had to try to fight it. Furthermore, because Miami was full of tourists, they could not find a place to live in the area that they could afford. They decided to return to Havana, where they remained for about a year. During this time, John started a five and dime with one of Elena's uncles, but it was not successful.

Broke, they returned to the States and went to live with his parents in Milton, where Elena worked in one of their dime stores and John taught civics at the high school. They decided that since she was a Catholic and he a Methodist, they should both be in one church together. There was no Catholic church in Milton, so they visited all the other churches and found that they both felt "at home" in the Episcopal church.

They weren't to stay in Milton beyond the year, however—John was unhappy teaching and he and Elena were eager to continue their education. They decided to go to the University of Florida, in Gainesville, where John would enter law school and Elena would finish her last semester in college before joining John in law school.

They moved into a two-room apartment on the second floor of a duplex that John's father had found for them. They had to share the kitchen and bathroom with another tenant, a retired Navy man, and almost immediately it became a problem.

"I am a morning person," Elena explained, "and, anyway, I always had school early. This man," she laughed, "would say we walked like elephants at six, seven o'clock in the morning. He was so unhappy. Then we found out that instead of paying half the utilities, we were actually paying the whole thing. He denied it, and of course we couldn't afford it. So we started looking where to move."

They rented a house near the University. "It had a kitchen, a dining room, a little yard, and two extra rooms we could rent to students."

When one of the students they rented to moved out, however, they rented the room to a traveling salesman and his wife. But it immediately turned out to be a mistake. The couple would get drunk and fight most of the time. John and Elena managed to get rid of them, and swore that from then on they would rent only to students. Elena, meanwhile, joined John in law school.

"Our home became a place everyone would come to." She had become a good cook, but the thing she would remember most of all about the parties they gave: "I love to bake, and I would bake cakes, and people would bring over steaks and wine. We had such wonderful times."

One of their friends was a former faculty member of the law school whose wife didn't let him drink. So he would keep his whiskey at John and Elena's, and would stop over not only for a drink, but for the conversation and food as well.

"He would also help us cram for exams," Elena said. "He would hold 'class' for six or seven or us, and he would make everything so clear."

John, meanwhile, the young man who wrote M.C. on his letters to Elena, took his first step in national politics in 1948, when he campaigned for conservative Senator Strom Thurmond in his run for the presidency.

As John Amos was to recall, "Basically, I have always been a liberal. I have always believed firmly and absolutely for civil rights. But this was just a lark. It was a last chance to holler, 'Dixie!'"

There was to be a big rally for Thurmond in Gainesville, where General Jonathan Wainwright, the "hero of Corregidor," was to be the main speaker.

"Johnny wanted me to be on the platform," recalled Elena, "but I couldn't go because my dresses were out of fashion. Women were wearing short skirts, and all I had were long ones."

She stayed home doing schoolwork, when about five or six o'clock that evening she heard a key in the front door. She got up to greet John and there, standing next to John, was General Wainwright. John had brought him home to have something to eat before he left town.

"Everyone in Gainesville would have loved to have the General in their home," said Elena. "And here he comes to my house, with nothing in there. We didn't even have plates or silverware that matched."

But she did manage to make something for him.

"This was something Johnny never stopped doing," she related. "No matter where we were or whatever was happening, he always enjoyed having people in. Sometimes when I wouldn't want to have somebody over, just wanted to be alone, he said, 'Well, I have it in my blood.' And he told me the story of his grandfather who would always yell out, 'All who ain't go someplace to go, come to my house for dinner.'"

When John graduated from law school, Elena needed only six more hours of credit to get her law degree. But she saw how anxious he was to get started in practice—and to find an area of the country to practice in. She gave up law to help him.

Over the years, many people asked her why she did this.

She always said, simply, to be with him, to help him get started in his career.

It was as though that should be very easy to understand.

"I've always been myself, though I didn't show it," she once explained. "I've always had a mind of my own. I wasn't in John's *shadow*. We were always *together*. Getting a law degree didn't matter that much. And we do things that matter."

6

THE NEW LIFE

They drove through the Florida Panhandle looking for a community where they would like to live and which would offer him a good opportunity to establish a practice. Though John felt the need to explore someplace new, he wanted to be close enough to his family in Milton so that he would still be able to get referrals from there. He and Elena finally settled on the small "frontier-type" seaside town of Fort Walton Beach in Okaloosa County, on the Gulf of Mexico.

It was a town of about five hundred people, with mostly dirt and sand roads, and without sidewalks. There were only two paved streets, Highway 98 running east and west and Elgin Parkway north and south, a two-lane road that connected the town with nearby Elgin Air Force Base. The Air Base was the town's main "industry." According to a neighbor, Margaret Reese—who lived there before the Amoses came—wild goats and cows from outlying farms used to wander through the streets until the town put up special kinds of gates to keep them out. Although there were places in town where people could buy such household things as groceries, up until just about the time John and Elena arrived the townsfolk had to go to Pensacola, about forty miles away, to do "real shopping," such as for clothes. At one time it had been a harbor for rumrunners. Also adding to the frontier atmosphere, though gambling was illegal in the state, Fort Walton at that time had open gambling, with slot machines in just about every place from filling stations to launderettes as well as other types of gambling in two beautiful supper clubs. Although it was a tourist town, it did not attract the richer tourists as Miami did. Though the beach was beautiful, the housing was crude and basic.

John Amos saw a future here. He was the only lawyer in town and could draw clients from Eglin Air Base and from other counties. Elena fell in love with it for another reason.

"Being from an island," she recalled, "I was so glad to see water again. It was like a little bit of Cuba. I thought I could never live where I wouldn't be able to see the water and hear the sounds."

With a $700 loan from John's father to help set them up, they found an office for John above an old ice and fish house. They moved in on February 7, 1949. That same day, even as they were putting away John's books and were literally in the process of putting out his shingle, John got his first case. A man who had heard that a lawyer was in town had rushed to the office to file for bankruptcy. Soon after that a woman came in to have John write her will.

"I was the typist," recalled Elena, "and I had no professional typing experience. I did it with one finger, two fingers. I got so many things wrong I had to do the will fourteen times." In the meantime, they had just rented a house in town, and while she was struggling with the will, John leaned over to say something to her. She would remember, smiling, how he said "in that teasing way of his—it got me so *mad*—'After you finish the will, you can start unpacking and getting the house ready for people.'"

They rented a little cottage from an elderly man everyone called "Captain." "He had a lot of property," said Elena, "and I wondered how a sea captain could have accumulated that much. Then I learned it had nothing to do with him being a captain. He *wasn't* a captain. An elderly person they respected was always called 'Captain.'"

She learned soon afterwards how much they respected John and her. "We had one car, an old one that was always breaking down. I remember having it pushed to a service station, where someone asked me, 'Are you Judge Amos's wife?' I said, 'No, my husband is not a judge. He just got out of law school.' They were just very nice."

The two of them grew to love the area more and more, one of the most beautiful places being the fishing village of Destin, about six miles away, where they would go to buy fresh fish off the ships at the docks.

Elena worked full-time in the office. "I was the telephone operator, filing clerk, cleaning woman, stenographer, legal researcher—everything. At the beginning when we got there, it was a community where just about the only other people who had ever been to college—or even graduated from high school—were the doctor and priest. And we were very, very close to them."

But she made other friends—lots of them—easily. Margaret Reese, for instance, would remember how much she enjoyed playing bridge with Elena, who loved bridge, and what a good hostess she was. "I remember Elena barbecued a whole pig. It had the apple in its mouth and everything. She was very traditional, a good hostess. And a very unselfish person. She always thought of the other person, would do anything to make anybody happy. I believe if I was to call Elena right now and say, 'Hey, I need some help,' she'd come to me or do something."

Elena also met a woman very early on who, in Elena's words, "was the wealthiest woman in Fort Walton, and she kind of protected me and I became her protégé." Elena came to know her through having attended the Methodist school in Cuba. The sister of one of the missionaries at the school was this woman's secretary. The woman who took Elena under her wing "was a beautiful, lovely lady with a lot of business interests. She introduced me to all her friends, and her business gave Johnny a good entrée in the community."

John's practice not only began growing, but even at his young age—he was still in his mid-twenties—he *looked* the part of a successful lawyer. He was becoming prematurely gray and had taken to wearing white tropical suits—which he was always to wear the rest of his life, except in bitter cold weather—but this was not, as some people might have thought, an affectation; he simply *enjoyed* wearing white.

Soon after John and Elena came to Fort Walton, he was appointed City Attorney for the nearby city of Niceville. He then became City Attorney for a number of other municipalities in the Panhandle, as well as associate City Attorney for Fort Walton. One of the first things he was called on to do was go to New York to complete a bond issue that had been stalled and was, therefore, preventing Niceville from establishing a water system.

His associate City Attorney for Fort Walton was, according to John, "an elderly, very fine, aristocratic lawyer from North Florida" who had represented Fort Walton "from the day they started. I don't know that he ever charged them. So they named me Associate City Attorney to keep from appearing ungrateful to him. But he and I never had any problems. We always worked very closely together."

John recalled how the elderly man used to call him "Amos." In the South in those days, as John Amos would tell it, you didn't call a person by his last name unless you didn't feel close enough to call him by his first name, and didn't respect him enough to call him "Mister."

"One day he and I were going to Tallahassee on a case soon after he and I became joint counselors for the City. As I said, he was very aristocratic. We were driving and he said something about Amos this or that, and I said, 'Would you mind pulling off the road?' And he says, 'What's the matter?' And I say, 'Well, it's obvious that you and I come from different sides of the track. You can't call me 'Amos.' You may either call me 'John' or you may call me 'Mr. Amos.' You may take your choice. And he said," related John with a laugh, "'Let's drive on, John.'"

But that wasn't the end of the story. As they were driving, John remembered thinking that "though I was not jealous of him, I just wondered when I was going to come into it...on my own, you know? And I thought, 'Well, he's seventy-five; he can't live forever.' But on this trip to Tallahassee that day, he told me he had to get back because he had promised to drive his mother to the mountains in North Carolina that weekend. So I came home"—and again John Amos was laughing— "and I told Elena, 'Elena, we're going to have to move and find us another place to practice law. This man is going to bury both of us.'"

John began getting cases of almost every kind—criminal, divorce, custody, business matters. Although John and Elena never had anything to do with the gambling, a number of gamblers came to him to represent them. But as he told the gamblers, he hoped to enter public life one day, and so he would represent them on anything other than gambling—divorces, legitimate business problems, and so forth. He became partners with another lawyer, Frank Hendrix. Also, whenever he thought it beneficial, he would work with co-counsel from Pensacola, specialists who not only could help him do the best for his clients, but also enabled him to charge higher fees.

"He got experience in everything," said Elena. "He found out early on that he was an important part of the community.

People instinctively liked and trusted him. And it happened almost immediately. For example, right after they had moved to Fort Walton

Beach, John had to try a case in the thriving town of De Funiak Springs, some forty miles away. He hadn't even had time to buy a briefcase, so he walked into the courtroom with a shoe box under his arm. When John's case was called, the judge stared at this skinny young man dressed in white, then stared at the shoe box, then back at his face.

"What's that?" he asked, pointing at the shoe box.

"This is my briefcase. My papers are in here."

The judge frowned slightly, but then his face broke into a smile. He told John he would like him to help him prepare his own papers. A little later, when John asked the judge why he had selected him out of all the other lawyers in and around De Funiak Springs, the judge said, "Because you're going to go places. You're going to get ahead."

Because for a long while he was the only lawyer in Fort Walton Beach, John was constantly referred cases that were already "lost"— cases for which it was literally impossible to get an acquittal. For example, there was the case of an Asian man who drowned one of his children in a toilet, while supposedly intending "only" to discipline him. John tried the case without a jury, hoping that the judge would better understand what might be mitigating circumstances—that the man was mentally deficient and that both he and his wife had horrendous childhoods, had many children, and were expecting another. The man received a very light sentence of perhaps two years, though later on he wrote to John that he would have been acquitted if he had had a jury!

But though the defendant did not appreciate him, the fact that it had been an "impossible" case helped establish John's reputation.

John was also forever volunteering to help defendants throughout the county who showed up in court without representation. He never stopped this, even when his growing private practice required all his time. And sometimes the advice he gave was quite "practical" in that it had nothing to do with his legal background, but rather with his down-to-earth, rural Southern background.

One day, for example, a very old man who owned several acres of timber came to him with a problem. He had signed an agreement with his neighbor in an attempt to settle some problems they had been having concerning their adjoining properties. But despite the agreement, the neighbor was still fighting with him.

"I don't know what to do," the old man said. "I just want to stop it, but I don't know how."

"I'll tell you what to do. You got yourself a knife? A whittling knife?"

"Sure," the man said, puzzledly.

"Well, John told him, the next time your neighbor comes over to quarrel with you, just take out your knife and start whittling on something, whittling slowly. But make sure," continued John, who had always carried a pocketknife since he was a little boy, "make sure you look him long and hard in the eyes as you're whittling."

Several months later, the old man was back. A couple months prior to this, his neighbor had come over and begun verbally abusing him—until the old man took out his knife and, with his eyes hard on the man, began opening and closing the blade. Then he started to whittle with deliberate slowness. His neighbor hadn't been back since.

"From now on," the old man said, "you're gonna be handling all my legal work."

"They were exciting times," said Elena. "It was an exciting place to be. I met people I would ordinarily never have met."

She became particularly close to many of the fishermen at Destin who "would get drunk and pawn their nets and just come over and get money from me to get their nets back. They were very, very sad cases, and I had more than they had."

There was also a small number of blacks, most of them from Birmingham, Alabama, who worked for people in the community and whose welfare Elena became deeply interested in. When she became busier in John's office, she hired one of the women as a maid.

One day a warning came through that a potentially lethal hurricane was heading their way.

"People around there," she said, "would have big 'hurricane parties.' But I came from Havana where a hurricane was a very, very serious thing. They weren't fun at all."

Just before the hurricane broke, her maid showed up at her door with a large group of her friends. Knowing Elena would welcome them, she had brought them because Elena's house was sturdier.

"Also, some of their husbands were in jail," Elena explained, "and they were afraid for them, that the jail wasn't safe either. And they wanted to be with their husbands. So I asked Johnny to go and get them out under his custody. He did. People were sleeping everywhere—the floor, the beds, the chairs. When the hurricane hit, it *really* hit, breaking windows, tearing things away. And those people were wonderful helpers."

One of the women also came to him for a divorce, a case that opened his eyes wider to what had been going on in this community without a lawyer.

"Oh, Mr. Amos," the woman said, "I want to get a divorce and the sheriff doesn't give divorces any more."

"The *sheriff*?" he repeated. "The sheriff gave divorces? Did he ever give you one before?"

"Yes, sir."

"How did he 'give divorces?'"

"Oh," she said, "he got a broom and I would jump the broom and my husband would jump the broom. Then the sheriff would say, 'You stay away from him, and you stay away from her, and now you are divorced and I don't want to see you any more.'"

John said, trying not to show his amazement, "How would you get married?"

"The sheriff. He would ask our names and then he would just hold our hands and say, 'Now you're man and wife and behave like that.'"

"Did he charge you for that?"

"No, sir. There was no charge."

She joined the many other clients John Amos didn't charge.

John and Elena worked so closely in his office that they established a rule that, because they were together most of the day, they would never talk business at home (nor would they ever go to bed mad at each other). But some of his experiences were hard *not* to talk about.

There was the time he was in court, waiting for the case he was handling to be called, when suddenly he saw a buzz of activity a few feet a way. Men were gathered in a small, tight circle, talking quickly to each other. Then a few of them started to break away, to hurry to the door.

"What's the matter?" John demanded. "What's happening?"

"Some black kid—the boys're goin' after him!" one of them exclaimed.

What had happened was that a boy of about twelve had just pulled into a nearby service station in a Cadillac with a Louisiana license. He had gotten some gas, then sped away.

Knowing that chances were that this would end up in a lynching, John immediately ran to the service station, where a large group of men were clustered. They were about to split up and get into their cars when John ran up.

"Hold it there, hear?" he cried. "You just hold it!"

The men whirled at this young figure in white.

"Don' you try interferin'," one said. "Stay outta this. He stole gas, and he sure as hell musta stole that Cadillac!"

"You just hear me," John shouted. "Anyone touches that boy, I swear I'll see they get the electric chair! Let the authorities get him!"

But some of the men still hurried to their cars and sped off. John ran to the phone in the service station and called the State Police, hoping they would find the boy first. He then put through a fast call to his closest friend in town, the physician, Dr. White.

They began contacting surrounding police departments, then hospitals in the hope that boy had been brought to one of them—alive. After about an hour they located him in a small hospital in the county. He had been shot, but was still alive.

But John and the doctor were aware that this didn't mean a lynch mob would let him stay alive. The men could rush into the hospital or might even grab him whenever the local police tried to take him from the hospital to jail.

With the cooperation of some of the police, John and the doctor smuggled him to safety in a large hospital in another section of the county.

Another time, John was riding through the countryside when he saw about a half dozen men running with guns along the highway. He pulled in front of them and jumped out.

"What's going on?"

They stopped, one of them yelling, "Mr. Smith's nigger just took off for Alabama!"

"What do you mean 'Mr. Smith's nigger?'" He was dumbfounded. It was as though they were back in the days of slavery.

"Mr. Smith's nigger!" he repeated. The men stared at John as if he were from a different planet. "I'm tellin' you, he just took off for Alabama!"

John knew the only way he could reach them was to use their vernacular. "How can anyone be anyone's nigger anymore?"

"He was from Alabama and the governor give him to Mr. Smith. And he just took off."

In an instant, something registered with John. He had heard of this happening, but had never actually experienced it firsthand until now.

In those days, in parts of the South, a man serving a long prison sentence could be released in care of a family and serve as their house servant.

"He jus' now run off! He's somewhere ahead!"

John tried to think fast. If only he could delay them...

"You know," he warned, "if you do something to him, if you kill him, you can go to the chair."

They looked at him as if he were crazy, as if they were thinking, Go to the chair for *that*?

"You jus' min' your own business," one of them threatened.

"I'm telling that you can go to the chair. If you kill that man, I'm gonna say I warned you! Why don't you just call the police?"

"And I'm gonna say to you right now, Mister, you're looking for a lot of trouble!"

"And I'm saying to you, "Call the police.' You think you can't get the electric chair? I'm telling you, things are changing. You can!"

He had no real hope of stopping them—just *delaying* them. Each moment that passed, he kept thinking, was a precious one for the fugitive who would have no chance if these people caught him.

The men seemed confused. Then, with quick last looks of anger, they began running down the highway again.

But as John was to learn later, he apparently *had* given the fugitive enough time. They did not catch up to him.

Another incident, a different kind this time, took place when his physician friend, Dr. White, called John to tell him that he had just received a phone call at his clinic from a man he felt might be an impostor. The caller, who said he was passing through Fort Walton, claimed he had heard so many good things about the doctor that he would like to visit him and see his clinic and his operating room. But there was something in the way the man spoke that made the doctor feel he might be a con artist. And so he had stalled him and was calling John to see if he had any ideas about how to check on him that wouldn't be an affront to the man if, in fact, he turned out to be a physician. The man was calling him back soon.

John gave it some thought, then came up with an idea that fit right in with his own sense of fun and adventure.

He told the doctor to say that it was impossible to meet with him today, but that maybe they could get together the following day. In the meantime, the doctor should ask him if he'd like to have dinner that evening with a good friend of his, John Amos.

John met the man at a local club and they sat at the bar. Suddenly, while they were chatting, John bent over. When the other asked what was wrong, he said he was in terrible pain.

"I-I'm sure I have appendicitis," he muttered.

When the man asked where it hurt and what other symptoms he might have, John mentioned a number of things, almost none of which, he knew, were symptoms of appendicitis.

But the man didn't need more than that to make a diagnosis.

"There's no question. You're right," he said. He would contact the hospital, he said, and if they would give him operating room privileges, he would operate that night.

Almost "miraculously" John found himself getting better. And, though the man didn't know yet, he was just beginning to get in deep trouble.

John had the authorities investigate the man—and word quickly came back. He had a record in another town of passing a bad check, using the name of a doctor he had met there.

But this was just the beginning of what would become an even more bizarre story.

John saw to it that he was in court when the impostor, who had been kept in jail after failing to meet bail, came to trial. John looked on as the man, who had no attorney, pleaded guilty. At that, John immediately stood up.

"I would like to represent this man, your Honor. And I want to change his plea."

While the judge looked on with astonishment, John made a plea for mercy, saying that this was the man's first offense and that he had suffered enough. And the judge, so moved by John's eloquence, let him go.

But this was still not the end.

One day several months later, John was in the same courtroom, awaiting the start of another case, when he was startled to see the same man brought up on a far more serious charge. As the man stood before the bench, the judge's eyes sought out John, then looked back at the defendant.

"I believe," the judge said, "that Mr. Amos is your attorney."

John Amos quickly rose to his feet.

"No, your Honor," he said, "I've never seen him before in my life."

And that was that.

He was a deeply compassionate man who gave people more than one chance—if he thought more than one chance would help them.

Another example, not only of compassion but of a kind of fearlessness, was the case of a woman in a nearby town. A young mother of two children, she had served as the bank's bookkeeper for several years even though she did not have training. During that time, the officials of the bank apparently never examined the books carefully. When they finally did, they found that thousands of dollars were missing. Suddenly, according to headlines and peoples' mouths, she was no longer that lovely young woman whom everyone knew and liked, but simply a crook.

It was a case that attracted John, that not only called on all of his legal acumen, but his compassion as well. On the surface, it was a crime without a defense. But to John the defense was clear. Basically, the officials of the bank, brilliant business-men, had hired someone who was untrained, and then had not practiced the most common-sense measures to keep an eye on what she was doing, or even to audit the books thoroughly. And there she was, with two children to look after and all this money all around her.

His course of attack was to cross-examine the bank officials to bring out their carelessness, and all the while he would have the defendant bringing her children to court every day, so that they would always be there for the jurors to see and sympathize with.

At the same time, since this was a case that drew wide attention, before he called the bank officials to the stand, he spoke with a number of other officials of the bank as well as local businessmen who were not directly involved in the case. He knew that his defense would be so harsh that it might bring him enemies in the business community—something that, as an attorney, he could hardly afford to do.

He told these other people, in brief, that it would be a good idea if they were not in the courtroom when he conducted his cross-examination.

"You're not going to like what I have to say, so my advice to you is that you don't stay around for it."

The trial went on—and John Amos went on to win an acquittal.

Another case took even more courage, since it not only involved a threat against him, but also set him up against the vested gambling interests in Fort Walton.

Having been arrested for resisting arrest, a major in the Army contacted John from the local jail. He had been with a male friend of his in the gambling room of one of the clubs. When he saw that his friend was losing his entire paycheck, the major tried to talk him into leaving. The friend put up an argument, but the major still tried to get him out of there, at which time an officer arrested him, claiming the major had put up a struggle.

One of the things that drew John to the case was that the major would lose his West Point commission if convicted of a felony.

Although, according to Elena, gambling was as "visible" as it could possibly be in the area, at the same time it was "invisible." It was supposed to be something no one "mentioned" out loud—certainly not in a court of law. Furthermore, when anyone was arrested, say, for a brawl or drunkenness in a gambling room, the police might put that person in jail, but then they would quietly release the prisoner.

Afraid for the major's commission, and angered at the injustice of the arrest, John went straight to the sheriff's home. He told him that not only did he want the major out of jail, but that "I'm going to start this case right in the gambling room where it began."

The sheriff frowned. He knew what John meant by starting the case "right in the gambling room." John wasn't about to hide where the arrest took place; he was going to say the "unmentionable" word in a courtroom, was going to describe what the judge knew was going on, but didn't want to hear— "gambling."

The sheriff said, "You got better sense than to do something like that."

"Do I?"

In the days that followed after the major's release and the time of the hearing, John heard several warnings from friends: "You're foolish if you go ahead with it." "I wouldn't if I were you."

No one spelled out for him what would happen if he did, whether it meant he would be in physical danger, or that he could simply forget about maintaining a flourishing practice in the area. Word that kept coming back to the Amoses was, "He's not going to last here long. He won't play ball." But as John told Elena, "I want to live my whole life in this community, but I want to live it honestly."

He went ahead with the case

In addition to being a West Point graduate, the major had volunteered to fight in the Spanish Civil War, had been a prisoner there and undergone horrors. John related it to the jury with subdued eloquence. He knew that the facts themselves were eloquent enough, and the major was acquitted.

The following day, the sheriff came to his office. John had no idea what he wanted. It could mean anything, something bad, something—

The sheriff stuck out his hand.

"I want to be your friend," he said. "And I'm going to send you clients."

One day in 1952 John told Elena he was considering running for state's attorney of a four-county area of Florida that included Fort Walton Beach and Pensacola. John would always talk over his plans and projects with her as they sat together at the kitchen table. It wasn't that he felt he needed her permission. If his mind was made up on something, he would go ahead with it anyway. He was, and always would be, an "idea man." Once he had thought things out, he never hesitated in making a decision. But she was his sounding board.

She and John not only shared everything with each other, but there was even a sense of something "lacking" when they were temporarily apart. As John once put it, "I don't necessarily want to spend twenty-four hours a day talking to Elena, but I want to know she's on the couch asleep in the next room or in her bedroom. I just want her within hollering distance."

So it was not that he was asking her permission to run for office, or that he doubted for an instant what her answer would be. She wanted for him what *he* wanted. And state's attorney could be the beginning to the governership, the senate...

One of the biggest obstacles to his winning, they realized, was that one of his two opponents was the son-in-law of a powerful congressman.

John immediately called on his friend from his teen years, Donald Beck. And Beck, who was working for a railroad, didn't hesitate. He came down and headed up the campaign in Pensacola, going from house to house to solicit votes. Elena knocked on doors too, sometimes each of them working a different side of the same street.

The night of the election, when the last of the votes seemed to have come in, he went to bed thinking he had lost by twelve votes. Elena couldn't sleep at all. Then at about five-thirty in the morning, he received a call from a newscaster that he was now three votes ahead.

"He had gone to sleep crushed," Elena related. He had cried. John, she said, never had any macho hangups about hiding his emotions from her. "But now with the call, he was excited, happy."

But this was not to last either. The result was that he had lost by three votes.

Because there was suspicion of tampering, however, a judge ordered one of the ballot boxes thrown out. But then he reversed himself.

Looking back on the election many years later, John said with a laugh that it had been a "dirty tricks" campaign on both sides. "But I'd say this: There were two reasons I lost. One was that I didn't have any money to spend at the polls, and there were certain precincts where they waited around all day for the candidates to come with some money. And so I chose to go fishing instead. And number two, my wife and my mother-in-law"—who was visiting them from Cuba at the time— "weren't citizens yet."

Elena's mother, Teresa Baña, actually had no intention of staying in this country, despite Elena's pleas and warnings of a Communist takeover in Cuba. Though she and Elena were very close, she simply had her work—and her way of life—there.

But though John often laughed about losing the election because he'd "gone fishing," the loss was hardly anything he laughed about at the time. This was the end of his dream of going into politics. And what was to make the hurt even more painful was that his opponent was eventually to be recalled from office.

Politics, many people have said, was always his first love, that his true ambition was to be a senator. And yet, they have said in almost the same breath, how fortunate it was that he lost.

Although John Amos was never to run for public office again, he was to have a tremendous impact on legislators, presidents, and other heads of state. And the work he was to do as founder of an international mega-corporation was to ripple out and affect the lives of millions of people.

But for those three votes, there would never have been an American Family Corporation.

7

Making the First Place

John and Elena were in debt from the campaign, but Fort Walton Beach—and indeed the whole Panhandle—kept growing, along with John's reputation and practice. One of the area's most pressing needs was a gas line to keep up with the booming population, and John was hired by a gas line company to do the legal work in getting the right of ways and to help develop the financing.

The plan was to build a 60-mile pipeline from north of Pensacola that would include such towns as Crestview, Niceville, Valparaiso, Shalimar, Mary Esther, and Fort Walton Beach. It would be called the Okaloosa County Natural Gas District and would be composed of all the municipalities. John, who became General Counsel of the District, was instrumental in turning the plan into a reality.

"Among other things, " he explained, "my job was to entertain the bond buyers or prospective bond buyers and sell them on the feasibility of the plan, because the word 'Florida' and gas for 'heat' didn't go together in their minds. They didn't realize what our temperatures were, that we did get cold. And it was also sort of considered a part-time thing, something that might be a good investment only for the winter.

Although John presented facts that disputed these arguments, banks and stockbrokers "weren't as interested in *facts* as they were in *appearances*, that this might not *look* like a good investment even though it was," John once explained. "Some investors and institutions simply wouldn't buy bonds from towns with certain types of names. They either *sounded* too 'touristy' or were tourist towns. They stood for towns that were unstable, without industry." And then there was the albatross of past experiences with Florida, of booms that had gone bust and ended in bankruptcies. "So the idea of building a gas line into homes in Florida wasn't anything they wanted to consider. They'd say, 'Show me something else.'"

Before they could sell the bonds, John related, they first had to have a permanent customer for the gas line. They found it in Eglin Air Base in what was called the "Climatic Hanger." It was a hanger used for testing temperature, where they could bring it down to the temperature of the North Pole one day and up to that of Equatorial Africa the next.

The Air Force, explained John, was willing to buy what was called "interruptable gas"—that is, they would use gas when no one else was using it, and you could also cut them off temporarily if there was a domestic need for it. But there was a roadblock in all of this: The Air Force did not have the authority to contract for the gas for more than a year or two.

So John did something he was to do again and again in his career during the coming year. He went to people who could do something about it—the government. And it opened the way for the Okaloosa Gas District to exist not just in name but in fact.

"I went to Congress," he explained. "I got them to pass a bill that gave the Air Force the authority to enter a contract for, I believe, twenty years. They had the gas whether they used it or not, whether they kept the Air Force there or not."

In 1954, after helping establish the gas district, John became General Counsel to the Southern Governors Conference and Special Attorney to the Governor of Florida.

But it was his fee for his work on the gas district—some $40,000— that enabled him to start working on another dream.

It was the dream of owning an insurance company, a dream that, almost unbelievably, he had shared with his father when only a little boy.

But why would he, a successful lawyer, act on it now?

One reason is certainly the fact that while in Fort Walton Beach, he had had an insurance company as one of his many clients, and he had seen firsthand the great amount of money that could be made. But, it can be speculated, something else—a phenomenon that had been taking place in the South—might have played a role. At the time, literally hundreds of insurance companies proliferated the South, many of them folding, others becoming successful, some set up by shady operators. So, he wouldn't have to "sell" the *concept* of a new company. The opportunity was there for a good, honest product. And so was the opportunity for a challenge—something John Amos always seemed to need in his life.

Looking back on their years in Fort Walton Beach from 1949 to 1954, Elena smiled as she reflected upon their experiences. She could have very easily, she said, spent the rest of her life there.

The area couldn't have been more beautiful. She was by the water she loved; they had dear friends; they had long moved out of their rented house and into a house that John's father built for them and which she would always remember with fondness. "The only blue, blue house in the neighborhood." Elena was also doing things she enjoyed, not only helping John in his career, but also charity work, the extent of which only a few people knew. And it was while they were in Fort Walton that they adopted two beautiful babies, who were just a few days old—Shelby (John Shelby) in 1952, and Maria Teresa ("Sita") in 1954.

In 1954 they moved to Jacksonville, Florida, where John started a casualty insurance company—the Presidential Insurance Company— with a partner who served as president, since John, who still had to practice law to support his family, could not devote full time to it. But after about six months, dissatisfied with the direction the company was taking, he realized that if he was going to succeed in the insurance business, he had to take a *complete* gamble, had to sell his interest and start a company of his own. The question now was: Where?

"After Jacksonville," Elena said, "I think I would have gone anywhere. He was very unhappy there." After a lot of research, he focused the search on Georgia. "He didn't have any connections in Georgia," she explained. "He chose it because it has a very respected insurance department."

The next thing he had to do was narrow it down to a city. Among other things, he wanted to choose a city that did not already serve as the headquarters for an insurance company. With their two children, they traveled through Georgia by car, looking for a city that not only would be a potentially fertile base for an insurance company, but also one where they would want to live. John spoke to businessmen, bankers, members of chambers of commerce; Elena researched as well for the quality of schools—and the quality of life each area offered.

Columbus, a town of about 100,000 people on the bank of the Chattahoochee River, held everything they were looking for. It had industries and cultural activities. Fort Benning, the infantry base, stretched away on the outskirts, a huge, potential source of insurance customers. The Panhandle, where John was known, was just a couple hours' drive away. An, when needed, Atlanta was only about a hundred miles to the north.

Elena had never been to Georgia before, let alone to Columbus.

"I liked it as soon as we drove through it," she said. "It looked like a city that had roots."

It was a new venture, but it was the "old" John Amos—as family-oriented as ever. One of the first things he did was call his father and brothers in Milton, and he got together there with them. By now, his father had retired and John and Bill each owned a five and dime store. He told them what he was about to do and gave them the opportunity to come in it with them.

"He said, 'Here's what I'm doing," Paul recalled. "'If you want to go into business with me or want to get involved, then I want you to come.' And of course we agreed."

John's father and mother moved to Columbus at about the same time as John and Elena, in October 1955. According to Paul, he and Bill joined them on January 1, 1956, though they didn't sell off their businesses for a number of years. Paul then left in the late 50's and returned in the mid-70's.

What John and Elena didn't know until after moving to Columbus was something quite startling that their research somehow hadn't revealed: There *had* been another insurance company in Columbus, but it had gone out of business—only the year before.

8

THE NEW BEGINNING

John and Elena probably weren't aware of the stir they started in Columbus when they first showed up there.

Mrs. Nancy Vaughn, Jr. was working for Dun & Bradstreet, the credit reporting firm, at the time. Mrs. Vaughn, whose husband, Glenn, was editor of what is now the *Columbus Ledger-Enquirer*, was in her office on the third floor of the Swift Building—which no longer exists—in downtown Columbus when "our phones started ringing off the hook."

Who, the callers wanted to know, is John Amos?

What had happened, she recalled, is that he had gone to one of the major banks in town and made a large deposit, then had come to the Swift Building and rented offices on the fifth floor. Now "bankers and all sorts of people" were calling to find out just who he was and why he was in Columbus.

"We didn't have one word on him," said Mrs. Vaughn, "and so we spent the whole afternoon looking for him. We finally found his daddy, but we never did find him that day. There were four or five of us in the office, and we all went home that night just worn out, tired and frustrated, really frustrated."

The next morning at about ten o'clock John walked into the Dun & Bradstreet office.

"He had on a white Palm Beach suit," said Mrs. Vaughn, "and you could see his shorts through his linen pants. They had red polka dots on them, though Elena told me later they were hearts. I always teased him about that."

John sat down and told them he was starting an insurance company, and he gave them full financial information. In the meantime, since some of the people in the office had their cars parked on the street and they had to feed the parking meters every two hours, Mrs. Vaughn had to go down and take care of their debts. That was when she had her first glimpse of Elena, who was parked in front of the building with some small children. They were all speaking Spanish.

Meanwhile, the office phones were still "going crazy" with people still trying to find out who the stranger was.

Not long after this, John himself supplied answers to the business community. He approached a man named Eben Reid, executive director of the Chamber of Commerce, who was to become an associate at the company.

"He said he wanted to start an insurance company," Mr. Reed recalled in an interview after John's death. "I was impressed. I arranged a meeting at the country club over lunch for him and invited some of the city's bankers and other businessmen...We talked for an hour or more. He was," Mr. Reed continued, describing the man he would come to know well over the years, "a man of great foresight. A genius, really...But he was a friend to the lowest man in the firm. He was fair and just to everybody."

American Family Life Insurance Company—the name was changed to *Assurance* Company later, so as not to conflict with another company by the same name—was chartered in November of 1955, with John as President and Chairman of the Board of Directors.

As capital, it had just about the same amount of money—approximately $40,000—that John had gotten as a fee for his work on the gas line.

And this was a problem—the first of so many in the years to come.

Before they could start selling insurance, the company needed to raise $300,000 in escrow.

While the Amoses looked for a house to buy, they put their furniture in storage and leased a furnished house that was up for sale.

"The owner," explained Elena, "had built this big, beautiful home, and then had a call for the ministry and left to study to be a preacher. But I didn't want to buy it. I didn't like it. It was made of concrete blocks and the windows were high. It was hard to see outside. It had a swimming pool and a music room and a family room, but it was not my dream house."

Six months later they purchased a home they fell in love with—and would come to love even more. It was nearby on Steam Mill Road—a frame cottage, with fields and woodland stretching beyond their own two acres. It had only two bedrooms at the time, but the house was to become legendary in its growth. It would keep spreading out like roots as the Amoses would tag on room after room as they needed them. And the house was to become legendary for another reason. The Amoses did just about all their entertaining there—business as well as social—with Elena doing the hostessing and most of the cooking, though John also enjoyed cooking and became famous for his pig and turkey barbeques.

"I built the house partially so that when my kids got older," John expplained, "they wouldn't have to go to dives and what-not. They could come back here, where they had the patio and the music and the pool, all of it."

But that lay years away. Right now they had an insurance company and a board of directors, but it was a company that wasn't allowed to sell a product.

The first thing they had to do was try to raise the $300,000 through the sale of stock.

The initial offer was for 80,000 shares at $11.10 per share. John and his father were largely responsible for the selling of the stock through commission salesmen who went from door to door. They sold it in an ingenious way, on the installment plan—often for just 50 cents down and 50 cents a week—to farmers, small businessmen, even bootleggers. At times the cash was wet, having been buried in the ground. But if there was any single thing that helped lift the stock sale over the top, it was when they advertised the offer on a local broadcast of a national football game. John, in his notes, also paid special tribute to Jewish merchants: "They are investors, and they gambled on me."

By March, of 1956, they had the $300,000.

They began enlisting commision salesmen to sell low cost, weekly-payment life insurance and hospitalization policies, some at a premium of only five cents a week.

The people who bought the stock and held onto it would one day become millionaires. But it wasn't long before John was aware that if the company wasn't to go broke, they had to make a drastic change.

Mrs. Frances King Lolley came to work for the company in January of 1956. She started off working for the father, primarily to help him keep track of stock sales; they were still selling the first issue of stock. Then when Amos senior died in 1965, she worked for John as his appointment secretary, then went back into stock transfers and became a vice president of the company.

She had applied for the job about the middle of December, at which time Paul Amos was the one who interviewed her

"About the first thing he asked me that day was, 'How do you feel about working on Saturday?' and I very 'subtly' told him, 'I do not like to work on Saturday. I have three children.' Anyway, his daddy was looking for a helper in his office, not necessarily a secretary, but someone to help keep track of stock sales. He was the stockbroker for the company at the time." They were ready to offer a second issue of common stock to the public, she explained.

She was interviewed while they were still in the Swift Building, where they had three little offices on one floor and a little office on another floor. They also had a print shop in the basement where they printed their policies.

The day she came to work, though, they were moving to offices in a new building on 13th Street; they had about eight employees. John's office was at one end of the large suite, his father's at the other, but "Mr. John was in and out of our office all the time. He was very close to his daddy." He also always remained close to his mother, a quiet little lady who died in 1990 at the age of 92. For the rest of her life, even when she was in a wheelchair, she would like to pay visits to the office.

"His mother was just like him," Mrs. Lolley said. "He loved politics, and she was so politically motivated. She had her opinion of every politician who came across the scene. She was interested in the national scene as well as the local." She would also voice her opinion freely if she ever heard that one of the employes wasn't being treated in the way she would like. "She'd say, 'Johnny, I don't like that. Do you think you treated him fairly?'"

If the telephone rang and his secretary said his mother was on the line, he would excuse himself and take the call. Said Mrs. Lolley, "He talked to his mother three and four times a day. He never refused to talk to her. I don't think any of them did."

Thin and already white-haired when he started the company, John hardly looked old enough to be out of high school, let alone running an insurance company. "He was so energetic," Mrs. Lolley said. "He could just run circles around us." He walked like he was always in a hurry, generally in his shirtsleeves; was a perpetual coffee drinker; and almost always had a cigarette in hand. "He had things to do and had to do it right now. He never did slow down, it seemed. He had a mind that was always, it seemed, five years ahead of anybody else."

One of the funniest things Mrs. Lolley recalled ever happening there was the day the girls in the office began giggling as "Mr. John"— they called the father "Mr. J. S.," the others "Mr. Paul" and "Mr. Bill" to differentiate the Amoses in conversation—would walk back and forth to his father's office or to the water cooler. Finally he couldn't contain his curiosity. He stopped at one of the girls' desks.

"Can you please tell me what you girls are so happy about today?"

"Mr. John," she replied, "if Elena buys your clothes, you need to tell her to buy you something besides polka dot shorts to wear under those white suits."

"He just chuckled," Mrs. Lolley said, "and when he went home he said, 'Elena, the girls are laughing at me!'" When he came in the next day he wasn't wearing the shorts anymore. "He was always such a good sport. He was always so nice."

He was also a very patient, soft-spoken man. Said Mrs. Lolley, "He never stood over me and waited for me to do something. He was a beautiful man to know. If I ever complained about anyone, I might say, 'You know, I don't believe they're doing a good job. They're just ripping you off.' He'd say, 'Oh, Frances, let's live and let live. They'll shape up. We'll take care of that.'"

He would bend over backwards to let you straighten yourself out. But he knew when to be hard, too. "He'd say, 'Joe, I'm sorry you're not doing a good job. You're not doing near what you're capable of doing, and if you don't straighten up and fly right, we're going to have to make some changes.' It was amazing how many straightened up."

One salesman, for example, was making a lot of money, but was also spending a lot of the company's money hand over fist. John called him in, and said, "It's all right for you to spend your money, but when you start spending my money, it's going to be stopped. I'm not going to fire you. You owe me too much money. I want you to go back home, straighten yourself out, and pay me back." And the man not only changed his ways, said Mrs. Lolley, but he also became one of their top employees.

Even at the beginning, when funds were limited, John always found some way to give the employees a Christmas party, either by taking them out for dinner or to his home. "He always thought of his employees. They were good friends to him—good buddies—and they just really did love him."

The brothers, she continued, were always pulling jokes on each other, like the time Bill Amos walked out of the building to his car and found that they had jacked up the back wheels. And they loved teasing their father. "Whenever Mr. J. S. thought there was any disagreement between the brothers," Mrs. Lolley said, "he would say to me, 'Miss King, I don't want to be disturbed. I'm going to talk to the boys.' They'd come back to his room and they'd just hug him and kiss him and pull his hair and take his cigar out of his mouth. They might come in and wonder what Dad wants this time, but they would leave just laughing and talking."

Meanwhile, Elena was seeing another side of the picture. It wasn't that John wanted to worry her; it was simply that they shared everything. He told her it was clear that the company would not survive if it continued as a weekly premium life insurance company, that they had to do something. But what?

John was always a night person, sitting up with his legal pad until two and three in the morning, sometimes breaking off to watch on old movie on TV for relaxation. She knew that most of those late nights, most of the scribbled notes, were focused on how to save the company. She wasn't worried that if it collapsed they would have nothing; after all, he was still a lawyer. He had lost none of that talent; in fact, he was still tying up loose ends on some matters for old clients. But she *was* worried in the sense of wanting him to be happy.

He discussed a number of options with her, among them that the company might do better if they concentrated on health and accident coverage instead of life insurance. That same year, 1957, through a stock deal, American Family sold the weekly debit business to another insurance company and began to offer health and accident policies. But here again they were bucking competition from the giants in the industry, as well as from the little companies that were scattered throughut the South.

Soon afterward he came up with a new idea.

What, he said to Elena one night, was the one dread disease most people feared and that could also devastate a person financially? Without waiting for her answer, he said, "Cancer. What about insurance against the costs of cancer?"

She looked at him, then said it sounded good—*great*, in fact—and then she asked if many companies sold such a policy.

He had already researched that. Few companies even offered it as a sideline, and none specialized in it.

His idea *was* to specialize in it. But he would do it only if he could offer an inexpensive policy that would truly lift the additional suffering of the expensive cost of treatment from cancer patients and their families.

Many people he discussed it with tried to discourage him. After all, wouldn't the "big boys" go into it on an large scale if it could be done profitably? Come *on*. And cancer itself—what would happen to this company when they found a cure? After all, there was bound to be a cure right around the corner.

John went back to the "drawing board," so to speak, and did further research. The Lord only knew, he told Elena, how he wished for a cure as badly as did the next person. But from what he was reading—he was an extensive reader on a wide variety of subjects—and from what cancer specialists he spoke to told him, there was no evidence that there would be a cure for the ravages of cancer in the near future.

John oversaw the preparation of a cancer policy that was not only inexpensive, but uncomplicated. Now, it seemed, "all" they needed was enough people to trust it—to trust *them*. But as Elena was to recall, even with *that* trust they were to have so many ups and downs.

9

COLUMBUS, GEORGIA

John was not one of those men who become successful at the cost of his homelife. He truly enjoyed his home and family and was always able to balance his family life and business life.

After their son Shelby had come into their lives, John didn't want Elena to work any more, but in a very real sense she was always a big part of his work. Walter F. Barton, who would join the company about 1961 and eventually went on to become a vice president, echoed so many people's thoughts when he said that Elena had "an awful lot to do with his success. As long as I knew him, John basically entertained at home. People would feel more relaxed there, and it enabled him to expose the people to Elena, and Elena to the people. I happen to know they used to talk a lot after functions and things like that—he would say to me, 'You know, I sat and talked with Elena a long time about this person or that person or this situation.' He entertained people from the lowest to the highest in the spectrum. He had that ability and Elena, of course, also had that ability, regardless who it was. The two of them would give you the feeling that they really cared for people."

A young man named Brooks Massey, for instance, lived on a farm about two miles from the Amoses. His father also owned a Sinclair service station down Steam Mill Road from the Amoses, and Brooks worked there part-time while he went to school. His father became good friends with John, did a lot of work for him, and also shared a love of politics with him. A county commissioner, he introduced John to a lot of people in Columbus.

In 1958, Brooks Massey graduated from Columbus High School and wanted to get a summer job before starting college. But he didn't want to stay in the city. Since he knew John had been an attorney in Florida, he asked for his help in getting a job there.

"I graduated on a Wednesday night," said Massey, "and in about two days Mr. John called me and said, 'Brooks, I want you to pack your bags. I want you to go to Florida with me. I've got to go down and do some work.'" John explained that he still had one more legal project to do for the Okaloosa County gas line.

Massey told him he would need to take his own car if he would be staying on there, but John said, "No, you just come and ride with me instead of driving me down there, and we'll get you a car down there in some kind of way."

That, related Brooks Massey, was how "Mr. John always was."

Here was a man with a new business and under a lot of pressure, Massey continued, yet he was willing to take the time to help a kid find a job.

"All the way down he was telling me about his past, the history of his school, how he didn't finish high school but got into college."

Massey worked with him in Florida for about a week, staying in motels with him, doing typing for him and "general flunky-type work." Recalled Massey, "I finally said, 'Mr. John, I'm tired of this. You told me you were going to get me a job and now I need to go to work.' So he called someone at Columbia National Chemical Corporation—I'm eighteen-years-old, remember, and I don't know much of anything— and he asked the man if he had anything for me to do. The man must have told him no, because I heard Mr. John say, 'Well, I guess within the next thirty minutes you can find him something to do because he's on his way over there.'"

John loaned him his car—it was about a twenty mile drive—and by the time Massey got there, the man had a job for him as a mail clerk. What's more, John let Massey keep his car until he, John, was ready to drive back to Columbus. Then he had Massey's car sent down to him.

And all of this was during a time when things were touch-and-go with the new business, when he had enough things to be concerned about.

In the meantime, John's longtime friend from his teenage years, Donald Beck, joined the company. John had called on him when he had started the casualty insurance company in Florida, and Beck had sold stock in the company on the side while he continued working at his job with the railroad.

"It opened my eyes that there was more to life than railroading," Beck reminisced, "because I made more in commission in six months than I would have in two or three years of railroading."

Beck recalled how John, during a subsequent visit to his home in Pensacola, told him he had sold the casualty company and was starting a new company and that this time he would be president.

"I said, 'John, you're a damn fool'—those were my words. And, of course, later on I did go to work for that 'damn fool.'"

John sent him a certified letter inviting him to come to Columbus to look over the company and offering him a job. Beck and his wife, Bea, came to Columbus where John and Elena "entertained us royally at their house on Steam Mill Road, which was a very, very modest home. We had a meal that night and partied in a garage that had been converted into a party room."

Beck decided to cast his lot with the company. But he wasn't there a week when, at a Monday morning meeting—they held a meeting every Monday—John made the announcement that he was thinking of selling out.

"And here I'd resigned my job, had given up my seniority of sixteen years, and now the company was having hard times," recalled Beck. "John could hang up his shingle and practice law, but Bill wasn't about to go back to the dime store business and I couldn't buy a railroad." Paul Amos, he explained, had already gone back to Milton, Florida, with his wife's family—not to return until 1974—and Bill Amos was senior vice president. "Bill and I, who, remember, had married sisters, said to him, 'No way. We're going to make it work.' And together we just sort of created a common bond and just worked our butts off to *make* it work."

Several times over the next six months, at these meetings John would say something like, "There's just no way we can get there from where we are." As Donald Beck put it, "Who's to say that he wasn't saying that to motivate us? I don't know. But it sure motivated *me*."

Beck's first assignment was to go out out and recruit salesmen in north Georgia.

"The first week I drove with Bill Amos and he showed me where each of our offices was located. We had just four or five people in the whole northern part of Georgia. He would say, 'I fired this fellow last week,' or 'This one was a crook.' And that was all the training I got.

He said, 'Your job is to make these rounds every week, help us recruit and train and motivate these people to do a good job for us.'"

Basically, there were two types of salesmen, those who sold stock in the company and those who sold insurance. They worked only on commission, as independent contractors. This eliminated the expense of salaries, let alone benefits, when business wasn't going well. Beck, of Georgia, pointed out that in general the original salesmen were far from as qualified as the people they got later, since it was hard to recruit high-caliber salespeople for a new company. The ones they got at the beginning were primarily people who needed jobs. But Beck had the talent of being able to recruit good people as well, to convince them that the company was on solid ground and that this was an opportunity to get on the ground floor.

Still, though the company was admitted to two more states— Florida and Alabama—it continued to flirt with insolvency.

One day after the company was licensed to sell insurance in Florida, Beck and his wife, who has a doctorate in education, were in West Palm Beach, where she was honored as Lady of the Year by a woman's organization. Driving back to Georgia, he got into a traffic accident and smashed up the car. By now, John had bought a half interest in an airplane, and Beck called him and asked him to send the plane down for him. But John had grim news for him.

The previous night about midnight, the treasurer of the company had called him to say that he had made a mistake in calculations. Instead of the company having a $25,000 surplus as he'd thought, it had a $25,000 deficit, and that left the company $50,000 impaired.

The treasurer had told John that he'd been up walking the floor before daring to call him.

John told him that was all right, that he should go to bed, and that he, John, would walk the floor instead.

"He got up," said Donald Beck, "got dressed and went into the office, and in two or three days he raised $50,000 to keep us in business. I don't know how."

He got it through a man named Matt Metcalfe, who was to play a particularly close role in his life as a dear friend, colleague, and confidant.

When John and Matt Metcalfe met, Metcalfe—who was about six years younger than John—was a clerk with Loyal American Life Insurance Company in Mobile, Alabama. (He retired as Chairman and Chief Executive Officer of Loyal American and Laurentian Capital Corporation, a billion-dollar company he created as an umbrella for several life insurance companies.) One day, about a year after John and Matt Metcalfe started in the insurance industry, the Alabama insurance commissioner called Metcalfe and said, "Matt, there's a fellow over in Columbus, Georgia, who has invented a new little insurance policy, and he calls it a cancer insurance policy."

The commissioner, recalled Metalfe, wasn't really sure what the policy was, only that John Amos was "writing so much of it he's broke."

In the insurance business, it costs more the first year to put a policy on the books—maybe 125% or 150% of the first year's premium. Consequently, you can literally write yourself out of business. "John was writing so much of this product that he was out of surplus," explained Metcalfe. "So the commissioner said to me, 'Now your company has got a little surplus, but it's not writing any business. Maybe you two ought to get together and do some sort of surplus relief treaty that will help him and help you, too.'"

Surplus is a company's net worth above its liabilities. A surplus relief treaty, which is unique to the insurance industry, is a reinsurance treaty whereby one company will, in effect, bank the reserves for the other company and carry those reserves on its books, depleting its surplus so that the other company's surplus remains higher. In brief, it is a way of raising capital.

Metcalfe called John and arranged to meet him in Birmingham, Alabama, at the offices of Loyal American's law firm. But John did not like the partner in the firm who was going to draft the treaty for them.

"He was a very intelligent, very successful guy, but he put John down," Metcalfe said. "So John asked me to step outside. Incidentally, the minute John and I met, we knew the chemistry was right. We just liked each other."

John told him he didn't like that lawyer, but he did like Dick Schweitzer, a young ex-partner in the firm,. So Metcalfe went back into the office and said to the first lawyer, "Why don't you just let

Dick and John and myself sit down and draft this thing out and you look it over afterwards? And he said that was fine. And that began a lifelong friendship. We called ourselves the trio—the three musketeers—John Amos, Dick Schweitzer, and myself. Dick remained my lawyer for many, many years. And he remained a consultant to John all his life, because Dick Schweitzer is probably the most informed lawyer in America on reinsurance treaties, and in particular those international reinsurance treaties such as between U.S. companies and Lloyds of London."

Now, Dick Schweitzer's memory of the meeting is a litle more graphic, though it has the same ending. His recollection is of coming back to the office after a long trip and being called into the conference room where the partner "was sitting there with his feet propped up, and this kind of silver-haired fellow was sitting over to one side and Matt was sitting over on another."

The partner was giving John a hard time as Schweitzer walked in. "He said to me," Schweitzer recalled, "'Dick, Matt wants to reinsure this guy's business. He's got some cockamamie cancer insurance policy. I told him there's no way you can reinsure that kind of thing. You can't insure cancer, so you can't reinsure.' He was really bad to him."

Schweitzer took the papers out of Matt Metcalfe's hands and asked him what it was that he wanted to do. Then Schweitzer turned to the first lawyer and said, "Isn't today Thursday?"

The other said, 'Yes, it is. Why?'

"Today is the day you're supposed to play golf, isn't it?"

"Yes, it is."

"Well," Schweitzer said, "why don't you get the hell out of here and play golf? I'm going home to take a shower and sleep for about an hour, and I'll come back and I'll put the deal together."

And they did.

The reinsurance gave John the surplus to survive and continue to write more business. "By the same token," Metcalfe said, "the additional interest that Loyal American earned from the arrangement gave Loyal a profit for the three years we maintained the treaty in force."

But not long after that, John called Metcalfe and said, "Matt, I'm broke. I can't 'make' a statement."

What John was referring to was that on December 31 of every year, insurance companies have to file a statement with every insurance department in every state they are licensed in. It is a very strict accounting statement, the "purest of the pure," as Metcalfe has described it, because it deals with the company's liquidity, its ability to pay claims. Its assets are valued on the basis of whether the company can pay a claim with it; thus, such things as airplanes and automobiles and office furnishings are not considered assets. It has to be an asset that can be converted quickly to pay claims.

"John was coming up to December 31st," Metcalfe said, "and he realized that he would be insolvent, that he would not have sufficient surplus. He said, 'I've got to do something.'"

Metcalfe came up with an idea of forming an insurance company, putting together enough assets in it, and merging that into John's company for stock; stock was all that John had to offer. He found a "shell insurance company." He knew someone who had an Alabama insurance charter, and Metcalfe got investors to put $200,000 into this little company, which would be merged with American Family.

"The deal was—and this was John's offer—" he said, "that they would get stock for this $200,000. John told me, 'Matt, if you can pull this off, I will redeem your shares in American Family after a year and give you 100 % profit.' Sure enough, we merged the company, he was solvent, he made the insurance statement, and a year later he redeemed every share for 100% profit. Now," reminisced Metcalfe with a smile, "if I had kept the shares that I got out of it, I'd be worth $50 million today. But I was a clerk and was probably making $600 a month, so 100% profit was a lot of money. I was happy with it, and all the investors were happy with it."

There was never a gap in their friendship after that, Metcalfe continued. They would talk or see each other at least about once a week.

"We'd go fishing together. We both loved to fish. We'd play together. The great thing about when we were together is we'd always laugh. It was always fun, just good fun. And that's something you don't do much anymore. You don't find people you have fun with. I mean *real* fun, not just this phony party business where you go to a party and stand around with a drink in your hand and try to make a joke or something."

Just as Metcalfe helped John, so did John help Metcalfe.

"One day I was in dire need of financial help personally. I had to have $100,000. That was a lot of money. I called John on the phone and I told him, 'I've got to have $100,000 and I don't have any collateral.' I commenced to tell him why, and he said, 'You don't have to tell me what you need the money for. What bank do you want it in?' I said, "First National, in Mobile,' and he said, 'Okay, anything else?' I said no. In an hour the bank called me and said, 'Mr. Metcalfe, $100,000 has been wired to your account here. Are you aware of it?' I said that I was. John never asked me for a note. He never put a letter in writing. He never mentioned it, and not too long thereafter I sent him $100,000."

At John's 65th birthday—so many years away, then—Matt Metcalfe would say in a toast: "To John Amos, who has taught all of us here the lesson that, in order to have a friend, you must be a friend."

And that *was* John, Matt Metcalfe emphasized. "John was always there when you needed him. If you were his friend, you were his friend. He would stick by you. And if you were wrong, he'd still stick by you. He might straighten you out later, but you were family."

10

FAMILY AND FRIENDS

When John moved to Columbus, the city government and the Muscogee County government were constantly at each other's throats. As Lennie Davis, who served as City Attorney of the City of Columbus for ten years, has described the bickering, the county government would meet one day and make all sorts of resolutions regarding how the city government was wrong, and then the city government would meet the next day and pass resolutions blaming the county. And it was this way, said Davis, throughout Georgia.

In 1961, John was asked to be chairman of a citizens committee to try to abolish this antiquated form of government. With all his experience in consolidating various municipalities in Florida into a single gas district, John found this to be an even greater challenge. Too many vested interests were involved. In brief, he came up with the concept that, as in the past, there would be a city government and a county government, but the commissioners would be the same on both bodies. Although his plan did not go through, it was like a seed that needed the exact time and climate to blossom.

"The idea was good," said Davis. "I mean, the main thing was that there was a need for change and John tried to do something about it. That did not work, but it was the forerunner of what happened two years later when we did put through a consolidation bill."

According to Davis, who went on to serve as City Attorney for the Consolidated City-County Government of Columbus, they were the first city in Georgia to consolidate. "You've got to give John credit for being one of the original dreamers of consolidation, even though he was not the author of the bill that ultimately passed. He was a dreamer—a *real* dreamer." Davis recalled that when John first moved into the community, "he was this guy nobody knew. But all in the world they had to do to love him was to have an idea and expose him to it and he'd take it and run with it for you."

Ordinarily, John was not a "joiner." He preferred working behind the scenes, whether it was in giving charity or supporting political candidates and issues. But that same year, 1961, he agreed to become president during the fundraising and organization of Goodwill Industries of Columbus.

Carol Royer, who was his secretary from 1957 to 1964, described him as coming into the office each morning with a yellow pad filled with jottings of "things you know he had been thinking of during the night. I don't think he was a person who slept a lot. He always reminded me," she said affectionately, "of an overactive child—just real busy, busy all the time."

He was the kind of person, she said, whom you meet just once in life; no one, no matter how interesting, would ever be anything like him. "He was driven, he was dynamic, he was interesting. You never knew what was coming next, and that made it fun because it was a challenge."

When he gave you a job to do, he not only expected you to do it, but you found yourself always trying to do a little bit *more*. "He liked people who were smart, but he also liked people with 'horse sense,' because he had a lot of it. It always seemed he couldn't have enough of it."

Like just about everyone else who had known him, she talked about his jokes, his pranks. She hadn't expected this when she had come to work for him, and so she hadn't known how to take him at first "because I didn't understand him. And a lot of it had to do with the jokes and the things he would say and do, because you really did not know sometimes if he was serious or not."

He often whistled absently to himself as he worked; and though he had a temper—something many people who knew him could not remember ever seeing—for instance, being known to toss his yellow pad across his conference table, "sooner or later he would start laughing," Carol Royer said. And he almost had to be protected from his own generosity. He never turned anyone down. "I've seen people who needed money, and if they wanted $2,000 and he had $1,000, he'd go to the bank and write a note. He'd tell them to come back the next day and he'd go get the money and bring it back and give it to them. He was that way."

Linda Bowick, who worked for him from 1965 to 1974, also spoke of his love for jokes, which at times were on her. One of the things he enjoyed doing, sometimes in conspiracy with her husband, Herbert—who came to work for the company a year later and became one of its chief executives and, with Linda, a close friend of the Amoses—would be to set quietly something as calorie-sinful as a banana split on her desk. John would then walk off, like the famed cat who swallowed the canary, and bet that she would not be able to resist eating it. Said Linda Bowick, "I've always gone up and down in weight. I loved food. He always won the bet because I always ate it."

John Amos was someone who inspired great loyalty, she continued.

"He *was* the company," she said, "and when he had an idea and said to do something, I think everybody just believed it was going to work. And it was fun working there. It was not a nine to five job. You might be there on Sunday afternoon, but you didn't mind for some reason. His door was never closed; it wasn't like he was the head of this big corporation. Anybody could talk to him. You didn't have to go through this long chain of command. You could also buy stock, so you really felt like part of the company, part of a family. And it was really like family the way they made you feel."

At home, he rarely showed the tensions and stress of a busy executive. In fact, quite the contrary was true.

At his and Elena's urging, her mother had finally left Cuba to live with them. He also got other members of her family out of there, helping to finance their way over and to support them until they could support themselves. This included an uncle and aunt, Mr. and Mrs. Antonio Sarmiento, who had owned a restaurant in Havana, had come to this country with just five dollars—all they were allowed to bring—and lived with John and Elena until they were able to get on their feet.

Her mother, who lived on Steam Mill Road with them until her death, added greatly to their lives. Her mother, Elena said frankly, hadn't liked John when they had first gotten married, but came truly to love him. She used to tease him that he would "die a Catholic," a prophesy that turned out to be true.

One of John and Elena's hobbies from the time they had come to Columbus was making ceramics. They used to attend classes in which John was often the only man in attendance. Another thing he enjoyed doing was carving little figures out of soap. Now that Elena's mother was living with them, they got her interested in ceramics, too. She set up a workshop in the basement. And, as did Elena, she also enjoyed playing bridge. But once his mother-in-law became involved in ceramics, John claimed, that was when he stopped.

"I quit when her mother came in," he once said laughingly, "because she wanted everything in its right place and I wanted everything where I left it."

It was a family that loved animals. They always had dogs, and the children rode horses. As an adult, their daughter Sita's laugh still had a touch of amazement to it as she recalled how they had once had a pet pig, and her father had told her he was going to train it to climb a ladder into a playpen, and then he went ahead and did it.

John loved to fish, and so did Elena and their children—Elena had enjoyed it since she was a young girl, when sometimes she would have to carry her fishing pole on public transportation. John also liked to hunt, a hobby Elena did not share with him, but he would often go hunting with Shelby and Sita. As a father, he was always around when the children needed help.

"Every time I had a problem," Shelby said, "he would take great interest in it. I could go to him with anything. One of the things I loved him for was that he didn't have any prejudice. He could sit down and talk with everyone. He found everyone of interest."

When Shelby was old enough to work, he worked at American Family in the stockroom and doing odds and ends. But then there was a time he thought he wanted to be a mechanic. Shelby, who eventually went on to head up American Family's operations in Alabama, did enter a vocational tech school. "Daddy," he said, "just let me go ahead, didn't try to talk me out of it. That's the way he did things. 'If that's what you want to do,' he said, 'go learn it and do it right.' But then after about six months I saw on my own that it wasn't for me."

Elena made it a rule to take at least a two- or three-week family vacation every summer. She and John had done quite a bit of traveling before they had children. Once Castro came to power, they had not been able to go to Cuba anymore, but they had done a lot of traveling through Mexico because, said Elena, "I wanted so much to speak Spanish."

Now, with the children, they took their vacations by car, but then found that the children would barely eat when they were taken to restaurants. So they began to go camping, then got a trailer—one of John's hobbies became the canning of food—and eventually a Winnebago, traveling throughout the country and Central America. John took to wearing a cowboy hat on the trips, the better for the children to spot him if—as happened with Shelby, once, in Mexico— they wandered off. It had taken them most of a frightening day to find him.

But the trips, the good home life, the steady growth of the business—none of this reflected the uncertainties that lay just beneath the surface of what looked to be a successful company. Every step forward, it seemed, was followed by something that threatened to bring the company down.

One was a complaint that the regional office of the Securities and Exchange Commission filed against them. It wasn't a complaint filed in court, Dick Schweitzer explained, but was an order for John to appear before the Commission for a possible administrative type of disciplinary action. The Commission claimed that the stock salesmen out on the street, who were under John's father at this time, were misleading the public in the way they were trading the stock back and forth, for which they were getting a commission.

This was a kind of "country trading," Schweitzer explained, that was absolutely unknown to the SEC, who were used to brokers selling stock. The salesmen, they were sure, *had* to be doing something tricky.

"I went to the SEC people, I talked to the enforcement people, because to me it was just totally unfair." John did not even have the money to pay him.

After a long time John, not wanting to fight anymore, having simply too many other things to do, made a settlement with the SEC in which he agreed to accept a consent order with the Commission. They agreed that they would not find that his violation was willful, that it was unintentional, and that the negligent practices would be corrected. But, said Schweitzer, "When they finally wrote the order, they put in the words they said they would not put into it, including 'willful,' 'intentional.' John was very angry. I told him that if he ever wanted that thing expunged from the records, he could because they had violated the basic consent letter which I had prepared for him which they had accepted. They had entered the order as though he had consented to more than he had. Anyway, he just wanted to let it go, and to get on."

And there was so much to get on with. The company by now had spread into other states in the southeast, and the stock was being handled by brokers and was being purchased by major investors.

In 1964, the company also took a major step forward in its sales approach, based on a suggestion by Donald Beck. Instead of selling policies just to individuals, it began "cluster selling" to groups—businesses and organizations. This triggered a burst of growth. Still, most people observing how the company was growing would not have guessed that it was still not showing a profit, that it would be a good many years before it did.

Over the years, meanwhile, Elena had stayed in touch with her old classmate from the Methodist school in Havana, Anita Stone. Anita Stone, who had returned to Cuba after attending the University of Florida, had kept in contact with John and Elena through the periods in which they were in Fort Walton Beach and when they came to Columbus.

Recalled Anita Stone: "I was very impressed when I went to visit them in Columbus and John pulled out a paper on which he had set up a series of rules that would govern this big enterprise that he was just initiating. I was so taken that he had all these prognostications that later on actually became a reality."

At that early date, John had even forseen the company being so successful that they would need to own their own plane.

Anita Stone went on to say that she and her then husband, Mario Stone, M.D., left Cuba after the Castro take-over and settled in a small town in West Virginia. John and Elena came there right away to see if they needed any help, but the Stones didn't need financial assistance at the time, since Dr. Stone had been made chief of orthopedics at the local hospital. But then, after the debacle at the

Bay of Pigs in 1961, they did need help, and once more the Amoses were right there.

"My husband," explained Anita Stone, "was supposed to leave on a hospital ship for Cuba, which never left Miami because the landing had been unsuccessful. Now there we were, with no future we could see, so John offered my husband a job as medical director of the company, which was well established at the time. We purchased a house right across from the Amos's, and we were there a little over a year."

Enough for them to get on their feet, and for Dr. Stone to move on and pursue his specialty in orthopedics.

"I can tell you," said Anita Stone, "that John and Elena each contributed something different to their marriage. I think she was John's reason for living, really, and vice versa."

Following the Bay of Pigs invasion, too, there was an influx into Columbus of about 500 Cuban officers and their families who had been ransomed out of Cuba. The officers—the United States had given the freedom fighters the rank of captain—were housed in Fort Benning, but there was no housing for their families. The Amos home was filled with refugees, sleeping on floors, sofas—just about everywhere; they kept coming and going for more than a year, while Elena led a gargantuan effort to find places for them to stay. She also started a Latin America Studies Group, and conducted weekly lessons in Spanish and Latin American culture to give people in the area a better understanding of these new refugees.

So many people of all faiths came to the Amos's aid. But years later, in discussing the role of the Jewish community in purchasing stock in his company, John also spoke of their role in helping the Cuban refugees. He was doing it, he said, not so much to single them out, but to express what he called an "affinity" he had with Jewish people. "Elena," he commented, "was a foreigner and had been raised in Cuba in a Methodist school where at least 50% of the children were Jewish refugees from Hitler. So they understood what it meant to be a refugee." He also spoke of his enjoyment in going to functions—weddings, bar mitzvahs and bat mitzvahs—that his Jewish friends gave. Indeed, though still not a "joiner," in later years he became the first gentile member of the Harmony Club, a local country club.

The fact is, he and Elena had an affinity with all minorities. As Julie Ellis, the acclaimed novelist who was born and raised in Columbus, said, "They didn't have a biased bone in their bodies." John, as a force in the community, was a pioneer there in developing relationships with blacks, in bringing whites and blacks together in his home and in politics.

"I was the first man that I know of," he said, "to ever hold a caucus, you might say, of blacks and whites in Columbus, Georgia. I feel that I have done more to integrate this community than any other man because I was willing to step out first."

Two men who stand out prominently in this regard are George Ford and Judge Albert W. Thompson.

11

POLITICS AND GROWING PAINS

Judge Thompson was elected in 1965 to the State House of Representatives from the southern part of the county, the first black to run successfully for political office in the area since Reconstruction days. He has always attributed his success to advice he got from John Amos.

John Amos never lost his love of politics. While it is conjecture to say, as some people have, that he would have preferred being a senator to anything else, what is absolute fact is that he enjoyed the excitement, intrigues and power of politics, and was always involved in it in some capacity. He founded a group in Columbus called the Fish House Gang—Democrats ranging from precinct workers to judges—who met every couple of months at a fish house or at his home for a barbecue. And, something which sounds ordinary today, but was far from that then, he always invited blacks.

Judge Thompson—who was to serve fifteen years in the House, then became a State Superior Court judge, and finally retired as an administrative judge with the State Board of Workers' Compensation—was a young lawyer then, hoping to represent a district which at the time was predominately white. He would be opposing a white candidate. A mutual friend, George Ford, a funeral director who was the unofficial "mayor" of the black community, suggested that he see John Amos. First, Ford spoke to John about him.

John's advice to Thompson was to stay off television. This was an off-year election, there wasn't much interest in it, and John, who was to play a key role in raising money for the campaign, didn't want him to create any unnecessary waves.

"He wouldn't allow me to get into a debate with my opponent. He wouldn't let me put my picture on advertisements. It was strictly low key. He said, 'Your one job is to get out in the black community and arouse interest and get black people to the polls.' And I followed his advice. I respected him as a very intelligent politician, and I knew nothing about politics—this was my first real effort. It was difficult because I'm sort of feisty and I'm an attorney and I think I'm as smart as anyone else, and it's difficult to hold an attorney back. But he said, 'I think you'll be elected that way.' He was right."

The next time Judge Thompson ran, however, John turned him loose, said, "Go get 'em."

In that election and subsequent ones, his reputation as a good, astute representative having been established, Judge Thompson was able to run normal campaigns, went on television and debated and ran ads.

John always supported him, but once told him candidly, "Al, I tried to get my mother to vote for you and it was just impossible." But, said Judge Thompson as he related the story, "I'm a Southerner. I've been here all my life and I understand motivation, particularly among people in this area. I hope I've been big enough that I have not let that impact on my thinking and how I feel about people."

Over the years, John was to help him in other ways. Judge Thompson, who actively practiced law in Columbus while in the General Assembly, bought an old frame house in the historic section of the city, for use as offices. He renovated it, but then found that he had made a mistake—he had put too much money into it, in fact all he had, and it did not increase the value of the place. Consequently, he could not get financing.

Desperate, he called John and told him the story, that all he had done was bring the building up to standard rather than increasing its value. "John laughed and said—this is exactly what he said—'I'm not going to let you fail because if you were white this community would be behind you and they wouldn't let you down. So I'm not going to.' He told me who to call to get the financing, and I did. It was successful. That's the kind of person he was, and that's the kind of thing he would do for a friend."

John, he said, helped in many other ways. For instance, the first night he was in the General Assembly, the members voted to refuse to seat Julian Bond because of statements he was associated with that were against the Viet Nam War. Judge Thompson did not vote to seat him, but instead abstained. He felt he could not vote for him because his father had been in the military for thirty years. Furthermore, as a representative of the district in which Fort Benning was in, and as an attorney who was handling the estates of people who had died in Viet Nam, he couldn't see how he could support someone who had spoken out so openly against what the United States was doing in Viet Nam.

Subsequently, Bond took it to Federal court, and they made the General Assembly seat him.

When Judge Thompson came back to Columbus from Atlanta after the vote, he had a conference with John. John told him that he had hurt himself in the black community. "He said, 'Al , you've really got to figure some way to overcome this.' So he arranged for me to go on television and express my view about the thing. I said to the people what I felt—that I'm a local product, I'm military, I've handled estates of people who have died in Viet Nam, and I could not see myself espousing a cause which would be opposed to this.' John paid for it. And he had a tape made of so it so that I would have it and be able to present it to protect myself in the future."

Although he and John were good friends, he said, it was not like the friendship—few friendships could be—between John and George Ford .

"He and John," said Judge Thompson, "were almost as close as brothers. It just happens that George was black and he was white."

George Ford had met John in 1964, the year before Judge Thompson had first come to John for advice. At that time, Ford himself was running for the county commission, the first black in the area to run for public office. He knew he didn't have a chance, but felt that it was time for blacks to enter the political arena. John, with his great interest in politics, contacted him and said he wanted to see him.

When Ford got to his office, John told him some things about his own background, then said, "Well, I guess I better tell you that I'm supporting your opponent."

Ford, a man who never took nonsense, said, "Well, hell, I ain't got no business here. I've got to go out and get somebody to support me."

Ford turned and started to walk out. A man who was serving as John's secretary at the time followed him to the door and said, "Mr. Ford, you're talking to a fine man, I wish you would hear him out."

"Let him hear me out, another time."

Not long after Ford got back to his funeral home he got a call from John's secretary, pleading with him to come over again and talk with John. Ford went to his house on the weekend. John explained to him that the reason he could not support him was that he owed his opponent a debt for having helped stop the construction of a highway that would have gone through his house.

"I told him," Ford would recall, "that I understood it—and I did. I can understand anybody who wants to be honest and pay a debt."

After the election, which Ford lost as expected, he and John got together, at which time John began talking about the Democratic party, that it had a great future in the county but it did not have leadership. It did not take Ford long to realize that John wanted to be head of the Democratic party in the state.

Ford, recalling their conversation, said, "You can't be a leader in any party, unless you've got some minorities kind of swinging your way. So I figured it out right quick, that that's what he wanted me to do." They agreed that they would work together to build a strong party, first in Muscogee County. "And we did that. We built one of the strongest Democratic parties Muscogee County has ever had, truly integrated, whites, blacks, Jews, gentiles, everything. From that point on we stayed friends. We had our disagreements, and that's what I like—I knew we were friends because we could disagree to the point where we'd cuss each other out and go home, and I'd call him or he'd call me."

One of the things they disagreed on was the advice John gave Thompson about staying off television during the first campaign.

"I told John I didn't think anybody should hide their identity, but if he felt that way and if Thompson went along with it, then I had no reason not to."

George Ford had been the one who had approached Albert Thompson to run in the first place. But Thompson had been hesitant. "He told me," Ford said, "'I don't think these people are ready to vote for a black man.' I told him, 'Well, it's your time. You can do it.

You're clean, you're a good man. If you weren't clean I wouldn't fool with you.'"

Thompson asked for some time to think about it. In the meantime, Ford spoke to John and told him it was time to get a black person to run for office, and to get the Democratic party to support him. "He agreed, and he said, 'Who do you have in mind?' I said, 'I've got one of the cleanest guys you can find.' And I told him. He said, 'We'll take him.' And then Thompson called me to say he had decided to run, but he didn't have any money. I said, 'That's all you need to say.' I knew John could raise the money."

Judge Thompson's election paved the way for other blacks to be elected to office in the City Council and the General Assembly. Ford, who was chairman of the local NAACP in the sixties, said, "John and I picked every black that ran for office. We always made sure we picked folks who were clean. And we kept pressure on everybody to make sure no racial mess got tied up in it. John had a way of keeping folks quiet. It was a skill. A man like John will never be born again. I loved him, I miss him so much."

George Ford, whom John would one day nominate to American Family's board of directors, recalled how John helped him buy out his partner's share in the funeral home. His partner had died, and Ford needed about $25,000 to buy out her family's interest. He approached John, who said, "Oh, George, I think we can work that out."

John, who was going out of the country, typed a letter to his bank, stating that anytime Ford needed some money he, John, would be responsible for it. "He wrote that I might need somewhere, I believe, around $50,000 or $100,000. I didn't need that much, but that's what he said."

Ford gave the letter to an attorney, a friend of John's, and went with him to the bank. There, the officer he handed it to, said Ford, "tried to make fun of the letter." The lawyer told him, "Now, I wouldn't make fun of that letter. If you've got a doubt about it, I've got stocks and bonds here at the bank—I'll use my bonds until Amos gets back to town, because Amos signed that and wants it done.' And the fellow realized he was making fun of the wrong man, and he said quickly, 'Well, I don't mean that, that's a joke.'"

John, he went on, was to show his friendship in so many ways. One night years later, for instance, Ford would be at a meeting of the Fish

House Gang which John could not attend, when a came through to him from John. He was flying to Germany on business trip and he asked Ford to come with him.

"I said," recalled Ford, "'John, I can't go to Germany, I've got to take care of this little one-horse business I've got.' He said, 'George, this will be the time of your life. You don't need anything but some clothes to put on your back. I'll take care of everything else.' I said, 'John, I don't have a passport,' and he said, 'Don't worry about passports.'"

Ford told him that he would let him know. "The whole story was that I never traveled on an airplane, I'm scared of airplanes. So that's what my problem was."

When George Ford got home that night, his wife told him to call John. I said, 'What's up?' 'I want you to go to Germany with me, this will be the time of your life.' I said, 'Okay, I'm going. What about a passport?' He said, 'You be here at the office at eight in the morning.'"

The next morning John actually flew with him to Washington D.C. in his private plane, to get him a passport that same day. Flying back to Columbus, where they would leave the next morning for an eight-day trip, Ford said to him—a few words that barely encompassed his deep feelings—"John, you're something else."

Although Ford accompanied John on numerous business trips, he would never sit in on the business discussions, because if any part of what was discussed came out, he did not want John to think he was the one who had revealed it. One night, while they were on a trip, John came to Ford's hotel room and "cussed me out" for leaving a meeting. For the first time, Ford explained why he would not sit in on them. And John's words were just as succinct as Ford's had been to him on the plane—"George, you're one helluva guy."

John tried hard to get Ford to buy $5,000 worth of shares of stock in his company when the price was still very low. Recalled Ford: "I said, 'John you know I'm just getting my business started, I'm trying to get it off the ground—I haven't got any money.' He said, 'Well, go over to the bank and I'll co-sign with you and get your $5,000.' I said no, I didn't want to do that. He worried me about a week or two with that thing." But Ford didn't buy any until sometime later, when the price of the stock was much higher. "I would have made, I guess, a couple of million. John laughed about it until the day he died, almost."

John, continued George Ford, was always in the forefront of supporting black causes. He was instrumental, for example, in paying for groups of local blacks to attend the black caucus that is held every year in Washington, D.C. He did this, explained Ford, "To get the folks exposed to some of the things that are taking place in Washington." He saw to it that contributions went to black churches and to such organizations as the NAACP and Urban League. He even did such things as buy up blocks of tickets when Jesse Jackson came to town, so that local blacks would have a chance to hear him and meet him.

John and George Ford were to share many experiences over the years: political campaigns, disappointments—John would feel one day, for instance, that Jimmy Carter let him down—and all the joys.

"Most everything he would attempt to do," said Ford, "he would tell me about it and ask me what I thought about it. He said he and I thought alike, more than any other person he ever knew. Every Christmas and every New Year, we'd call each other. Most of the time he would beat me to it. He'd call me and say, 'George, I love you.'"

12

POLITICS AND RACE

John had a ten year lease on the 13th Street office, and long before it was up he bought land for a new headquarters on Wynnton Road, in Columbus, the site of a homestead called Five Oaks. Leaving as many of the oaks as possible, he built a two-story building. The company moved into its new headquarters in 1966.

George Jeter, who was to become executive vice president and chief financial officer, joined the company shortly after they moved. The building, he would recall, was half empty—no more than a hundred and fifty people were working for them then.

At the time the company was licensed in eleven southeastern states, and one of Jeter's first assignments was to get them into additional states. By then, he said, other insurance companies had come to realize the potential of cancer insurance, and John was afraid that bigger companies would capture the market in those states before American Family could even get licensed in them.

"John bordered on genius, if he wasn't a genius—I guess it's a matter of definition," said Jeter. "He left the day-to-day operations of the business to others, which was good. He was an innovator, a visionary, a genius. He came up with ideas that were unbelievable."

Sometimes, he said, it made you feel kind of stupid when you worked with John. "He was a night person—he stayed up all hours of the night, and he slept a lot in the morning. So as a result, you might get a call at two or three and the morning, and this was John, wide awake. He'd get you out of a sound sleep and he'd say, 'Hey, what about so-and-so?' And that might be the first time you ever knew that this thing even existed. And John may have been thinkiing about it two or three months. So it did make you feel awfully stupid to wake up, half asleep, and get hit with something like that, when you wanted to be able to respond intelligently."

But though the company was expanding, finances continued to be a problem. John moved his account to a new bank, the Trust

Company of Columbus, founded by Frank Morast. Morast, who became a close friend, was able to get him financing at one particularly perilous point in the company's existence- "They had," Morast recalled, "one drawer of bills to be paid and one drawer for receipts, and they made them balance out the best they could."

No one who was unaware of the financial intricacies of the business would have guessed at that—not from John's manner, not from the way he and Elena entertained and enjoyed life

As Paul Amos said, "John was an individual who never worried about money. He had such confidence in his ability to make money that he felt there was no need for him to worry about spending money. He always told me, 'You're never going to save yourself out of debt. You're going to have to work hard enough to earn enough so that you can live the style of life you want to live.' And of course he was a fighter."

And there was his wild sense of humor that never changed, from the years of struggle through the years of wealth.

Once, as an example, he went on a hunting trip to South America. When he came back, he announced to his employees that they were all invited to a barbeque for lunch. This was not unusual—he often held barbecues on the grounds.

What made *this* one "unusual," however, was his announcement— which he made with a straight face—that he had been very fortunate to kill a lot of monkeys, and they were having barbequed monkey for lunch.

Frank Morast, who was with him at the time, said he and John walked down the back stairs from his office on the second floor.

"We were behind a couple of the top people, and they didn't know John was back there. They were talking about this luncheon. And one of them said, 'God damn, that son of a bitch ain't gonna make me eat monkey.'"

Worried that the giants in the insurance industry would get into the other states before he could, and knowing that he did not have the luxury of simply waiting to be licensed in state after state, John made in an ingenius move to enable the company to go national. He made a deal with another insurance company, Globe Life, in which he rented their license in other states and sold cancer insurance under their name until American Family could get its own license in those states. This meant recruiting more salespeople; it also meant he needed more money. He got the money by selling a block of stock to a man named Fred Carr who ran a mutual fund called the Enterprise Fund. John was eventually able to buy back the stock. At about that same time he set something into motion that in the years ahead would have a great impact in helping turn the still-fledgling company into a giant. He set up a stock bonus fund, where the salespeople—as part of overall incentive—would receive stock in the company in accordance with their production.

But meanwhile still another in the seemingly endless series of problems rose up to confront the company. It came under a harmless-sounding name—"coordination of benefits." But it could have meant the life of the company itself.

Simply, the major insurance companies, who wrote general medical health and accident policies, did not like *specific* illness insurance—insurance for one type of illness. They had a clause in their policies stating that they would pay a policy owner on his claim after other carriers with whom he had coverage for the same claim. They called this coordination of benefits, claiming that a person should not be paid twice for the same illness. So, if a person had a total claim of $10,000 against a major carrier, and was paid $5,000 by American Family, the other company would pay only $5,000 instead of the full $10,000. This could have been devastating for the company. Why would anyone with a general medical policy buy a supplemental policy from American Family when all it meant was that the benefit would be subtracted from the primary company's benefit?

The companies claimed that by not paying people twice for the same illness, they were serving public interest, since double-payment would encourage malingering, would result in people staying in hospitals or at home from work for longer periods. This might be true of certain types of illness or injuries. "But nobody," as Dick Schweitzer put it, "gets cancer to collect *insurance*."

The insurance industry, said Malcolm A. Hoffmann, a friend of John's and an attorney specializing in antitrust matters and litigation, acted in a frightened fashion now that John's company was really catching hold. They came up with a small study, the object of which was to show that the more policies you had, the longer you stayed in the hospital. John and Hoffmann, who represented him in this, argued that the study didn't really show that.

One of the things that happened was a congressional investigation. John appeared before the committee, where he was so convincing in his explanation for the need for a cancer policy that one of the congressmen actually asked him whether he himself could buy a policy.

"John was a very powerful convincer," Hoffmann was to say, admiringly.

Hoffmann brought suit against the major companies, claiming that these insurance carriers, by agreeing on a system of coordination of benefits, were in essence economically boycotting the single-risk policy. The case, with its various ancillary aspects, was to last for years. In one aspect of the case, they filed suit in Miami, Florida. Although they lost this case in the end, said Hoffmann, "the result became unimportant, because the insurance carriers didn't want these cases pending everywhere. It took the bloom off the rose." The companies began just not invoking coordination of benefits against John's policies.

Through all of this, as always, John tried not to let the burden of business problems affect his homelife.

One of his daughter's fondest memories is how openly affectionate he was. "He was as free to say 'I love you' just as he was free to say 'I don't like what you're doing.' I remember how much I liked it when he would put his arm around me and sing 'Let Me Call You Sweetheart.'" She and her father, she said, were alike in that they were both strong-willed—at times with each other. "But I was always his little girl, regardless."

She spoke, with a smile in her voice, of his jokes. "Sometimes when one of my friends would call me and he answered the phone, I'd be sitting right there and he wouldn't just put me right on. He'd say, 'Sorry, she's out possum hunting.' That was just him, that was his sense of humor."

He taught her early in life how to fish, how to bait a hook, and even how to clean them in a way that he preferred. Where most people cut off the head straight across, for some reason he preferred doing it in a V, from one gill to the other.

"He always would let us have friends over," Sita continued. "And when we'd go camping, he'd always let us invite over whoever we met at the campground. He'd tell them, 'Come on, let's fry fish together,' or whatever."

"Probably my first recollections of my father," added Shelby, "have to do with the camping trips. I remember that every time we picked up a pull-trailer or motor home or whatever, he had to modify it to meet his needs. He would always rig it up somehow with generators, extra water, whatever. We were always running out of water, there was never enough for everybody to take showers."

One trip that Shelby was to remember in particular was the time they drove from Columbus to the Panama Canal, taking a circuitous route since John intended to hunt along the way. "What really complicated everything was that Daddy decided to bring his own hunting rifles. He chose the M-1 carbine, the Army rifle."

They were stopped at the Mexican border, but John was able to talk the guards out of confiscating the rifles. But the guards at the border of Guatemala, who carried machineguns since there was guerrilla fighting going on at the time, insisted on keeping the rifles.

"Boy, did Daddy get mad," said Shelby. In fact, recalled Elena, the commandant said to him, "Mr. Amos, I have a jail just for people like you."

But before John gave up the guns, he had a quiet, "side-bar" conference with a young man whom they had taken along on the trip. "He was somewhat of a firearms expert," Shelby said, "and knew how to field-strip weapons. I remember Daddy pulling him off to the side and saying, 'Before we turn these over, can you fix them so that they won't work?'"

The young man didn't—but that was just a sample, a tiny sample, of John Amos's stubbornness when he thought he was right.

To John, those camping trips and motor home travels with the family were the best way of truly being with them; it cut out the rest of the world. Business trips, which he was doing more and more of— with Elena when possible—was not really "travel" in his mind; it was basically to and from an airport. What brightened the family motor trips even more was that upon entering an area they wanted to see, or sometimes before, they would buy local histories, and one of them would read aloud from it as they drove. They didn't simply buy these books for souvenirs.

Then, in the mid-60s, he came up with an idea for another sort of "vehicle" that the whole family might enjoy.

A pontoon boat—but one so different, so characteristic of John Amos at his most unique, that it just might have been a one-of-a-kind.

But not a *fancy* one-of-a kind. Just the opposite.

His secretary, Carol Royer, would see him as his desk, trying to sketch a boat that looked like something from the "Beverly Hillbillies."

"He couldn't figure out how he wanted to do the floor of it," she recalled, "and he'd sit there and he'd draw and he'd work on it and he'd get mad. He searched all over to try to find pontoons. He finally found somebody to help him."

That "somebody" was the father and uncle of Brooks Massey, the young man John Amos had gotten a summer job in Florida.

"Mr. John wanted a houseboat," he said, "so they built it behind my dad's service station."

It was something Huckleberry Finn would have loved. They got 55-gallon drums and welded them together, then set a trailer—with an awning on it— in the middle. Called the "John B," the jerry-built houseboat had a bumblebee painted on the side, and was powered by an outboard motor.

John docked it on the Chattahoochie River, and would take the family out on it. But they weren't all "happy campers" on that craft. Sita would still remember, as an adult, how embarrassed she was by it, especially with all the yachts and slick speedboats on the river—"It was funny-looking," would be her to-the-point way of describing it.

All the while, the Amos home was gradually growing into what the Amoses themselves would call the house "that Jack built." As people came to live with them, and grandchildren appeared, the house would take its final form. It would have four bedrooms, six baths, three pantries, two dining rooms, two studies, a living room, a music room, a children's playroom, an exercise room, and a room they called the "museum," since it housed their mementoes. Outside were terraces, a covered pool, a fishing pond and richly-flowered gardens.

He wanted, he had said, the house to be a place where his children would want to bring their friends; and it was that, but more: it was the center, in many ways, of the Amos's lives. Every weekend, it seemed, they would entertain—sometimes hundreds of people.

Frank Martin, who knew the Amoses for years, and was a mayor of Columbus, said that Elena was a counter balance to John, a decompression chamber. "He was a very direct person and she was a wonderful hostess, kind and generous. Seeing what a generous person she was, what a gracious hostess, she softened up a lot of situations at times that could have left bruised feelings. She was always able through parties and social gatherings to mend a lot of fences that he had broken down."

13

BECOMING ESTABLISHED

Commenting on John's giving up the debit insurance business to concentrate on cancer policies, Matt Metcalfe said that most American businessmen seem to try to be all things to all people. The smart ones are those who can put all their attention and emphasis on the one thing that can make their company successful and forget about the rest. John found a need and he filled it.

"He was amazing," continued Metcalfe. "He was always working. He was always thinking. He always had a yellow pad within arm's length and he would start to write and write rapidly and would not say a word until he finished it. It would be like Mozart writing a symphony. There wouldn't be one superfluous word. It would be as clear as a crystal drop. And he was that way when he talked."

John was a doer. "He always did *something* about a problem. He never did *nothing*. He never expected a problem simply to go away. He might make a mistake, but if he did then he just turned around and did something else."

He also had to feel "right" about whatever he did. Surely most people have had the experience of working or trying to reach a decision when "something else" takes over, a power—and you are almost set apart from it. "Well, that was John," said Metcalfe. "If he did not get that natural feeling—a spirituality if you will—he wouldn't do. And once something *felt* right, and as long as it continued to feel right, he would prosecute it until it either worked or failed. He would follow his instinct better than most of us. Some of us let conventional wisdom, peer pressure, fear of loss, greed, selfishness get in the way of that quiet, still voice. Not John. He'd listen to it. He had a superior sense of what is right. He would do the right decent thing, not anything sleazy." If he bent a rule, it was to get to the end product when the end result was right for everyone.

Dick Schweitzer spoke, too, of a force at work in John. "I think that something larger than John himself moved him. I don't mean to say that he was an ordained instrument of God, but I think he was an inspired person. Most people think of preachers, teachers, researchers, and so forth as being inspired. But I think John really was inspired, though what I can't identify is the full source of the inspiration. I know that part of it was his great love for his wife." He knew, Schweitzer reflected, what the two of them had been through over the years during the drastically-changing tides of the business. "I can remember her saying to me at their twenty-fifth anniversary party, 'Dick, I'm so glad you could come. Because you were with us through all of the bad times, I want you to be here for one of the good times.'"

Another clue to what inspired him came from John himself. When Schweitzer once asked him about it, he said, "I guess I'd have to say it was what my mother expected of us boys."

Schweitzer went on to say that John "could see the future, I'll tell you that. He could see things coming from way out, things that happened politically, sociologically, economically. He could sense it," Schweitzer said, adding poetically, "He could hear it was 'raining in the mountains;' he knew 'the creeks were going to rise.'"

John's sense of following his instincts extended, naturally enough, to an uncanny ability in picking people as his top aides, people who, in many cases, did not have the slightest experience in insurance or even in sales of any kind. One of many such people was George Othell Hand, Ph.D.

Dr. Hand was the senior minister of the First Baptist Church of Columbus, a beautiful, 3000-member, antebellum sanctuary, the largest church in Georgia outside of Atlanta. His service was also televised to an audience of hundreds of thousands of viewers.

John Amos entered his life unexpectedly one day in 1966 when Dr. Hand had been with the church about six years. It came in the form of a telephone call from John, saying he would like to take Dr. Hand out to lunch. John and Bill Amos came to Dr. Hand's study.

"Let's just talk a little," John said, "and then we'll go to lunch."

The reason John had called him, he explained, was that they wanted to invite him to become a member of the board of directors of the company.

"It was quite a deal," recalled Dr. Hand. "Very few ministers are ever on corporate boards. In his very perceptive way, John said, 'You may wish to consult your board to see that there will be no conflict of interests or any objections," but I said, 'John, that's very thoughtful of you to say, but knowing boards and churches and committees, I don't wish to consult the board because someone will say, 'Well, pastor, maybe don't.' So I said, 'Give me the problem and I'll work it out here.' And that was that. John said, 'Beautiful. We'd love to have you. We want your image, your prestige and the insight that you've demonstrated leading this corporate structure called a church. We want that insight for our company.'"

Dr. Hand discovered at this first meeting and lunch that John, in Dr. Hand's words, was very ingenious, that he lived and worked "in the range of ideas and visions and business acumen, and so he assumed that everybody else was in that range, too. So, talking to him even that first time we were together was almost like getting in on the second half of a sentence. He assumed you knew the subject matter and how the sentence was structured. And that never ceased. As close as we were, I never worked harder than when I sat with John Amos carrying on a conversation."

The upshot was that Dr. Hand did go on the board, and there was no objection to it from his church. Then four years later John approached him about a full-time position. As Dr. Hand described it, "John, in his perceptive, visionary, far-reaching, ideal world, saw that I would top out of that church—in other words, I would have lost my challeng. I would have done the things I wanted to do there." In an uncanny way, John had come to him when he was contemplating moving on, perhaps to go into academia or to become an industrial chaplain.

John told Dr. Hand, "You're still a very young man. You just turned fifty. And if you don't want to go to another church from here—and I can't conceive of another one you'd really like to go from here—come with us. I'll send you across the nation as an inspirational speaker."

Dr. Hand's answer was, "Okay, John, you are a prophet and the time is coming. I will let you know."

Nine months later Dr. Hand told him the time had come, that he would like to leave the church on Easter Sunday.

"When I announced my decision to leave the pulpit of the First Baptist Church to join this company of John Amos's, a lot of people thought I had lost my mind. Some said, 'Othell, I sure hope you got a contract.' Well, the truth of the matter is, I never had a contract. You know, in the ministry you use the word 'calling'—divinely led, called into the ministry. I was as certainly called into this work as I was to the pulpit of the First Baptist Church. And I knew that."

After Dr. Hand decided to come with the company, John asked him how he planned to maintain his relationship with the church since he would still be living in the city. Dr. Hand told him that he might be pastor emeritus, but John said he would prefer he not do that.

"He didn't want me to linger on there, and as a matter of fact I didn't want to either. He said, 'We really want to dilute the ministerial image'"—not to try to eradicate that Dr. Hand had had an illustrious career as a minister, but that "'I don't want my people to think I've imported someone who's going to preach to them.'"

Dr. Hand, who years later would retire from the company as Senior Vice President, Board of Directors, started out as Director of Motivation—John's choice of a title. His job was to go across the country giving inspirational talks to groups and seminars of American Family salespeople. Then there came a time when John decided he needed him more in Washington, D.C. He became Director of Government Relations, and as a representative of American Family he set about establishing relationships with people in government. As John put it, "I want you to be at the receptions, the dinners, the parties, the hotels—wherever they are, I want you there.'"

Dr. Hand never registered as a lobbyist—the company did have lobbyists— but when, for instance, an issue of interest to the company came up that they would want their lobbyist to discuss with a congressman, Dr. Hand would be the one to contact the congressman and ask to see the lobbyist. "That became a very strategic role, and that's what John envisioned," said Dr. Hand. Since the insurance industry was so regulated and there were so many rules and tax and trade issues involved, John "always said the company will rise or fall in Washington. It would be what happens in Washington that either sets us up for business or for insolvency."

The company now had a town house in Washington, and Dr. Hand would commute there, would generally go up on Monday afternoon and be back in Columbus on Friday afternoon. "So I would stay at the town house three or four nights a week. I would be relating to senators and congressmen, to the White House, to Cabinet members. It came to pass that I knew every senator and a great many representatives by their first names and had been in half of their homes."

John, he said—echoing what so many people said—was an incurable politician. "John breathed politics, he slept it, he ate it. Nothing did he enjoy more than to sit down and speculate about politics and politicians and government affairs. And if I didn't get to his office often enough, he would summon me there and he'd say, 'Tell me what's going on.' He'd ask the question and then he'd express himself."

John used to prepare for the board meetings, Dr. Hand said, "to perfection." He would anticipate every issue, every subject or question, and so the meetings "would just roll right along. His board meetings were very beautiful. The reports were always bullish. He could wrap it up in a few succinct sentences and then push his chair back and that was it. He didn't like long meetings."

Dr. Hand used to enjoy watching John's body language. "When John would call me into his office, he would say, 'Sit down, Parson,' or, 'Sit down, Othell.' If he ever said 'Parson,' I knew he was in a jovial mood, because he liked that. He liked to act sort of like I was a country parson. So he'd say, 'Sit down,' as though we were going to have a long visit. And I think he would think that, but then something else would come into his mind and I'd see him shuffle his papers and then start whistling. At that moment I would excuse myself. I'd say, 'Well, John, I'm going to have to go. I know you're busy.' I might not have been there two minutes. I have sometimes thought that he might have interpreted it as being impatient with him or preferring not to spend too much time with him. But I liked that better than the other way around. I wouldn't ever have wanted him to think, 'God, he never leaves. There comes Othell. Tell him I'm not in.'"

But Dr. Hand knew he was right in cutting it short. There was no sitting in his office just chewing the fat; John did not like that, wasn't comfortable with it. Nor did he like sitting through long speeches

"He knew I was a speech maker and he wanted a speech maker, but he didn't want to listen to them. It wasn't unusual for John to slip out when I'd be making a speech. God, that was hard to counter, because here sat your salesmen and there goes the CEO walking out on the speaker. But that was John."

Away from the office, however—on the trips John frequently took with Dr. Hand, or when at the town house—he loved conversation, especially late into the night.

"When we were in Washington we'd end our day at the town house, and we would be there in the late evening chatting. Now, he liked a night cap. He loved Canadian Club and Coke." Years later, his favorite drink would be vodka. "I can see him sitting in that chair, telephone within reach. And he would smoke a cigarette—he consumed a great many of those—and we'd be talking about everybody. We would have already exhausted politics, the Washington scenarios, and we would be going back through his childhood. We would be back down in Enterprise, Alabama, or Milton, Florida, and how he first got into politics, his courtship with Elena, their marriage. He idealized Elena, always. She was always the apple of his eye, the daughter of his heart."

John, he explained, never wanted to go to bed; he loved to talk into the early hours of the morning. "By about three or four o'clock I'd be trying to slip away, and he'd say, 'Well, a little bit more.' The only hope I had was when he said, 'You know, I'd like a glass of milk.' We always had chocolate candy there, and when he'd reach for the candy and the glass of milk, I would think, 'Oh, hallelujah, we're about to get to bed.' He was signing off the Canadian Club, and he would go to bed. He could just go right to sleep. It seemed that the candy and the milk following the cocktails just put him out."

Dr. Hand said that he often felt in awe of John. "I could never quite feel that we were on a par. We had different worlds. I felt like he was far superior, though he was my junior by four years."

Though John might have seemed outwardly irreligious, that was the furthest thing from reality. John, he said, was very devout in his heart, and mind, always wanted to do what was right. "He didn't care whether he was a Baptist or Methodist or Episcopalian or, eventually, toward the end of his life, a Catholic. It was all in his heart. The other were outward expressions, Like personalities differ, so churches differ. And I admire him for that, and I agree with him very much."

John, he continued, didn't go to church a lot—a little more toward the end of his life, a little more at the beginning of his career when he first came to Columbus. But there came a time when he did not go simply because it was laboring the obvious to John, and therefore it was a very arduous hour for John to go and sit through something "that was identical every Sunday, no changes, not a jot nor a tittle of a change.

"That bored John. The minister was usually either laboring the obvious or into some innocuous area that didn't speak to the here and now. John wanted the minister to relate the Bible or whatever is in the essence of religion to the here and now, to help us be better where we are. We don't know what the hereafter brings, and there's one thing for sure. We can't do anything about that now. John wanted to enrich life and he very much expected ministers to do that. I think the reason he invited me on the board was that I was more of a motivational minister. I always spoke to the enrichment of life. I didn't care to speak about Hell or Heaven or the hereafter. I didn't know enough about it. So I avoided those subjects."

But John never lost that "devout spark." It would come out in those long sessions they would have in the evenings, or it might come out when Dr. Hand would just walk into his office. Sometimes he would ask Dr. Hand, "Othell, what do you really think happens after we die? Are we like a cow or a horse or a pig?"

"I would say, 'John, there are intimations of immortality everywhere we turn, in nature, in the outreach of man's own spirit,' and so forth. We'd talk about that. He cared about that. He would speak about 'when I'm gone,' or 'in the next world.'"

They spoke, too, of sin and morality and ethics. John felt that there are things, such as drinking or smoking, that go against our body and that we would be better off not doing, but he felt that those things didn't hurt anybody else.

"It was hurting the other fellow or society that John recoiled from very much."

14

THE DRIVING FORCE

John breathed politics, he slept it, he ate it, Dr. Hand had said. *"Nothing did he enjoy more than to sit down and speculate about politics and politicians and government affairs."*

Almost every person with any importance in John's life, when talking about him, would mention sooner or later his deep interest in politics.

Mrs. Frances King Lolley described him as "the most political-minded man I had ever been around in my life. He was involved with local politics; he was involved with national politics, international politics. The first time he asked me to call the governor's office or the President's office, I just thought, 'I can't do that. You just don't pick up the telephone and dial the President's office.' But he did if he wanted to talk to whomever was in office. I realized for the first time that you could pick up the telephone and call the President of the United States if you wanted to. That was just something new for this little old Southern girl. He could deal with the little everyday worker and he could deal with the heads of state. He never ceased to amaze me."

Carol Royer was one of the people who felt that John would have wanted to be a United States senator more than anything else. "I think that if he thought he could have run for the office and been elected, he would have left American Family, because politics was his thing. One thing he learned from losing the election in Florida , he told me, was that no matter what project he had going, he would sit through to the end. He would never take off and go fishing thinking something's being taken care of, because that's when he lost his race in Florida."

Robyn Smith, who became his secretary in 1987, spoke of how "he gave me a much greater interest in my community, because he was very political. He was very involved and very caring about what went on everywhere, from the smallest job in government to the largest, to the President. I had always been interested in things like who became President. But I wasn't so sure I was so interested in who was mayor. But he taught me a lot more about that, and that what you do in your community can make a difference, that what you do with people around you can make a difference."

Glenn Vaughn, Jr., editor of what is now the *Columbus Ledger-Enquirer* (he retired as publisher and chairman of the board of the parent company) said that John got involved in politics soon after he came to town and that during those early years the two of them were on different sides on various political issues. Vaughn, who with his wife, Nancy, became dear friends of the Amoses, recalled an editorial he wrote in which he referred to John as operating a "political juggernaut." When Vaughn got to his office the next morning John was sitting in his office.

"He confronted me eyeball to eyeball," recalled Vaughn. "He said, 'This is really not fair. You know, you're too tough on me. I tell you, you just don't understand my motives or something, and I just wanted to be treated fairly.' He didn't sit by and take it. He was a scrapper." After a while, as they developed respect for each other, "It got to the point where John wanted to know what I thought about some political candidate or some issue. Sometimes he'd call me in the middle of the night."

The spectrum of John's friends in political life ranged, amazingly, from the left to the far right, both Democrat and Republican. It included, among so many others, Hubert Humphrey, liberal senator, vice president and presidential candidate, on the one side; conservative Senator Jesse Helms, Republican from North Carolina, and Alabama Governor George Wallace on the other; and somewhere in the middle Senator Sam Nunn, Democrat from Georgia, who might fairly be called a moderate. He was close to President Carter and President Johnson, as well to President Reagan. At his funeral, all his pallbearers were politicians, including such diverse figures as United States Senators Orrin Hatch, Republican-Utah; Howell Heflin, Democrat-Alabama; Strom Thurmond, Republican-South Carolina; Jesse Helms, Republican-North Carolina; and from the House of Representatives were Charles Rangel, Democrat-New York City, and Richard Ray, Democrat-Georgia. Among the mourners were President

Carter and his wife, Rosalynn, and Senator Ernest "Fritz" Hollings, Democrat-South Carolina.

As a group, they probably would have trouble voting on any single thing, but they were bound together by the deep respect and friendship they felt for John Amos.

Being in an industry that was heavily regulated by the government, it was, as has been pointed out earlier, only practical and certainly good sense for John to maintain friendships with people on both sides of the aisle in government. At one time, in fact, American Family supposedly had the largest Political Action Committee (PAC) in the country. But that only accounts for the fact that John had many widely-disparate friends on the political scene. What it does *not* account for is the *quality* and richness of these friendships. A large part of the answer to that lay within John Amos himself, the qualities within him that he brought to other people, the qualities that the friends he made in government—as well as the every-day-person he happened to meet—felt in his presence.

John once said of the congress and the senate that he not only considered them the representatives of the people, but of *all* the people, not just those in their own districts. "I have found them to be very conscientious. They have different philosophies from me and I can't always sell them. But in general I can at least get to see them and their staff." And he had no qualms about going into seeing them. "I had," he explained with one of his laughs, "the guts of a burglar when I was five years old."

After John's death, Senator Helms spoke of the very first time he had met John Amos. It was a day, he said, he will never forget.

"It was a busy morning in our office," he recalled. "Our receptionist signaled me on the intercom and said, 'Senator, I slipped away from my desk to let you know that the nicest man just came in. I know you have a full schedule of appointmemnts, but I think you'll want to meet Mr. John Amos. He's such a pleasant gentleman."

It so happened, continued Senator Helms, that the next appointment was a few minutes late. "I suggested that John Amos be brought in. As he entered John said, 'I'm just going to poke my head in; I know what a nuisance it is to have someone come by without an appointment.' I waved him in and for the better part of twenty minutes I was in the company of one of the most delightful men I've ever known."

Senator Nunn had met him much earlier in the late sixties. At the time, Senator Nunn was a representative in the State Legislature. He had heard of John Amos, but had never met him. They met at a function where the main speaker was United States Representative Jack Brinkley, a Democrat from Columbus.

"He had on a white suit, white shoes, and white socks," recalled Senator Nunn. "I'm not sure what color his tie was," he added with a smile. "He was a very appealing fellow, very attractive. You noticed him immediately."

John gave a speech introducing Representative Brinkley. "I remember," said Senator Nunn, "that though Brinkley's speech was pretty good, the introduction is what I remember about the evening. He made a speech that had a lot of humor in it, a lot of wit, and a reasonable amount of exaggeration. The salesman came through. But he gave Brinkley a great introduction."

Senator Nunn met John Amos after the speeches and would recall thinking at the time what an impressive person he was. Senator Nunn met John briefly several other times while he was in the State Legislature, then went to see John for help when in 1972 he decided to run in the Democratic primary for the United States Senate.

"I went to Columbus," Senator Nunn said, "and talked to him a long time. What appealed to me then about him was he was absolutely frank with me. He said, 'I'm going to support you and I'm going to support two other candidates.' Most people who do that don't tell you. And he named them. Then he said, 'If you keep doing well, I'll help you some more. I want to help you because you're a nice young man. You deserve to have a hearing."

John contributed about a thousand dollars to his campaign, which in those days was a generous contribution. After Senator Nunn did indeed do well in the primary—and, in fact, eventually won both the primary and the election—John supported him even more and got other people in Columbus to help raise money for his campaigns.

"John," said Senator Nunn, "was a very interesting combination. He would come up with an outrageous exaggeration, but on the other hand he was just very candid and laid it on the table. A lot of the times when he said something outrageous, he wasn't really being funny; it was to make a point. Sometimes he would go far beyond his goal and get your reaction and then back up to what his real goal was."

John and Senator Nunn were good friends from the time of the 1972 election; they would be in communication with each other at least seven or eight times a year. Whenever John was in Washington, he would usually come by and visit with him.

"I have known him and Elena over the years. I've been involved in two or three meetings with him that related to his business, but my major contact with him was more about what was going on in Columbus—helping Columbus, helping Georgia and the national economy. Most of the time—I'd say 85% of the time—that I was with John it didn't relate to American Family or any of his businesses. It was related to Fort Benning, to the School of the Americas. He and Elena were very involved and probably more responsible than any other people I know for getting the School of the Americas in Columbus and making it permanent. Or it was related to the general economy or the general political situation—he loved to talk about the national political scene and what was going on—give me his views and get my views."

Senator Nunn's feeling was that the essence of John's political philosophy was pragmatism. "He was conservative economically, but I would say on racial issues, and a lot of issues like that, he was very progressive. He did an awful lot for the black community in Columbus matter how much wealth he had, he never lost his understanding of those who didn't have it. That's what made him somewhat unique from a lot of people I know with a lot of wealth. A lot of them forget about how people who don't have a lot of money think and act. John made sure he never did that, either politically or economically or socially."

Elena, Senator Nunn went on, was a special person, too. "He was so proud of her and she was so proud of him. They loved each other. It was a great marriage, and they both complemented each other. It was so obvious."

John did not confine himself in his friendships, continued Senator Nunn, to particular people with particular philosophies. "I think he judged the individual more than he did the political party or the philosophy. But I would say that if he had a choice of voting for a good Democract or a good Republican, and he liked them both individually, he would end up being a Democrat. But he would have had no hesitancy supporting Republicans."

But *why* did he attract as good *friends* people of different political stripes? Why did these people, many of whom were so different from each other in so many ways, not only look on John as a friend, but as someone they loved? Said Senator Nunn, "Obviously in the political business, people who are generous with contributions certainly are welcome by politicians, since you need money to run a campaign. There's no doubt about that. But I think what people liked about John so much was the same experience I had with him. If he had a particular business problem, he would not hesitate to get in touch with somebody. I don't mean he was shy about it, but that really wasn't what he talked to you about most of the time.

"Most of the time he would talk to you about the general economy, about his concern about America, about where we were going. I had a lot of conversations with him back in the Watergate period; he was so worried about the economy then. He was not a person who came in and gave you a donation one day and the next day would call up and say, 'Now I want you to do this, this, and this.' He didn't approach it in that way at all."

1. John Shelby Amos and Helen Amos (parents) with sons Paul (left) and Bill (R; brothers to John B.)

2. John B. Amos as a teenager.

3. John Shelby Amos and Helen Amos.

4. John B. Amos as a teenager.

5. John B. Amos in the early 1940s.

6. John B. Amos and Elena Diaz-Verson on their wedding day, September 23, 1945 in Miami, Florida. Bill Amos is left, and Teresa Bana de Diaz-Verson, Elena's mother, is right.

7. John B. Amos in 1955 founded American Family Life Assurance Company of Columbus, Georgia, now AFLAC.

8. John B. Amos representing clients while a practicing attorney in Fort Walton Beach, Florida, in the late 1940s.

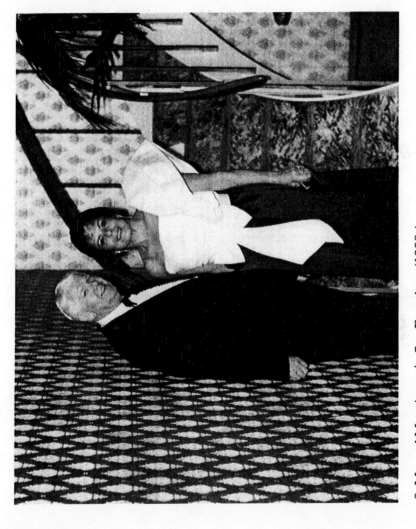

9. Mr. and Mrs. Amos in San Francisco (1980s).

10. Mr. and Mrs. Amos with Senator Orrin Hatch of Utah.

11. John B. Amos with Hubert Humphrey, then senator from Minnesota, and a long-standing friend of John's.

12. Mr. and Mrs. Amos with Senator Howell Heflin of Alabama.

13. John B. Amos with long-time friend Senator Strom Thurmond of South Carolina.

14. John B. Amos with Senator John Glenn of Ohio.

15. Mr. and Mrs. Amos with Congressman Charles Rangel of New York.

16. John B. Amos with Senator Hollings of South Carolina.

17. John B. Amos with Senator William Brock of Tennessee.

18. Mrs. Amos with Congressman Richard Ray of Georgia.

19. Mr. and Mrs. Amos with Senator Sam Nunn of Georgia.

20. John B. Amos when he received his honorary doctorate degree from Mercer University with Bob Steed (left) and President Kirby Godsey (right).

21. John B. Amos at the New York Stock Exchange when AFLAC, Inc. became publicly traded at the Exchange on June 14, 1974.

22. John B. Amos at the ground-breaking ceremony for the AFLAC Headquarters Building in Columbus, Georgia.

23. John B. Amos at the ribbon cutting ceremony for AFLAC Tower Headquarters Building in Columbus, Georgia, in 1974.

24. John B. Amos with Rosalyn Carter.

25. John B. Amos with the paddle wheel boat he built and named for his wife, the "Elena Queen of Hearts."

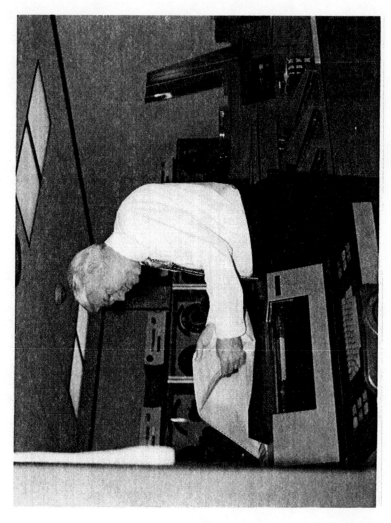

26. John B. Amos at work with the new company computer equipment.

27. John B. Amos with Governor George Wallace of Alabama and President Jimmy Carter.

28. Mrs. Amos with the award posthumously presented to Mr. Amos by the Emperor of Japan in recognition of his outstanding achievements.

29. John Shelby Amos II, son of John B. Amos, accepting the posthumous award, given to his father by the Emperor of Japan, from Japan's Ambassador to the United States, Ryohei Murata, at a special ceremony in Washington, D. C. held on January 31, 1991.

30. AFLAC Headquarters Building.

31. Mr. and Mrs. Amos with their children: John Shelby Amos II and Maria Teresa Amos, and Mrs. Amos' parents, Salvador Diaz-Verson and Teresa Bana de Diaz-Verson.

15

HIGHER IN POLITICS

John's first active interest in politics, as we have seen, had begun inexplicably when he was a boy when he not only urged his father to run for the state legislature, but was his campaign manager. Maybe, as has been suggested, this interest in politics came from his mother. But what-ever the source, it was *there*. It was almost as much a part of him as was his physical being.

In Columbus, one of the first campaigns he got involved in was Jack Brinkley's, when he had first run for Congress. Attorney Lennie Davis would recall that he, Davis, ran the campaign while John provided the ideas, planned such things as campaign breakfasts, and handled the printing of the campaign literature. And Brinkley won a seat he retained until his retirement to return to the practice of law.

John's friend George Ford mustered the support of the blacks in the campaign. And something happened the night of the victory-celebration that "tied John and me a little closer," he said.

Ford happened to go to the back of the room where the celebration was being held to get a cold drink. Two white men were standing together back there, verbally tearing John Amos apart. Ford touched one of them on the arm and said, "Look here, I'm John Amos's friend and I want to tell you something. If you don't say any more, I won't tell John a damned thing you said. But if you say one more word about John Amos, I'm going back and tell him every damned thing you said." Both of them said they were sorry; one shook his hand and walked straight out of the place. "I never did tell John, because they lived up to their part of the bargain. But somebody else went back and told him, and I think he appreciated it."

John also played a role—a most unusual one, to say the least— when Barry Goldwater, the conservative Republican, ran for the presidency. Someone, said Lennie Davis, came up with the idea of a campaign gimmick for Goldwater. They would manufacture and distribute a soda, which would be gold-colored and would be called GOLD WATER. The slogan, Lennie Davis recalled, read something like: "The Right Drink for the Conservative Cause."

Some people approached Lennie Davis with it and asked if he could think of any way to promote the drink. Davis answered that they would be able to promote it if they could get one man, John Amos, interested in it

They inquired, "Why?"

"Because he's an idea man. If we walk over to see him now, he'll either say yes or no. And if he says yes, he'll do something about it."

They spoke with John who, after hearing them out, said, "Well, what money have we got to run with this?"

"We don't have any money," Davis answered.

And John's answer to that was, "Okay, I can print some labels and put all that stuff on it. If you can get RC Cola® to manufacture one case of drinks for us, we'll glue the labels on it and we'll go see Mr. Goldwater and see if he will accept this as an official part of his campaign. If he does, we'll up and run with it."

John, Davis, and another man put up $100 a piece with which they printed some labels and put them on. They flew to Goldwater headquarters in Washington, where the idea was accepted and it was made an official part of the Goldwater campaign.

They then succeeded in getting RC Cola to manufacture the drink, though it was rarely used in the campaign.

"It didn't get Goldwater into office," Davis said with a smile, "but when Barry came to Columbus to give a speech, we got a picture of him drinking GOLD WATER. But the point is, in five minutes time John had made up his mind about it. 'Oh, yeah, I'll go with that.' And then he got us off and running, and as a result we ended up manufacturing that drink in eight different places across America by the time the campaign was over. Of course we didn't make any money at it. We broke even though. We sold enough of it so we didn't lose anything.

"If I were to say one thing, this kind of characterizes the type of person I think he was. He was a dreamer. But unlike most of us who have dreams, he tried to do something about them. He didn't just sit there if he had a dream. He made an effort."

☙

Hubert Humphrey and John were particularly close friends. According to John, he first met Humphrey at the 1948 Democratic Convention, when John—a student at the time—managed to get a job as a "runner" for the Platform Committee. But their friendship began in 1964 when Humphrey ran for vice-president under Lyndon Johnson. John was introduced to Humphrey, recalled Elena Amos, by a mutual friend, Morris Ernst, the attorney who won the legal battle to permit Joyce's *Ulysses* into this country. Ernst wrote to Humphrey that he felt that John could be of great help in his campaign in the South.

When John joined the campaign, he met a man who was to be another of his great friends. This was Patrick J. O'Connor, a lawyer who had been a longtime, volunteer fundraiser for Hubert Humphrey.

O'Connor, a founding partner of O'Connor & Hannon, with offices in Minneapolis and Washington, D.C., met Humphrey in 1943, when O'Connor was still in law school and Humphrey was running for mayor of Minneapolis. O'Connor worked for him more or less as a go-fer in several campaigns, a route that led to his becoming—among the long list of his titles—a director of the Democratic National Committee. It was Humphrey who in 1961 advised the Minneapolis lawyer to open an office in Washington where—though his practice spread to general law—O'Connor started off representing clients before Congress and executive agencies.

"John," explained O'Connor, "was in a unique position to help Humphrey. Humphrey's reputation in the South was that of a flaming liberal, and many people in the South were critical of Johnson for picking him."

This went back to a famous civil rights speech that Humphrey gave at the 1948 Democratic convention in which he said, "Let's come out of the darkness and get in the sunshine," and the Southern delegations walked off the floor.

John not only served as a fundraiser but he was a rarity in the sense that, though a lot of people of means contributed money to the Democratic party, there weren't many—if any—who were the political strategist in the South that John was.

"He knew the political organization in the Southern states," said O'Connor. "He knew the senators and the governors and he had a history of working with them. They respected him. This came about mainly because of John's love for politics. I would say there wasn't a day during the week that John wasn't on the phone gathering intelligence about various campaigns and keeping up his contacts with Southern senators, representatives, and chairmen of the state organizations. And he was shrewd in figuring out strategy. He also knew the importance of the media and was on a first name basis with many people on the Southern newspapers and TV stations. So John was invaluable in advising Humphrey how to proceed in the South. He also set up the appointments in many instances."

John would call people he didn't even know and say something like, "Now look, this guy Humphrey isn't so bad, you know. I mean, I know him quite well. He's coming down your way and I'd like you to get to know him a little bit."

Although John concentrated mainly on Southerners, he also had ties because of American Family in about forty-eight states, so he was able to get intelligent information about various issues in the different states and could advise Humphrey on what to come out strong for, what to avoid.

Both John's personality and Humphrey's personality—which meshed—were such that even many people opposed to Humphrey's civil rights stand welcomed and were friendly to him. Even leaders of the Southern opposition in Congress never seemed to take it personally. O'Connor recalled running into them occasionally and having them say, "How's that friend of yours, Hubert? He's been damning me lately," or they would tell Humphrey himself, "Hubert, you sure damned the hell out of us today, but we're getting back tomorrow."

There was, above all, a great camaraderie between John and Humphrey. Said O'Connor, "They joked a lot, talked politics a lot, would go out to dinner. I can't recall John ever lobbying Humphrey on a particular issue for American Family. He may have, or Humphrey may have asked him, but it was never a reason for the meetings. Mainly it was social, political. It was that kind of relationship."

Humphrey and his wife Muriel would visit John and Elena in Columbus, and the Amoses would visit them at their home. Parenthetically, perhaps as an example of the kind of down-to-earth man Humphrey was, Frank Morast told of a little incident when Humphrey was in Columbus and John brought him over to Morast's house, mainly because Morast was a collector of Indian relics, as was Humphrey.

"I didn't notice where he parked his car," said Morast, "because I didn't see him until he came into the house. But he parked it in the middle of the street. In fact, it was a dead-end street. A little old lady who lived there got in her car to go uptown, and this car was in her way. She started blowing that horn and blowing that horn. Humphrey goes out and sees what's the matter and walks over to her car and apologizes, introducing himself. 'I'm Hubert Humphrey.'

The little old lady stared at him for several moments, her eyes gradually widening, and then popping full-width. 'My God,' she gasped, 'You *are*.'"

John would occasionally visit Humphrey when he became Vice President. And John campaigned for him again when Humphrey ran for the presidential nomination in 1968.

When Johnson announced in April of 1968 that he wouldn't be running again, said O'Connor, it didn't give Humphrey much notice to start his own campaign before the convention in Chicago. Again, John was both a fundraiser and a strategist. One of the things Humphrey had going against him was his loyalty to Johnson's position on the Viet Nam war. Another, again, was Southern opposition to him.

John would recall a very pertinent bit of advice he gave to Humphrey if he hoped to win in the South. "What we need to do in the South is to attend all county commissioners' conventions and all sheriffs' conventions we can get to and let them know you are a real human being and don't have horns, because the black folks have forgotten what you did for them, but the traditional Southern hasn't forgotten what you did to him."

Humphrey, of course, lost to Richard Nixon in 1968 by about 500,000 votes, and then failed to win the Democratic nomination in the 1972 election, losing to George McGovern.

An interesting footnote to this is a call that Matt Metcalfe received from John during Humphrey's run for the nomination.

John told him, "Matt, I've had a call from the Humphrey camp and Humphrey says that the only way he can win is to have Governor George Wallace on his ticket as Vice President." Wallace, though a Democrat, was ideologically on the opposite pole from Humphrey!

John went on, "He wants to meet Wallace. But you have to appreciate that this has got to be so insulated that if it gets out and either candidate is asked the question, he can deny it."

Metcalfe got to Wallace in a "super-confidential" manner, then called John. "I told John to fly to Bay Minette, Alabama, and see a mutual friend of ours, Jimmy Faulkner, who was a close friend and confidant of George Wallace's. I said, 'Jimmy will handle it from there.'" Arrangements were made for them to meet, but then Wallace, campaigning at a Laurel, Maryland, shopping center, was shot on May 15, 1972. Wallace went to the convention in a wheelchair. But it turned out to be moot as far as Humphrey and Wallace were concerned. McGovern won on the first ballot.

Not long before Humphrey died in January, 1978, a fundraising meeting, with Humphrey and John in attendance, was held to form the Hubert Humphrey Institute at the University of Minnesota. It took place at a Washington, D. C. hotel. Everyone knew that Humphrey was dying.

John had to leave early, just as they were serving Humphrey's plate at the head table. John went over to him, crouched down to keep from being conspicuous, and whispered that he would have to leave.

"Hubert," John recounted, "said, 'Just a minute.' He got up and called for 'Fritz' Mondale and Senator Anderson, former governor of Minnesota, to come over. And he put his arms around us and says, 'Fritz and Wendy, John Amos has been for me when it was dangerous to be for me in Georgia.' And he said, 'Y'all take care of him.' And that was the nearest to his last will and testament that I can possibly remember."

One of the things that broke Hubert Humphrey's heart, John once said, was that he loved "the Southerner" and could not understand their rejection of him.

"A total American" is the way John Amos described him. "I think he would have made one of the greatest presidents in history. And, of course, we've missed many great presidents. I think that Hubert Humphrey stands in history along with the Daniel Websters and the Henry Clays, with those who made great contributions but were never quite at the right place at the right time."

According to O'Connor, John did not get involved with McGovern, because McGovern was too liberal for him. But he spent a lot of time working on congressional and senatorial campaigns. Then when Jimmy Carter emerged as a possible nominee in 1975, John—since Humphrey was still alive then and was considering running again—was faced with a dilemma. He supported Humphrey until Humphrey withdrew, then gave his full support to Carter.

But the story goes further back than that.

In the early 1970s, John had become chairman of the Democratic party in Muscogee County. He wanted to become state chairman, and was assured that his friend Jimmy Carter, who was governor at the time, had promised to support him. As it turned out, Governor Carter did not come out in active support of anyone, and John did not become state chairman. He broke off with Carter, feeling that he had reneged on him.

One day, said George Ford, he got a call from Governor Carter. Carter was coming to Columbus on a tour, and he wanted to meet Ford at a local country club to talk to him.

"I told him," related Ford, "I don't think I could make it to the country club, because they didn't have blacks in the club. They didn't want us over there. He said, 'Well, you come on. If you can't come in the country club, I won't go in there either, George.' I said, 'You promise me you won't go in there?' He said, 'I promise you. If they don't let you in there, I won't go in.' And I and maybe ten other blacks went over to the club and met with him there."

During the meeting, said George Ford, Governor Carter told him, "I need your friend."

"What friend are you talking about?"

"John Amos."

"Alright. What do you need with John?"

At that time, Governor Carter said, "My plans are to run for President of the United States. For me to do that, I need John Amos. I need his help."

One of the things Ford suggested was that perhaps the Amoses would give a party at their home for the Carters to which Ford would invite "my black friends and John would invite his white friends." Rosalynn Carter called Elena and told her that they were in the last quarter of Jimmy's term and they wanted to make a tour around the state to renew old friendships and to bury hatchets. She asked if Elena would give a reception for Jimmy and her. Elena, of course, said yes, and they fixed a date. Rosalynn, according to John, gave them a guest list of about twelve hundred people. Some eight hundred showed up at the reception, the first for the Carters on his road to the Presidency. Elena, with the help of some friends, did all the cooking.

John not only supported Carter in the election and during his presidency, but remained his personal friend and contributed to the building of the Carter Center. But just as he could be close friends with such ideologically opposites as Representative Rangel and Senator Helms, he was to support and be a personal friend of Ronald Reagan's.

John Amos, as we have already noted, considered himself a liberal, certainly when it came to human rights in this country. As he told an interviewer, while he had a great deal of respect for George Wallace, "I was much closer to Humphrey because I believed firmly and absolutely in civil rights. I had seen vehemence that followed the Civil War come right up to the Second World War. I had seen the blacks who quit their jobs and were charged with stealing. The sheriff would go get them and bring them back.

"I remember a tale Daddy told me one time about the early twenties when he was trying to sell sewing machines. He went around in a buggy. He went out on this plantation and it wasn't long before either the owner or the foreman showed up on a horse with a shotgun in his saddle. And he said, 'Young man, what're you doing here?' 'I'm selling sewing machines.' And the fellow said, 'My niggers don't need no sewing machines. Get out of here.'"

John, said Elena, became close to the most conservative politicians, such as Senator Helms, because of their stand against Cuba. "We were conservative because of Communism. We knew what Castro was."

An excerpt from a talk John gave to the Kiwanis Club of Columbus in 1960, titled a "Prophetic Appraisal of Castro's Cuba," offered insight into how his feelings and fears for the future of that country had evolved.

"I do not speak as an expert on Cuba," he said. "I speak only as an ordinary citizen who has been interested in and watched the political and economic life of Cuba over the past fifteen years. During those years, I have been married to a very intelligent Cuban girl, and Cuba and its family squabbles have been everyday conversation in my home. I lived in Cuba for one year and have visited there often. I have harbored in my home refugees from both Batista and Fidel Castro and have patiently listened to the tales of intrigue and of personal woe. In fact, I could qualify as a conductor on the underground railroad...."

A humanitarian "conductor."

16

MORE OF POLITICS

Even in "little things," John Amos was an individualist. There were the white suits, of course, usually held up by suspenders. He never carried a watch, but was uncanny about knowing what time it was. In fact, he almost always got to appointments early, which was as much a result of his inner drive and personality as it was his ability to sense the time. He never carried a billfold for two reasons, he claimed. One, he didn't like "bulk" in his pocket. Two, wallets were too easily snatched. If he were held up, he joked, he would just throw a handful of bills at the culprit "while I run like hell." He enjoyed dining "in style" as much as he did eating suckling pig from his barbecue, but he ate little. He didn't wear jewelry—not so much as cuff links—and hadn't even wanted Elena to buy him a college ring after graduation. She did buy him one later on, and he lost it. One of the things he did always carry from the time he was a boy was a penknife, and it would save him from harm one day when he was attacked by a drunken employee, and he was able to hold the man at bay.

The only exception he made about jewelry was his wedding ring. He always wore his wedding ring.

"He loved Elena with a devotion and intensity and sweetness that I don't think I've ever seen in a husband," said Matt Metcalfe. "We'd go off on a trip together and the porter would open the door to the hotel room and John would walk straight through to the telephone and call Elena and say, 'I'm here, Honey. What's going on?' And he might call her a half a dozen times that night. Such an absolute closeness and love."

Salvador (Sal) Diaz-Verson, Jr., Elena's half brother from her father's second marriage, and one of the top executives in the company, added that when something major happened in the office, John would usually pick up the phone to let Elena know about it. "John," said Sal, "might say something like, 'I want to tell you that the loan I told you about last night for the company came through.'

He'd give her news so she wouldn't worry about it. She'd say, 'Great, Johnny' or whatever, and he'd say, 'I'll talk about it when I get home. I'll tell you about it.'"

This was especially true when it concerned dealing with personalities, whether family or people in the company. He might, for instance, tell her he had to fire someone because of something that person had done. Said Sal, "She'd say, 'Well, Johnny, you know you should get his side. He's been loyal. You can't tolerate this, but you should hear his side.' And he'd usually say okay. She didn't agree with everything he did. He didn't agree with every comment she gave, but they shared their thoughts very openly."

Many times, John would call Sal Diaz-Verson to his office first thing in the morning and say, "Your sister's mad at me today. I told her last night I was going to do such-and-such and she doesn't like it. She disagrees with it."

Sal would ask him what he was going to do about it. "He'd say, 'Well, I'm still thinking about it.' A lot of times he'd decide to do it, and a lot of times he'd come back and say, 'Well, no, I think I've changed my mind. Maybe Elena was right.'"

If Elena was really upset at him, John would usually tell him, "Your sister's upset at me and I want you to go talk to her. Give her my side of the story."

Sooner or later, continued Sal, he would sit down with Elena, perhaps have coffee with her. "She'd ask what brought me and I'd say, 'John sent me,' and she'd say, 'Well, he's wrong about so-and-so.' So I'd go back again and John would ask did I talk to her and I'd say, 'Yeah, I talked to her.' 'What did she say?' I'd say, 'It's the way she really feels, John. You can't blame her for feeling this way.' He'd say, 'Well, maybe I should do something differently if she doesn't understand.'"

John Amos was also a collector of friends. But not just friends, emphasized Matt Metcalfe—*lifetime* friends. And none could have been more remarkable than an elderly man with whom John took a trip around the world in 1970, a trip that was, through John's foresight, imagination and creativity intended to change the face and direction of the company dramatically, and thus the lives of so many of the people it reached. That man's name was Mark T. McKee.

John met Mark McKee, who was about seventy then, through Matt Metcalfe. This was at the time when John was was suing ten major insurance companies because of the problem of coordination of benefits.

John called Matt one day and told him, "Matt, I've got a real suit against these people, but the damn problem is that the president of Metropolitan Life, for instance, doesn't even know this suit exists. It's buried down there in their legal deapartment and he's not aware of it." And he said that he only wished he could get to meet the president to discuss the problem.

Metcalfe's answer was, "Well, John, I can get you to meet the president."

"The hell you can. How?"

"Through Mark McKee."

"Who's he?"

Metcalfe explained that Mark McKee was on the board of directors of his company, Loyal American, and that he was "one of the most interesting individuals in America, one of the original moguls of American industry." McKee, a lawyer, had helped found such companies as American Airlines, Pan American World Airways, Greyhound Bus, AT&T, and later on Holiday Inn. Matt arranged for the three of them to meet at Pan American's restaurant in the Pan American Building, in New York City.

"John laid out his problem to Mark," said Metcalfe, "and Mark said that of course he could help him." He served as a consultant to John in the case and subsequently became a member of American Family's board of directors. They were to remain very close friends until McKee's death at the age of ninety-five.

Because McKee loved to fly, he would often call John and say, "John, let's take a trip." And John, reminisced Metcalfe, would drop whatever he was doing and they would get on a Pan American plane and, at times, fly around the world. "And play gin rummy," Metcalfe added. "Mark was a notorious gin rummy player. He loved it."

Mark McKee had a creed, a five-part creed concerning business ventures that could only have given John a feeling of kinship with him: 1) It must be substantial; 2) it must have a large potential; 3) it must be difficult; 4) it must be profitable; 5) it must be fun! He was also an astute politician, as was John, which was another great basis for their friendship. McKee had been responsible for getting Pan Am routes into many countries, including Russia. Said Metcalfe, "I asked Mark one time—this was at the height of Pan Am's day—'Why is it, Mark, that even though there is a coup and a government change in a country, that it never interrupts Pan Am's flying? They just keep right on, regardless of who is in power?' He thought a minute and then said, 'Because the new people want a way out, too.'"

McKee also owned some ore boats on the Great Lakes that went between Cleveland and Duluth; and in the summer he would put together a group of his friends, usually including John and Matt Metcalfe, to go on cruise. Once, John invited Dr. Tebeau—John and Elena had remained in touch with their former history professor. Mark McKee was like John—"all brain," said Metcalfe. "He wasn't one for small talk either. It was always a subject of substance he discussed. Never gossiped. Never heard him use a swear word."

One of the people Mark McKee introduced John to was a man named Hashem Naraghi. Naragi, said Metcalfe, had come from Iran in the early forties and went to the West Coast with only several hundred dollars. He was in the San Joaquin Valley before it was developed agriculturally, when he noticed a house that had an almond tree growing next to it. Iran was a great almond growing area, and Naraghi had been schooled in agriculture. He began buying up desert land, Metcalfe continued, and since became the largest almond grower in America and perhaps the world.

The way John and Naragi met was that Mark McKee called Matt Metcalfe and asked that the four of them get together. Naragi, said Metcalfe, had gone to school with the Shah of Iran.

"The Shah was trying to rebuild Iran," explained Metcalfe, "and bring it into a Western culture. He was trying to make it an industrial state. He had built a modern hydroelectric dam on a river where a dam had existed in the days of Alexander the Great. He called Naragi and said, 'Hasham, I know what a great farmer you are. If you will bring your talent and the capital, I will give you and your group fifty-square miles immediately in the valley below this dam. It was once the breadbasket of the Middle East and I want it again to be the breadbasket of the Middle East.' So, Hashem, John, and Mark put up the money—I didn't have the money—and they got together and developed this farm."

121

Hashem Naraghi became a member of the board of American Life, and John, Elena, and the Naragis became good friends.

It was on a round-the-world trip that John took with Mark McKee in 1970 that was—though McKee had no way of knowing it at the time—to have the greatest impact on John's business life. McKee, who was eighty-one at the time, was especially interested in going to the Expo in Osaka, Japan. John had never been to Japan before.

They spent some time in Osaka, Tokyo, and Kobe.

"While I was in Kyoto," John was to relate later, "I heard a Japanese businessman say that he believed Japan's standard of living would equal if not surpass that of the U.S. in ten years. As Mark and I traveled throughout the country, we observed great activity, evidence of production, and other economic indicators that Japan's standard of living was on an upward spiral. It occurred to me that the Japanese would have the money to purchase supplemental cancer insurance, AFLAC's major product."

But he also saw something else on a cold, rainy April that a lot of people have seen, but he saw it in a different way than anyone else would.

Many of the Japanese wore surgical masks to prevent other people from catching their colds.

Most people observing this would think, How thoughtful. How sensible. Or perhaps, how *quaint.*

John may have thought some of this, too. But, far more important, he thought of something else, too.

These were a health-conscious people, people who might buy cancer insurance if it could be made available.

Before leaving Japan, John did a little research which revealed that though the Japanese had a national health plan, it was very limited. Moreover, supplemental insurance of any kind was unknown there. But the questions that faced him were formidable. Would the Japanese government permit an American insurance company to operate there when it hadn't done so since the war? How could American Family transplant its techniques and philosophy into such a different culture? And, as he was to learn, one of the many other problems they were to face was that the very word "cancer" was so frightening to the average Japanese that it was just about a synonym for death, to the point where many doctors didn't tell cancer patients the diagnosis for fear the patients would simply give up. How, then, could you possibly sell *cancer* policies?

Soon after John got back, he dispatched Walter Barton to Japan. Barton's goal was to see if a Japanese insurance company would consider going into a 50-50 joint venture with American Life. Barton contacted about eight of the larger insurance companies, but in every case they said no, that it would never be successful.

"When I got back," recalled Barton, "John and I sat down and I said, 'I'm really disappointed. It just doesn't look like we're going to be able to joint venture. They won't even talk about it.' He said, 'Well, why can't we get our own license?' I said, 'I don't think it's ever been done before.' He says, 'Well, so what?' Only John. Nobody else in the world would have said that. So I went back and we got to work."

Ahead of them were four years of roller coaster-type hopes and frustrations and discouragement.

They made their first contact with the Japanese Minister of Finance in early 1971, but it wasn't until 1972 that they were formally invited to *apply* for a license. It then took until 1974 before they were licensed to do business in Japan. But those four years had not been spent simply in *waiting*. They used the time to research the Japanese market, to develop ways in which to mold American Family concepts and techniques to blend in with Japanese culture. One of the most important things they learned and built upon was that in Japan, unlike the United States, companies were allowed to own an insurance agency and to receive a commission on policies it sold to its own employees or those of its suppliers. This opened the door for American Family to adapt its cluster-selling technique, whereby Japanese companies could serve as its agents. By the time American Family received its license, it had already had over a hundred agency contracts with major companies ready for signing.

Still, even after receiving its license, American Family found itself confronted by what seemed like insurmountable problems, much of it stemming from cultural differences between Japan and the United States. John and Elena went to live in Japan for six months to immerse themselves in Japanase culture. The Japanese branch, he realized, had to be run according to Japanese practices and customs—and *by* Japapese. During this period he was able to resolve the last of the major obstacles.

Years later, in 1985, John was honored to be invited to testify before the Ways and Means Committee of the House of Representatives of the United States at a hearing on international trade. He was there as a success story, as an example, it was hoped, for other American corporations to follow. He said, in part:

"I felt it was my duty to tell our story of success in contrast to the many horror stories about trade with Japan that we read and hear about daily. Possibly we are an exception to the rule, but somewhere between the story of our success and the stories of frustration and failure may lie the true situation...

"Possibly I was better prepared to meet the challenge than some others might have been because I have had to work and fight every inch of the way through life. As I began to climb the ladder of success it seemed that at every run someone standing by would decide to knock me off the ladder for no good reason or for no reason at all, and I had to stop and fight a few weeks, a few months, and even several years—without regard to the comparable size of the combatants...

"I said before, it has not been easy. We do not speak Japanese. We have had to learn "the Japanese way" the hard way. We have had our ups and downs with the Ministry of Finance and at times have reached impasses. We have not totally understood them, and they have not totally understood us, but we have had some distinct advantages also. All Japanese industry is subject to ministerial guidance from some ministry. It is always oral and never in writing. Many times it is reading you a regulation or reading a chapter of the law. The Ministry of Finance is composed of the top graduates from the universities of Japan, but being the brightest. They can sometimes be the most unyielding.

"When a Japanese insurance executive is called to the Ministry of Finance for guidance and receives that guidance, he accepts it and goes home, because that is the Japanese way. We go back to the hotel, think it over, and come back the next morning and ask, 'Why?'

Often they have no 'why' because no reason must be given for guidance...

"The Ministry of Finance considers its first responsibility in Japan to be the policyholder, which will take care of the country, and secondly to insure an orderly insurance market and industry.

"By patiently coming back to the Ministry of Finance week after week, sometimes month after month, we finally have been able to convince them of the merits of our position or to reach a compromise that we can both live with...We were granted a monopoly on the underwriting of supplemental cancer insurance for a period of three years at the outset. The monopoly was extended from year to year for a total of eight years, and then in the interest of an orderly market in the insurance industry only a few of the small to medium-sized companies with limited agency forces were allowed to compete. This was not a gratuitous favor to us, but was designed—in total accord with Japanese custom—to insure the success of our undertaking. Japan does not like the failure of a foreign company in Japan any more than it does a Japanese company..."

"Mr. Amos," said the Honorable Sam Gibbons, of the Ways and Means Commitee, 'I wish every member of Congress, the House, and Senate could have heard you. I wish every American businessman could hear you. Yours is the most inspiring story about perserverance in Japan that I have ever heard. I commend you."

John Amos had expected to write about $3.5 million in premiums in Japan the first year. Instead the Japanese branch wrote $25 million, and its assets at this point are $5.5 billion—and growing

As Matt Metcalfe put it, John Amos was the first American businessman to do a "reverse Toyota."

17

ONWARD AND INTO JAPAN

As one of John's secretaries, Carol Royer was one of those who watched a dream—a *specific* dream—grow from an abstraction to a reality.

She saw a new, towering building transform into house company headquarters.

Not long after the company had moved into its two-story quarters, John was already thinking and planning something on a far grander scale. Over the years he had various types of sketches and plans drawn. Then in 1973, while the venture in Japan was still perilously rocky, the license still not having been granted, the new building was started. It opened in 1974. An eighteen-story tower adjoining the building on Wynnton Street, it rose far above City Hall, until then the tallest building in Columbus.

Elena designed John's office and helped design the board room, both on the nineteenth floor (there is no thirteenth floor). The magnificent, mahogany u-shaped board of directors table, modeled after one in the United Nations, was so massive that it had to be built within the building itself, since it could not be lifted in through windows from the outside.

Frances King Lolley would recall how John's mother, a widow since 1965, could look out her window where she lived and see the tower. "How I wish," she would say, "that Daddy could have lived to see it."

This was a great era for the company in many ways. In 1973, American Family Corporation, with John as Chairman of the Board, was founded as a holding company, with American Family Life Assurance Company as a subsidiary. In 1974 the corporation was listed on the New York Stock Exchange. The company was now licensed in forty-seven states.

But once again clouds formed. As John said in his talk to the House Ways and Means Committee, "As I began to climb the ladder of success it seemed that at every rung someone standing by would decide to knock me off the ladder for no good reason or no reason at all...."

This time trouble came in swarms.

One came in 1972, from the Pennsylvania Commissioner of Insurance, Herbert Denenberg.

By an unfortunate coincidence, recalled Malcolm Hoffmann, American Family had been licensed in Pennsylvania only about a year before Denenberg became commissioner. And this short period of time, as will be seen, worked against the company.

"Denenberg," said Hoffman, "looked at the figures of payout under the policies and he saw that American Family had paid, I think, only one or two claims in the year it had been in business in Pennsylvania. Now that in itself was remarkable, because you're not supposed to have cancer when you get the policy. So you would think the payout would be zip because usually it takes a year or two to discover that you have cancer."

But Denenberg, continued Hoffman, didn't take any of that into consideration. Instead he pointed to the tiny fraction of a percentage of the premium that the payout represented. "He thought," said Hoffman, "this was a con."

Denenberg tried to outlaw cancer insurance in the state, which could have started a wild-fire in other states. As it was, headlines began to appear in newspapers throughout much of the country. "CANCER INSURANCE CAN BE MALIGNANT," "CANCER INSURANCE FLAWS CITED IN REPORT," "TOP EXPERTS REVEAL CANCER INSURANCE IS A BIG RIP-OFF," "CANCER INSURANCE SELLING PUBLIC FEAR."

John debated Denenberg on the TV show *Good Morning America*, but he did so under the disadvantage that he had had teeth extracted the night before but, fighter that he was, he came on the program with brand new dentures and bleeding gums. As it turned out, the policy was not banned in Pennsylvania. The way Hoffmann eloquently described it, the whole thing ended "like everything else in our political, social lives. It seeps into the muck, and the circles which it makes as it seeps down gradually dissipate. Nothing happened."

The next problem, in 1975, involved the Internal Revenue Service. American Family Life had been reporting their taxes as if they were a life insurance company, and the IRS wanted them to file as a casualty company, which would increase their taxes dramatically. In brief, the issue revolved around the amount of reserves the company was holding to pay out claims, the IRS claiming that they were "over-reserving" money and thus withholding income. The company finally won on all major points.

Now, it wasn't as though with one problem over John could simply concentrate on another. Problems didn't "separate" that easily; a problem didn't wait until the one ahead moved on completely before taking its place. Sometimes the problems were like multi-layered storms.

In this almost "meteorological" swirling was a hearing before the House of Representatives, another before the Senate, and a devastating television "documentary" on Family Life.

The House hearing, in the late seventies, was held by the Select Committee on Aging, with Representative Claude Pepper of Florida (he had formerly been a senator) as Chairman. The Committee dealt with general problems of the aged before focusing on cancer insurance. That it did, came as a surprise to many in the company, since cancer policies were mostly aimed at younger people—not the elderly—who are more subject to cancer.

"Claude," said Pat O'Connor, who had known him well, "became involved in 'catastrophe' insurance, and of course in that package is cancer insurance. He had a very active staff, and they were interested in all these topics that would create media attention. One of the crusades they had was that cancer insurance was bad. It takes advantage of the old people; they pay premiums and get damn little coverage, and the sales techniques were outrageous. What this select committee would do would be to get the worst case scenarios and holding hearings and publish reports about how bad a rip-off it was of the old people."

John had known Claude Pepper from the time he was a senator and had seen him occasionally. But O'Connor knew him longer and better. John asked O'Connor if he thought Pepper was a reasonable person or, at least in part because of the ensuing publicity, if he be prone to lambast them.

"I think he's a reasonable guy," O'Connor assured him.

128

"Well, I think we ought to set up some meetings with Claude to talk about these issues."

"You've got to realize something, though," O'Connor said. "Claude's up in age. That staff runs him. They conduct all those investigations and they prepare his statements beforehand. He accepts whatever they produce and he goes with it."

John and O'Connor arranged a meeting with Claude Pepper in Miami.

Reported O'Connor of the meeting, "We went down and we went through these issues one by one with Claude, pointing out where a lot of this stuff was fallacious and a lot of it had two sides to it. John would say, 'There have been some abuses by people in this business, and I have no argument about that.' We came away feeling that Claude could see that side of it, that he was fair."

Since their hope was that the next hearings would be fair, they wanted to get directly involved in them. But from newspaper accounts they read prior to the new hearings, they could tell that their meeting with Claude Pepper had had no effect. Said O'Connor, "Claude had said to us, 'Look, I'll talk with you and go over with you what my views are and take your input.' He never did. As a result, John said, 'I don't think we ought to try and work with Claude anymore, because the staff determines this and writes this."

The hearings, continued O'Connor, were strictly a bashing—"They knew what they wanted to do beforehand, and they would call just people that they wanted to call." John and O'Connor considered whether they should talk to other members of the committee, who apparently weren't as involved as Pepper. "But we never did try to offset it by getting other members of the committee to refute or disagree with what Claude did. John just concluded it wasn't worth the effort."

But John appeared, well-armed with facts, at the Senate hearings. The public hearings on cancer insurance were held in 1980 by the Subcommittee on Antitrust, Monopoly and Business Rights. The Chairman was Senator Howard M. Metzenbaum, Democrat of Ohio.

"From talking to members of Metzenbaum's staff," recalled O'Connor, "I concluded that it was more or less that he had already concluded what the report would be before the evidence went in. And of course he had lined up people to testify whom we knew had

129

testified on the House side, and we knew pretty much what they were going to say. I have known Howard for a long time, and I went to him and said, 'Now, is this going to be just a kangaroo court deal where you have already decided what you want, you're going to get it in, and you don't care about the other side of it?'"

Metzenbaum assured him that it would be a fair hearing, and did say he would permit certain people who had been helped by cancer insurance to testify.

"Still, you could tell from the way the hearing was conducted," said O'Connor, "that Metzenbaum was interested in establishing what he called abusive practices. And he made an effort to do that through the testimony of various people. On the other hand a number of insurance customers of American Family came in and testified that they were happy with their policies, that it worked out for them."

In a very strong presentation to the Committee, John Amos said in part, "American Family is truly a family to me in every sense of the word. In 1955, I founded the company, along with my brothers Paul and Bill.

"I must admit that the early years were very difficult indeed. Today, however, I am proud to report that millions of consumers have chosen to protect themselves and their families with supplemental cancer expense insurance from American Family.

"Over 58,000 organizations have selected American Family's payroll deduction plan for their employees. These organizations represent a broad cross section of American business society. They include 866 hospitals and their employees. I point out, who would know more about the validity of payment of cancer plans than the hospitals?

"We have 6,748 divisions of state and local governments, 5,608 school districts, including colleges, universities, and I believe medical schools. These organizations and their hundreds of thousands of employees have chosen American Family because we provide a valuable service.

"Our company's product is low cost, supplemental cancer insurance. Our insurance is never offered as a substitute for basic, comprehensive or major medical insurance. It complements basic major medical and high deductible catastrophic health

130

coverages....Furthermore, unlike most other types of insurance, our policies are guaranteed renewable to life...

"Mr. Chairman, American Family believes that the best way to find out if consumers are satisfied with your product is to ask them. Thus, we commissioned on two occasions an independent survey by the Opinion Research Corporation of Princeton, New Jersey, a subsidiary of Arthur D. Little and Company.

"Their study found that 95 percent of American Family's claimants would recommend our policies to their friends and relatives. In their words, that finding represents "A very strong endorsement....""

And one of the members of the committee, Senator Orrin G. Hatch, Republican from Utah, broke in on John's testimony at one point, to say, "I don't know about other members of the committee, but unless we can bring out some more testimony that is strong, I don't know what in the world we are doing holding this hearing with regard to you."

As Pat O'Connor would say of the hearings, he and John were happy with the outcome, because "all in all I thought because of our efforts—John's, mine, Hatch's, and others'—we got a fair hearing` and fairly good publicity out of it, though "if you had your druthers as to whether or not you wanted the hearings, you wouldn't want them because, as always, a certain amount of stuff that goes in there is detrimental."

Meanwhile, at the same time as this was going on, American Family was undergoing further attack—this time on television.

Stemming from the Pepper hearings, ABC videotaped American Family Life sales agents selling policies to the elderly and then ran the program over a couple of nights. The company protested that the videotape had been edited and taken out of context in a way to make it look as if the company were using tactics designed only to prey on the elderly's worst fears. John sued them for libel.

Mark Veve of the firm of O'Connor & Hannon was part of the litigation team that was headed by Miles Ambrose. But John came to feel that the litigation would generate more controversy than it was worth, that going to trial would only continue the adverse publicity. And he decided to settle.

But something that could not be settled that easily was the horrendous damage that had been done to the company.

The stock plummeted. The company lost about $200 million. A big part of the problem was that a lot of American Family salespeople, having seen or heard about the program, did not want to be associated with the product anymore and refused to have any part of it. What had to be done now was a mammoth task—to try to rebuild the salesforce, to restore confidence in American Family.

One of the things John did was write an ad that appeared on a two-page fold in the *Reader's Digest*. It was headed: THE TRUTH ABOUT CANCER INSURANCE. The reason he wanted in the *Digest* was not only because it was so widely-read, but because the magazine made them prove every fact that was in it. In addition, the company bought almost untold numbers of reprints. It was a massive morale and "factual" booster for both for new customers and the salespeople themselves.

It was to be a long, very hard struggle, but gradually the company fought its way back.

18

REGULATORS AND POLITICIANS

When asked if John was ever openly "down" or depressed—especially during this era—Elena looked surprised at the question. Of course he was, she said, but he generally had a very good way of handling it. When he was depressed, it didn't show itself in long periods of frowning, curtness, or moroseness. He didn't walk around *looking* worried.

"He had a very good quality," she said. "When he got depressed, he could go to sleep for hours. It was very unusual. Most people lose their sleep, but he could just sleep and recover."

She worried that he was working too hard, was carrying too many burdens. But what eased her worry, and in turn helped him, is that he didn't let his business concerns draw them apart. They discussed complex business matters in their den, their kitchen, in much the same way, as back in the early days of their marriage. They used to talk about such things as selling sandwiches at the girls' dorm.

Neither did his secretary see a man at the office who looked troubled.

Kay Stover had become his secretary toward the end of 1979, when he was going through the Metzenbaum hearings.

"Despite all the things that were going on in the business and in his mind, I'm sure," she said, "he was always calm. He really was. Never, ever raised his voice about anything." Did he ever talk about the hearings to her? "Well, he would always make comments about Howard Metzenbaum, you know, but that was just Mr. John. You knew he was upset with him. But he never raised his voice or anything like that. He used to just go, 'Oooh, that Howard Metzenbaum,' you know. But he never yelled."

When Kay Stover had first met John, he was using a walker. John and Elena had bought a summer home in Florida—a fishing camp as they called it—on the St. John's River near Orlando. They had been entertaining a group of American Family Life contest winners, and the group was ready to pull away from the dock to go fishing, when a thunderstorm approached. John jumped from the boat to help the others off, and in doing so he fell on a slippery patch of grass and broke his ankle.

Kay Stover's first sight of John was as he came around the corner on the walker into the office

"This was the very first time I ever saw him and I thought, 'Oh, my goodness.' He scared me to death. I was young, for one thing, and had gotten this wonderful job. I was in the tower, and here comes John Amos, whom I've heard about all my life, that he's such a wonderful person."

She didn't have too much time to get used to him, because he went out of the country the first month she worked there. "So I had a month to get situated in my job and get the feel of the office, of the tower. By the time he got back it was almost old hat. And he was so easy to get along with. He just was very easy to get to know."

He would always ask, "How are you doing?" and was concerned about whether she was enjoying her job, if she had any problems.

"He told me after three months, 'I'm going to make you the best secretary in the world.' I don't know if he accomplished that," said Kay Stover, who worked for John until 1987, "but I'm still a secretary, I work for my husband. I'm very confident in what I do now, and it's because of him. It's because of all the things he taught me about business, how to deal with people."

Although he was free with his compliments, if you made one little mistake he also let you know about it.

"One time I remember, he had a very important letter that needed to go out Federal Express, and I guess I didn't touch on it with as much importance as I should, because it was late. And he called me at home and wanted to know where his letter was and why had it not gotten to where it was going. And I just felt awful, and I don't think that ever happened again.

"He taught me so much. I could never, ever thank him enough. I was just a little person, still am, but he gave me this wonderful job and I got to travel all over the world—conventions, Japan, Europe—which I probably never would have a chance to do."

She even got the opportunity to meet the man who became her husband. This was at the opening of the Carter Center, which Amos contributed to.

Then there was a company trip to Japan—a "President's Club" trip—that exemplified the sense of fun it was working for him. She went shopping with a group of ladies and bought several dresses to wear to the office.

"I came in to work with one that I thought was very pretty—not super, but pretty," she recalled. "And he said, 'That is the ugliest dress.' Since he said that, I said, 'Well, good. I'll just have to go buy me a new one.' So I went and bought a new dress and I sent him the bill. It was funny. I told Elena about it—I was wearing the dress at the time—and she laughed and said, 'I have a dress just like that.' And she said he'd done that to her, too. He'd say, 'Oooh, Elena, I don't like that outfit.' And she'd hang it up and never put it on again. And I never worn that dress again either."

She had been able to joke in this way with him, because that was *his* way. "He was always making jokes. He would call me into his office and tell me stories. When I would leave, I would say to myself, 'How could that possibly be true? Is he *really* telling me the truth?' Because he was always joking."

And then there was the matter of the "mouse."

One day, hearing the sound of a cry, she hurried into his office. And there he was on his knees on the floor, papers flying around.

"I thought," she said, "he was having a heart attack."

But he said he was looking for a mouse. And all at once, to her horror before she broke out laughing, he stood up with it.

It was a rubber mouse, the kind you could put your finger in and wiggle.

He always showed an interest in her welfare, Kay Stover continued. Though he never met her family, who lived out of town, he would ask about them, ask if she saw them often. He also helped get a couple of her nieces transferred to a school they wanted to get into. And there were many other people she knew of whom he helped. For instance, while he was away fishing with a friend, he met a fishing guide who happened to mention that he wished he could go to college. Further conversation revealed that he didn't have the money, and John gave it to him.

Although she was John's fulltime personal secretary, occasionally Kay Stover would also do some secretarial work for Elena.

"They had such a wonderful relationship. She would come into his office and they would always hug and call each other 'Baby' and 'Sweetie.' They did that the whole time I worked there. It never stopped. And if they ever got upset with each other, they would send each other roses."

One day, John was sitting at his desk when he called Kay Stover to come into his office. "I want to show you this."

When she came over to his desk, he pointed to the security television screen in his office.

"That looks just like Elena, doesn't it?" he asked.

Kay Stover stared at the screen. But all she could see, all she could *ever* see there, was a floor on the screen—and a shadow on the floor, made by a reflection of the sun through the window.

To her it was a shadow, but to him—

"Doesn't that look just like her?" he said again, shaking his head admiringly.

The Amoses have been, in as pure a sense of the word as could be, not only a family, but an *extended* family. At the core of it, of course, there are the children—Shelby, who after graduating from the University of Miami entered the company; Sita, who after high school spent a year in Italy as an exchange student at the University of Florence, then returned and got her degree as a pre-education and art major at Columbus College. And there are Shelby's children—John William, Jacob Oliver, and Chana Gail; and Sita's (Mrs. Donald Land)—William Donald, John Beverly and Elena Maria Teresa.

But in the Amos's case, the word "extended" goes far beyond aunts and uncles and cousins, beyond blood relatives of any kind or distance. It goes to people whom they brought into their lives— indeed, in some instances, into their home.

They met one of them, a youth of about fourteen, at an Alabama military academy.

He first came to Elena's attention because she happened to hear someone speaking Spanish.

19

INNER RESOURCES

They met him at Lyman Military Academy in Camp Hill, Alabama. She and John had come to enroll Shelby in the Academy when she heard a young voice speaking in Spanish. She turned and saw a short, red-haired cadet. She didn't know it then, but his name was Luis C. Garcia. He was a second year student at the Academy, from Puerto Rico.

Garcia was a cadet officer and a member of the committee welcoming new cadets. As he would remember it, he was speaking to another cadet in Spanish when all at once someone behind him laughed. It was a woman's laugh. Then before he had a chance to turn, he heard her greet him—in Spanish—with, "How are you, general?"

"My first thought," he recalled, "was that no one living in Camp Hill, Alabama, speaks Spanish. I turned in amazement."

That was the beginning of a friendship, between the two boys and between Garcia and John and Elena. "I told him," Elena said, "that if he looked after my son I would give him Spanish food on the weekends." They not only invited him to the house for weekends, but for holidays. Then, because his parents were going through a divorce, they offered to let him live with them. He was happy to accept. And when he graduated, he went to Columbus College and continued living with them.

But he wasn't the only "extended" family at the Amos home. They took in several more young people over the years, for varying lengths of time, one of them a youngster named Wingate Caro.

Said Garcia, "I really formed a loving bond with John and Elena, and that bond grew." They helped ease him through the pain of his parents' divorce. Elena was able to do so in a special way, having lived through her own parents' divorce.

"She would talk to me a lot about forgiving," said Garcia, "about not carrying grievances. There are several things we Hispanics do very well," he went on, smiling. "We are very emotional. We party very well, we cry very well, we are sad very well. We suffer really hard."

Just as John used to do as a boy with his own parents, Garcia enjoyed staying up until all hours of the morning with John. Said Garcia, "He and I were very close. We would talk until three and four in the morning. I cannot tell you how many times we were in the kitchen—which was the favorite place to talk—and we would see the sun rise. He would say, 'It's time to go to bed,' and I remember thinking, 'Oh, gosh, I have to go to school, but he can sleep a little more.'"

He was a fun-loving young fellow, who wasn't against getting into a little innocent mischief. One day someone in John's office noticed that somebody had been playing with the photocopying machine, had been running off a lot of copies and had jammed it. When they opened it to try to fix it, they found a photocopy of Garcia's face. He had placed his face against the screen and taken his own picture.

John and Elena were always so kind and compassionate to him. But at least once, John attempted some of his own special kind of "shock treatment." It happened when Garcia was about sixteen. He began having problems with his stomach and developed ulcers.

"I remember fairly late one evening, John said, 'Luis, I am very concerned about your health. You're a male and in this world a male has to be very tough. A male who gets sick very often cannot survive the business world.'"

John told him that he wanted him to know that he and Elena loved him and that he had a home with them. He also told him that insecurity was one of the worst things a person could feel, that he did not want him to feel insecure. He went on to say, basically, that somone who feels insecure might as well be dead.

Then John went over to a drawer, took out a gun, and put it on the top of the desk.

"I never found out if the gun was loaded or not," said Garcia. "I suspect it was not. I remember crying all night." Indeed, perhaps John had been secretly watching him. "Whether he had been watching me or not, what I mean is he had this fantastic ability to shock me."

Six months later, Garcia's x-rays were completely clear of every ulcer.

That incident, he claimed, made him decide to stand on his own two feet, to accept the security he was being given by the Amoses, and move forward in his life.

While he went college, he—as did Shelby while he was in school—worked part-time at the company, in his case as a mailboy.

"I was quite a bit of a challenge," Garcia reminisced. "Among the challenges was that I had a pretty bad driving record"—an understatement as it turns out.

John bought him an old Chevrolet Impala for about three hundred dollars. But a neighbor's young daughter got into it while it was standing on the driveway, the motor running, and accidentally released the gear. The car rolled down the hill and was totaled. Luis Garcia had had the car less than twenty-four hours.

And that, he said, was just the beginning of his "automobile saga." After that, he had eleven accidents in one year. What's more, he was using Amos cars.

"Elena got to the point that when she went to answer the phone, her blood pressure would go up, because it was a matter of where is the wreck this time?"

For the most part the accidents were relatively "minor." The big one, by *anyone's* estimation, took place a few days before Christmas.

Wingate, said Garcia, had a brother in Pensacola whom he hadn't seen several years. Garcia thought it would be nice to get them together for Christmas. He asked John for permission to drive to Pensacola, but John said absolutely not, because the weather was bad. But John had to leave for California, and soon afterward Garcia talked to Elena. Whether he told her that John had refused him is not clear, but according to Garcia, she gave him permission.

They got to Pensacola about three in the morning and located the brother. The three of them were driving across a bridge in Pensacola, Garcia at the wheel, when, according to Garcia, Wingate suggested that they show his brother how fast the car could go.

"I said all right," recalled Garcia, "and the last time I looked at the speedometer, it said 115 miles an hour." At the same time, the windshield began fogging. "But right before it fogged up, I saw a toll booth at the end of the bridge."

They hit a cement light pole, a wooden telephone pole and then the toll booth itself, fortunately after the toll collector had leaped away for his life. The car was so twisted and compressed that it had to be sawed apart to get to the boys. Miraculously, they didn't have a scratch on them.

Garcia ran crying and carrying on onto the beach, a policeman running after him. The officer grabbed him, and as he held him in his arms he began trying to console him, to tell him that "this wasn't worth it." And the officer felt so sorry for him that he reported the accident as "unavoidable."

"We went to a room to get some sleep," Garcia continued, "but I couldn't sleep. I knew this was it. I was going to get kicked out of the house. John had said not to go, and I knew when he said no to obey him. Otherwise, it was trouble."

In the morning, Wingate called Columbus. Elena answered the phone. John, meanwhile, had just gotten back from California. Wingate told Elena about the accident.

"He told her," Luis Garcia related, "that the car was not driveable, and asked her if we could catch a plane back home. In the meantime, John said, 'Who's on the phone?' She said, 'The boys.' I was standing next to Wingate, so I heard John yell, 'I told them not to call from downstairs!' And she said, 'They're not downstairs.'"

What had happened was that, long before this, John had given instructions that the kids were not to use the phones in the house as an intercom. Now Elena explained to him where they were, at which time John grabbed the phone. "You get your little tails home any way you can!"

They took a bus back, Garcia crying all the way. In the meantime, John and Elena began to worry. They had spoken to Wingate on the phone, but not to Garcia, and didn't know what happened to him. They contacted the Pensacola police, learned how horrendous the accident was, called hospitals all around.

"By the time we got there," said Garcia, "they were ready to go to Pensacola themselves. They were outside the house ready to get in their car to drive to the airport, when the taxi that brought us from the bus dropped us off. Elena just grabbed me and hugged me, and we were crying. John just looked at me and he says to Elena, 'If you think I'm going to be feeling sorry for that little bastard, you're...' He walked in the house, and the next thing that happened we were sent to our rooms."

John's instructions were that the boys were not to step into a car until further notice. On Christmas Day they had to walk to church, with John following behind in his car to make sure they didn't hitchhike. But he did buy each of them a pair of roller skates. And it was only a few weeks later that he let them drive again.

And then there was the matter of the thousands of fish in the swimming pool.

John not only loved to fish, he especially loved to fish for bream. And fresh fried bream was one of his favorite meals. He decided that instead of traveling any kind of distance to do his fishing, he would have a fish pond in the back yard.

As Shelby told the story, one afternoon John called a handyman who worked for him. "He said, 'McKinley, come on down to the house. We're going to build us a fish pond.' McKinley said, 'Whaaat?' 'Just come on down. We'll draw it out.' When McKinley came over and they paced it off and talked about it, McKinley looked at him and said, 'Do you know what you're doing? I've never done this before.' Dad says, 'No, but we'll get through it.' And they proceeded to get a backhoe or whatever they used to dig it."

The pond they dug had concrete sides and a mud bottom. There was an old well on the property, and they sunk a pump and pumped water into the pond. John bought a couple of aerators and other supplies and put through an order for about four thousand bream.

One day, said Shelby, "Daddy would actually bring people visiting from New York or wherever for lunch. They'd go out and catch their own fish and somebody would clean it while they had a cocktail, and Mama would fry the fish right there in the kitchen."

But that "one day" lay very much in the future.

Right now there was a problem. The four thousand bream he had ordered, John learned, were on their way—before the pond was actually finished!

Luis Garcia was in school when a messenger came into class with word that he was to call John Amos. John filled him in quickly, explaining that there was no way to stop the delivery. The only solution he could think of was to put the fish in the swimming pool—a beautiful, lagoon-like pool on the patio.

"But we've got another problem," John announced. "We've got to get rid of the chlorine. So get right home."

Garcia called the water department and got instructions for de-chlorinating the pool. They finished the job just about the time the delivery arrived. Hoping that they'd been successful, they watched as the deliverymen dumped the thousands of fish into the pool.

They checked the fish frequently. For about a week, everything seemed to be going well. Then three o'clock one morning, John woke Garcia.

"The fish are floating."

They hurried outside and sat helplessly by as hundreds of fish floated button-eyed on the surface. More were bobbing up. With daybreak, Garcia took one of the fish and drove as fast as he could to Auburn University to have them try to find out what was wrong, to see if the rest could be saved. But no.

Said Garcia, "They'd developed some crazy disease. In a matter of twenty-four hours we had four thousand dead fish."

What's more, the Amoses were having a big house party that night.

"Elena was working hard on the party," recalled Garcia, "and here were all these dead fish. All we knew is that they were going to stink like crazy."

There was no way of getting rid of all the fish in time, so all they could do was try to cover up the fish and the odor. They kept dumping chlorine into the pool, until the water turned white.

"It looked," said Garcia, "like we had a big green pea soup in there."

Garcia's job during the party was to station himself by the pool, to keep pushing the fish down so no one would see them. And, far from incidentally, to make sure no one fell *into* the pool.

Somehow the crisis passed without incident. But in a way, that experience was like a prologue to the day Garcia brought home a lion.

It was on a day that the Amoses were to have another party, this one even bigger and more important than the one that had been encumbered by dead fish. The guest of honor was to be attorney Malcolm Hoffmann, who was making his first visit to Columbus. Elena even used the occasion to put in a new kitchen floor.

Garcia was studying downstairs when John called to him.

"Luis," he said to him, "I've got a job for you."

John always liked exotic animals. But his request seemed unusual even for him. What had happened, he explained, was that a friend of

142

his had gotten a lion cub, and a neighbor objected to it. The friend asked if he would want it, and John agreed. He thought he would be able to pen it in the yard, where it would not only make an interesting pet, but would serve as protection. Now he wanted Garcia to pick it up.

"He said to me, 'Don't get scared when you see it. It's going to be sort of large, but it's only a cub and it's not going to harm you.'"

When Garcia got to the house, he found a cub all right, but it was a cub that looked to him to weigh about two hundred pounds. Garcia studied it for a while, walking around it listening to the owner, who gave him a leash and a choke collar.

"This guy told me that if he gets too 'rumbly,' I should just pull the choke collar and he will calm down. Well, on the ride the lion decided he wanted to look out the window, and I decided he was big enough that he should probably be able to do what he wanted. I remember being at a red light, and there was a Jeep next to me with some kids in it. The lion stuck his head out and went 'woooah,' and these kids ran the red light."

When Garcia pulled up to the house, John was waiting outside. Said Garcia, "He couldn't wait to see the lion. He was just like a kid."

As soon as the lion got out of the car, it climbed up a pine tree, with Garcia still holding onto the leash. "He was almost pulling me up the tree, and John was telling me, 'You've got to show him who the boss is. *Pull!*' So I pulled, the lion falls, the lion looks at me, and I say, 'Oh.'"

John, with his love of practical jokes, wanted to take the lion into the house, but every time they started pulling him there, the lion set his legs squarely—"and I'm talking *legs*," Garcia said—and they couldn't budge him. John, with Elena still not knowing anything about this, called the owner, who told him, "John, the only thing you need to do is pull on the collar hard and scream at the lion, and he will obey you."

John came back out to the yard. He put his arms around Garcia, pulling on him while Garcia pulled on the lion. They were able to drag the lion to the house, Garcia realizing every moment that he was *between* John and the lion. Then the lion started walking into the house on its own.

The lion accidentally knocked over some loose ironwork, at which time he let out another roar.

"It sounded unbelievable. I mean, he had a throat you wouldn't believe."

The housekeeper screamed. Some workmen in the kitchen ran in several directions. Sita came from her room just as the lion was heading into the living room; she lost her balance and slid across the floor, coming to rest under the lion, speechless. At that moment, Elena's mother came out of her room carrying her little dog.

"He went hysterical," said Garcia, "and stayed hysterical for two weeks."

The next on the scene was Elena.

She stared at the lion, a hand under her hair.

"I will give you five minutes to get that lion out of here!"

The lion stared at her. Then John looked at Garcia.

"I think," John said, "we'd better take it back."

The lion gone, the party the Amoses gave for Malcolm Hoffmann went without unusual incident. But a boatride Hoffmann and his wife were to take with the Amoses was to have an interesting, intellectual aftermath, one that provided further insight into John Amos's thinking.

The Amoses took Hoffmann and his wife on a ride down the Chattahoochee on a flat boat, with an Amos employee by the name of Hiawatha at the wheel and at times poling it.

"We pulled onto shore," recalled Hoffmann, "and tied up the boat and made steaks on the shore. We had a great day in the sun."

On the way back, they passed Phenix City, across the river from Columbus, where Hoffmann saw a lot of shacks in bad repair, with blacks sitting on the front porches. It looked, he said, like a "rural Harlem." At the time, Hoffman and his close friend attorney Morris Ernst were publishing a pamphlet called *Back and Forth*, in which they wrote essays on whatever topics were of interest to them.

Recalled Hoffmann, "I wrote about our trip on the Chattahoochee, and I said something about how those blacks sitting there did not have the chance at schooling or improving their social position which the blacks pent up in Harlem might have. I sent it to

John and said I'd like to get his response to this. John wrote one. And it was very brilliantly done, so I printed it."

Here was John's response as published:

"I know you to be intellectually honest and I believe that on your first trip South you tried to view with an open mind, yet your article proves that you are only human and subject to human weaknesses. What you had read and heard about the South had become so ingrained that when what you actually saw and heard yourself came in conflict with your pre-formed ideas. You rejected your own observations, as the body rejects foreign tissue...

"For a man who usually thinks logically, your article is a master-piece of illogic. How you can see my employee Hiawatha as a slave on the Chattahoochie and how you can distinguish between his role and that of your own colored maid and colored houseman on the Hudson is more than I can understand. If Hiawatha is a slave, he is indeed a fortunate one. He owns his own home, autumobile, and TV set. On Sundays he and his wife drive a hundred miles to Atlanta to watch the Braves take on some Yankee team. At the time he was with us on the river he was drawing time and a half overtime pay. He has hospitalization benefits, sick leave, adequate retirement benefits, and two weeks vacation each year. He would be insane to want to join you in the great states of New York or New Jersey. He would, I am sure, have an even greater fear of participating in the battle of Harlem or Newark than of having to face the enemy in Viet Nam...

"I wish you had included your bibliography so that I could read the novel from which you drew the 'red-necked sheriffs.' Was it published before or after 'Uncle Tom's Cabin?'"

Indeed, related his son Shelby, John loved playing on the conception so many people in the North have of how Southerners treat blacks. What he would sometimes do, in essence, was expose—through his sense of the absolutely outlandish and absurd—these people to themselves.

One time a group of insurance agents from the North came in town for a meeting. They called John at his home at night and asked if they could come over for a nightcap. He said, "Sure, come on out. Then he spoke to a young man who helped around the house.

"Daniel," he asked him, "are you claustrophobic?"

When he learned that Daniel was not, he then asked him if he would do something for him.

After the agents came over and had a nightcap, they wanted to call a cab.

"But Daddy," said Shelby, "told them, 'No, don't do that. Take my car. I'll pick it up or you bring it to the office in the morning.'"

After the salesmen walked out, they came right back in, saying that one of the tires was flat and that they would change it. John walked outside with them, saying, "Don't worry about it. I'll change it."

Said Shelby, "They insisted on changing it. They kept saying, 'We can't let you do that.' But Daddy says, 'Step back, boys, I'll handle it.' He knocks on the trunk and Daniel jumps out and changes the tire and puts it in the trunk and gets back in. And all these guys are just standing there staring at him. And Daddy says, really calmly, "You boys don't have that up North?"

20

EXTENDING THE FAMILY

Luis Garcia went on from having eleven accidents in one year to become a lawyer. When asked if John Amos played a role in his selection of a career, he said, "Remember, he was my hero. And he was a lawyer."

A lot of the long conversations they used to have were about John's experiences as a lawyer. And though Luis Garcia had always wanted to be a lawyer, it was John who instilled in him the "ultimate assurance" that that was what he wanted to be.

"I remember him telling me one time that he would be ashamed if I did not go to law school."

There were many other young people whose lives John Amos touched, perhaps not always as dramatically, but in his own way.

Katherine Hazouri Hess was one.

Daughter of the late Dr. Louis Hazouri, who had been John's friend and physician, she would go to him for advice after her father died. "I would just call the house and ask if I could come over. I was always welcome." What she sought, she said, "was more of a father thing. I wanted his approval of what I was doing, and he gave me his approval. He was a source of strength, someone I could lean on."

He was a very honest person, she continued—very sincere and very intuitive. "He saw people for what they were worth. I would say he was a very good judge of character instantly and didn't mind telling people so. That was one of the things he and my father had in common. And Elena was his backbone. She was a pot of gold, his rainbow. You will never meet such a lady. She is genuine and a good person from her heart to the surface of her skin."

Ira Meyers was another young person who, even as a small boy, found a common ground with John.

Ira's parents, Sam and Esther Meyers, residents of Columbus, knew the Amoses since about 1957. Esther Meyers had met Elena when Ira was about three or four, and Elena offered to lend her a piñata for Ira's upcoming birthday party. They became fast friends after that. Sam Meyers, a merchant, taught contract bridg , and at one time gave lessons to John and Elena.

Said Sam Meyers, "John only played to please Elena, who liked to play bridge more than he did. He would have been a marvelous bridge player if he'd spent the time with it."

"I just adored that man," added his wife. "There is nobody any better or finer than he was. My husband and I always said that when he was born, God made a mistake. He gave him the intelligence that he intended to share among six normal people. John got it all."

From the time Ira was about six or seven—he was a couple of years younger than Shelby and about a year older than Sita—he spent most weekends at the Amos home until he was about sixteen or seventeen.

"John," he said, "acted more as a friend and an equal than a superior person. We discussed everything from school lessons to national politics. John loved to tell the story from when I was about eight years old when he said to me, 'What are you going to do when you grow up? You don't want to be in a retail business like your dad, why don't you come and work for me?' And I said, 'No, sir, I think I will just start my own insurance company.' That got him tickled."

Often, when Ira was still in grammar school, he would ride his bike over to American Family's two-story building, lay it down on the front steps and go in to talk to him. "I would say, 'How's business? where are we going next, what's it look like, what's the stock doing?' and it intrigued him to have someone that young interested in things like that. And he was always full of jokes. He didn't mind a tall story at all. He loved to pull your leg."

John helped get Ira and Sita jobs as pages in the General Assembly in Atlanta. Ira also was in the party that went with John to Atlanta when he had gone there fully expecting to become State Chairman of the Democratic Party, only to come back deeply disappointed and angry at Jimmy Carter for having let him down.

If John had had any single political philosophy, said Ira, "It was 'Be involved.' It didn't matter what side you were on, but be involved. He didn't care who you voted for, as long as you voted. He believed very much in the system. He knew it had its faults, but he knew that you must work with it—be a part of it—to make it better."

148

Ira Meyers, who worked for a while at American Family, but then became the owner of a printing plant, said that he looked on John as a second father, that he was sure that John looked on him almost as a son. And Ira's parents treasured the relationship. There was the time, for instance, when Ira was going through a divorce.

"My son was devastated," said Esther Meyers. "Ira had always been like Mr. John's own son. They both loved each other very much. I didn't know what to do, so I decided to call Mr. John. I went into the kitchen—Ira was living with us then—and I called their home and Elena answered. She said to me, 'Don't worry. John will call him.' And I said, 'Please have him call.'

"A few minutes later the phone rang and Ira answered it and Mr. John told him, 'Ira, come on up here. I want to see you, talk to you.' Ira went up, and time went by, and the next thing I knew the telephone was ringing. It was Mr. John. He says, 'I sent Ira home with a security guard. I wouldn't let him drive the car because we had a drink, you know. I just want you to know he's a little better.' And Mr. John called me the next day from his office to tell me again about Ira, that he was going to be okay. Mr. John just loved helping somebody, and he loved this boy very, very much."

Ira was to be one of the very last people to sit with John through the night, as he lay dying.

Then, to name just one more young person, there was Sachiko Sakakibara Beck.

Or, as the Amoses nicknamed her, "Chiko. Or, as they truly looked on her, "Our Japanese daughter."

Chiko Sakakibara was working in the Japanese office as a secretary in the computer department when she met the Amoses. This was in 1975, when the company had a grand opening party in Japan. Among those who came over from the home office, in addition to John and Elena, were Bill Amos and his wife Olivia, and Paul Amos and his wife Jean. Chiko, who had been a member of an American missionary church when she had been in college, not only spoke English but had made a trip to the United States.

Each VIP at the opening was assigned a personal interpreter. Chiko was assigned to Bill and his wife, but she met all the Amoses at the party and they took a tour of Tokyo together.

"I guess Elena liked me, and I was so impressed with her. At that time we called her Mrs. Amos, but she asked everyone, 'Please call me Elena.' Everybody had been so tense beforehand, but then here comes the Chief Executive Officer's wife saying, 'Please call me Elena.' She was the first one and the last one who said that."

A little later, at a "ladies' get together," Elena and Chiko had a friendly conversation. Said Chiko, "She asked me all kinds of questions: What are your future plans? What are your dreams?' And she gave me the name 'Chiko.' Later I heard that when she got home and talked about Chiko, everyone thought that was a little boy."

Chiko had never met an executive's wife like Elena before. "She treats you on the same level. She makes everybody feel at home. Every time they came to Japan, she'd ask me to be her shopping companion, traveling companion, and just her *companion.* I was lucky, very lucky. I was working at the company office, but whenever Mr. John and Elena were in Japan, I was pulled away from my desk work and I was with them all the time. When they stayed at a hotel, sometimes they'd get me a room next door to them."

Chiko left the company in 1977 because she wasn't receiving promotions like the other girls were getting. She felt that it was jealousy. "They said I wasn't being promoted because every time Mr. John and Elena were in Japan I had to be with them."

She took a job with a travel agency, making sure to let John and Elena know where she was working. And every time they came to Japan she made up excuses to be with them. Then one day Elena asked her what she could do to reciprocate for the kindness Chiko had shown them during their trips to Japan.

"I said, without reservation, 'I want to go to the home office and work.' And Mr. John called me and said, 'Well, Chiko, you pack up and go pick up the airline tickets at the Japan office and come on." A few days later she was in Columbus.

She spent the first weekend at their home. In the meantime, they had found her a studio apartment. It was near the office, so she wouldn't have to worry about a car. She started off in the claims department opening mail (eventually she would help make audiovisuals). And every Friday Elena would pick her up or send someone for her to bring her to the house so she wouldn't be alone on the weekend.

Her parents had asked them to take care of her, and they did that and more. She was like a part of the family. And she looked on them as family. When Sita had her baby, Chiko went to Florida where Sita was living at the time to help her. Each time the Amoses bought a new car, they gave her the "old" one. It was rarely more than a year old. She always asked their opinion of her dates, and they were frank. And when she became engaged, they gave her and her fiance, James Beck, a wedding at the house, a simple ceremony, with the grandchildren as ushers and flower girls, but with about five hundred guests.

John liked to joke with her, tease her. But she was always in awe of him. "When I looked at him, it was like he knew what I was going to say. He had an authority about him. When he was home I was always careful to make sure I wasn't bothering him, that maybe he was thinking of something. And yet he didn't *show* that he was the president of a company."

But, in a sense, it was hard to think of John and Elena separately, as anything but a team.

"When they made a trip overseas, they were always together. Mr. John would take care of business. Elena would take care of friends and associates and wives. Every time she makes a trip, no matter where, she has a suitcase full of gifts. It's not because it's an obligation to give something to somebody—that's *her*. She wants to give. And she wants it to be something you like, that you can use."

There are many, many, *many* lucky people in this world, said Chiko, who have known Mr. John and Elena.

"One of them," she emphasized, "is from Japan."

21

AND MORE FAMILY

"It was a Siamese situation," said Matt Metcalfe. He was speaking of John and the company. "They were inseparable. But he always put the company first. He would always say, 'If we take care of the company, it will take care of the rest of us.'"

At the same time, he was forever spinning off ideas for other businesses, other projects, generally leaving the details of research and spadework to others. As person after person has said, he had no patience for detail, which in his case was a tremendous strength; the sluices stayed open to the free flow of creativity. As Metcalfe said, "To me, most people do not understand what an executive is. Most think that it is a manager. If you think that an executive is one who executes daily routines and follows through, he was not that. There is a manager and there is a leader. John was a leader. He was the tip of the arrow. He was always out front; he was singular. And everybody else followed."

Sometimes, it seemed, he gave off ideas for new ventures like a sparkler. As with any prolific thinker, many of his ideas never went much beyond the discussion stage. And many of those of substance had relatively short lives. But even those that eventually failed said something exciting about the man. He never did *anything* routine; there was always something about the projects that caught his interest that was out of the ordinary, that broke new ground.

When he threw in a hand, it was either because the project was ahead of its time or he didn't want to give it the concentrated effort he gave to his company, or he wanted to cut his losses. He was a firm believer in *that*. But there was one idea he came up with that didn't fall into any of these categories. It was an idea for a hunting preserve, and it enmeshed him in controversy.

First, about a man named Orestes Martin.

Orestes met the Amoses through a mutual friend in 1967, when he came back from Viet Nam but was still in the army. He did a lot of home decorating work for them on the side. One day, at a party at their home, John asked him what his plans for the future were when he left the army. Orestes said he had to find a job. John, who knew Orestes wanted to go into the interior decorating business, held out one of his hands to Orestes.

John said, "You see this?"

"Yes. That's your hand."

"You don't make money with your hands. You make money with your brain. I want you to go home and figure out how much money you need to start your business and come back at see me at ten o'clock in the morning."

When Orestes came to see him, he told John he would need $5,000. John called to his secretary to come into the office and he had her write out a check for that amount.

John also kept him busy. One of the projects he gave him was to build a house—the Amos's fishing camp in Florida—out of a beat-up, old trailer that was on property he had bought on the St. John's River. Another project, in 1971, started when John called him on the phone and said simply, "Would you like to take a ride with me?"

They drove some thirty-six miles to Pine Mountain. When they got to the top, John said, "What do you think?"

Orestes looked at him puzzledly. "What do I think about what?"

"I just bought this land. What do you think we can do with it?"

"Mr. John, I don't know what you want to do with this, because this is all rocks and mountains and things like that."

"How about a hunting preserve?"

"A *hunting* preserve?"

"Sure. I know how to get all the animals."

John had discussed this much earlier with Matt Metcalfe.

"John told me," recalled Metcalfe, "that he wanted a place where people could come and shoot exotic wild game, such as caribou or a boar, instead of having to fly great distances. He would have a hunting lodge and there would be good food, and the grounds would be totally enclosed in chain link fence." Metcalfe helped him finance the purchase of about six hundred acres of what was to be called the Royal Hunting Preserve.

What John wanted from Orestes now was to design the Royal Hunting Lodge on the very top of the mountain. Orestes came up with a design of two prefabricated units with five bedrooms in each, the units connected by a roof. By opening day, it looked far from pre-fabricated—more like a European hunting lodge, which is what John had in mind.

Animals were brought in, including buffalo, elk, mountain sheep, fallow deer, and Russian boar. Fees for hunting ranged from $60 to $2,500. But even before the hunting began, protests started.

Animal humane societies went to court to try to obtain an injunction against the preserve, but the judge ruled against them. That was far from the end of it, though. There were harassing calls, vandals poisoned a number of the animals, poachers shot a few others, a comic strip gave the preserve national notoriety.

John closed the preserve in 1972, though the first year proved, in fact, to have been financially successful. He donated the lodge to Mercer University in Macon, Georgia.

Did he, an interviewer asked him, learn anything from the experience?

"It taught me one thing," he answered with a smile. "Not to go in the hunting preserve business."

Once American Family was ensconced in Japan, One of his other ideas was to introduce a chain of outdoor hot dog carts in that country. It's unlikely he thought that this might be considered an unusual business, so to speak, for the founder of the only insurance company to be licensed in Japan since the war; he might not have gone ahead with it if he HAD. Rather, he saw a need to be filled, and he also saw what *he* always needed: another challenge.

He came to Elena's brother, Sal Diaz-Verson, with the idea. "What," he asked, "do people say are the best tasting hot dogs?" And he answered his own question. "At Yankee Stadium."

He told Sal to go to Yankee Stadium and try to find out how they made them. Sal called the people who handled the concession stands and they invited him to go back there during a game.

"I saw," recalled Sal, "how they were cooking the hot dogs, how long the hot dogs stayed in. I spent three days in New York studying how you do hot dogs."

John also wanted his carts to be totally different from any other hot dog carts, and he asked Sal to design one for him and get an architect to work with. "I must have spent several months designing that thing and finding out what the best hot dog was, how best to cook them."

Because of certain meat restrictions in Japan, John decided that his chain would sell chicken hot dogs. And the business began to take off. They wound up with about twenty-five stands in Tokyo. But then John, basically, was forced to shut it down. Word came back to him that the Minister of Finance was quite upset. A man of John's stature who was building an insurance company there, the Minister felt, should not have a side business of hot dog stands.

After that, he started a pizza business in Columbus called Pizza Square—the *pizzas* were square. "He learned of a modular pizza stand that a group was making near St. Louis," said Sal. "He wanted me to see it, to price it, to make projections. This is what he always did when he had an idea. Then I'd come back and tell him what the numbers were."

They operated two sites in Columbus, each on a different side of town. They did well for about three or four years. Then business at one of the places started slipping—the neighborhood changed—and John decided to give up the other as well.

Then, among others—for instance, he bought a part interest in a bull to breed. There was the goldfish business. During one of Sal's trips to Japan, he got a call from John in Columbus that someone was going to pick him up and take him back to his house. John told him nothing more than that. On the ride there, the man didn't explain what it was about; they spoke mostly about Japan.

"When I got to his house," said Sal, "there were about twenty ponds in front of his house. They were about five feet by four feet." In them were gold carp with huge, ugly heads. "Basically, they're mutated. They keep them in small ponds. They go for about $10,000 to $20,000 each. They're very, very big in California."

Sal spend the day learning about the fish. When he got back to Columbus, he wrote a report for John about the cost, about a feasibility study and so forth. Said Sal, "What this really told John was that it wasn't going to work very well over here. And of course he said, 'I think I found a better way to do it. If the cycle takes one year to produce these things, I think I can do the cycle in six months.'"

What John did was buy about forty bathtubs and sink them in the ground in back of his house. He began breeding the fish, but Elena couldn't stand them and he gave up the business.

Probably John's greatest interest, aside from the business he had founded and his love of politics, was the communications industry. The John Amos who had conceived and developed a new concept in health insurance still had within him the boy of thirteen who dropped out of high school to start a newspaper. Yet his love of politics, of his business, and of the media were not three separate things. He saw the media as a way of bringing his opinions—political, business, whatever—to public attention.

In 1973 he started his own paper in Columbus.

Up until then there were two daily papers in town: the *Enquirer*, a morning paper, and the *Ledger*, an evening paper, both of which were owned by the same corporation. Both were formidable competitors to come up against. They were old, established Pulitzer Prize-winning papers, the *Enquirer* winning it for taking on the Klu Klux Klan, the *Ledger* for leading a crusade to clean up Phenix City, Alabama. At the time John started his paper, recalled retired newspaper executive Glenn Vaughn, Jr., the *Ledger*, and *Enquirer* were still often on a different side of the fence than John on various issues.

In fact, said Nancy Vaughn, she used to do a financial column for the *Ledger* and *Enquirer*, and got a curious reaction from her publisher when she wanted to do one on John.

"John had gotten into different states but he hadn't gotten into Japan yet," she said. "I decided I'd do a column on him and I talked to my publisher about it. He wasn't real keen on it. He didn't like John at the time, though later he came to love him. 'Well,' he said, "before you do anything, I want you to go to the company lawyer out there and go through all those records. I think John is a little bit on the crooked side. I want you to check all those records and check all these states he's going into before you do anything, and see if he's breaking any laws.'

"Well, I went out and spent the day at the company, and they gave me all the information, all the records and everything. John didn't break any laws, and he was in like forty states then. So I came back and I wrote the column, and it was a favorable column. My publisher was sort of chagrined about the whole thing. He wanted me to find something wrong with him. He wanted some dirt. But it wasn't there."

The newspaper John started was a weekly called *Thursday*.

"He hired a lot of key people," said Glenn Vaughn. "It was a beautiful paper. It started out with some color. *USA Today* kind of reminds me of it."

Ron Feinberg, who was to become city editor of the *Atlanta Constitution*, was one of two reporters on the paper. He had been a police beat reporter on the *Enquirer* when he was hired away to join the new, still-unpublished paper. He was the first reporter hired; the editor was Ed Wilson, a broadcast journalist. Fineberg was young, unmarried, and ready for a new challenge. "This sounded like a pretty good challenge," he said. "I was doing just police reporting and I wanted to expand my horizons as a journalist. I wanted to do a lot of different things, and this seemed to be a perfect opportunity. And they did offer me a significant pay raise."

Thursday was a large-sized, handsome paper that John Amos visualized as outstripping the local papers both in the quality of the graphics and the writing. Recalled Feinberg, "I was somewhat involved in it from the very first day of the enterprise. When I went over there, they had just gotten a building and were sort of putting things together. They had rented or bought what looked like a warehouse, and carpenters were there, building offices. They were in the process of buying a press."

The paper, John hoped, would grow from a weekly into a daily. But the city was not ready for another paper, especially one that in graphics alone was ahead of its time. And John, with his many interests, did not have a lot of time to give it. Problems began developing almost immediately. One of the first things that happened was a breakdown in the press. John had to fly in a mechanic by Lear jet to meet the first deadline. Unfortunately, the first issue of *Thursday*, which of course was supposed to come out on Thursday, didn't appear until a few days later.

Thursday, however, apparently did have an effect on the local publishing scene. About three months after the paper came out, the *Enquirer* and *Ledger* were sold to another publisher, a sale which, in

Glenn Vaughn's opinion, was precipitated by the launching of *Thursday*. But it can take years before a new paper makes money, and gradually the paper underwent changes to cut costs. For example, color printing was dropped, And then after several months, the paper ceased publication.

Still, John had his sights set on being a newspaper publisher.

John called Glenn Vaughn about eight o'clock one evening and told him that the directors of American Family were meeting the next morning and were considering buying a newspaper in Patterson, New Jersey. They had gotten an evaluation of the paper from some financial group but, said John, "I just don't feel good about it. How about doing some research on the paper for me before the meeting?"

"Before tomorrow *morning*? My God, John," Vaughn said, "it's eight o'clock."

"Well, if you can come up with a report on this thing, I'll give you a thousand dollars."

Newspaper editors in Columbus, related Vaughn, were not making "huge money." He went to the office.

"It's incredible," related Vaughn, "how much information you can find if you really stick your mind to it. Within an hour I knew all about the Patterson, New Jersey, paper. I also knew how many papers the *New York Times* circulated in the area, how many the *New York Daily News* circulated. I learned all kinds of things, and of course John also had some information that he provided me. I developed about a ten or twelve page report. I worked all night on the thing, and had my secretary type it the moment she got in the office."

His analysis was that it was a "dog newspaper in a dog market"—do not buy it. And that was the end of that.

But it was still not to mark the end of John as a publisher. In 1981 he began publishing a national magazine.

Actually this is part of a larger story, a story that goes back a number of years and makes up part of the kaleidoscopic human being that was John Amos

One night in the late 1960s, a young woman named Beverly Greer, assistant news editor of the *Columbus Enquirer*, was at the news desk when the phone rang.

"Hello," a man's voice said, "this is John Amos and I have a very important announcement to make and I want it to go in the paper."

""Well, Mr. Amos," she replied, "we're closing out for the night. The final is on the press. And unless it is extremely urgent, would it be all right if it waited for morning? I'd be happy to take the information now or have somebody call you in the morning."

"I think it is important," he said. "I'm fixing to move the headquarters of American Family Life out of Columbus."

American Family was nowhere near the size of the company it was to become, was still in the two-story building, but Beverly Greer knew that it was important news if Columbus was losing a company like that. She told him to wait a minute while she got the press people to hold up on the final end. He then told her he was going to divide the country into four big regions, and that he would establish regional offices which would replace the home office.

He was going to try not to put anybody out of work, he said, but he had to get ready to make a lot of moves and changes. Any secretary or any other office person who wanted to move would be accomodated.

Recalled Beverly Greer, "I was frantically taking notes, and when he finished giving it all to me, I said I would do my best to get it in the morning paper. He said, 'If you do that, sweetheart, I'll buy you a new hat.' I said, 'Well, I don't really wear hats that much. How about one of those regional jobs?'"

She managed to get the story in the morning paper. After it came out, she got a call from John Coomdes, his public information man. And he was furious. He asked her where she got the story, and when she explained who had given it to her he told her that he would get back to her.

What was happening, as she was to learn, was that John wanted to expand the company into still more states, but that he was running into opposition within the company itself. Explained Beverly Greer, "He told me later that he was giving a message to the people who were standing in his way. What he wanted was that when all those people who were so complacent and happy with the company the way it was and were drawing down big paychecks, when they walked out on their front porches to bring in the morning paper the first thing he wanted them to see—in his words—was that they didn't have a job, that he was just moving the company completely.

"John used me and could very well have cost me my job because I didn't do any substantiating. But what do you do when it's the president and founder of the company? Fortunately, it worked out." The company didn't move and she came to work in the company's public relations office.

"I was Director of Agency Public Relations, which meant that I did the company sales newspaper and worked with agents in doing press releases—all kinds of things like that. I traveled a bit with John because he was in the process of building and going into a lot of states. There were sales meetings, presidents clubs, honor clubs, conventions."

John was so many-faceted that no one person other than Elena ever really knew him in his entirety. You would get to know some areas of him and maybe get glimpses into others, but it would still not have been the whole John Amos.

The idea of a magazine came up the way the way a lot of his ideas did.

"He was never one to linger over details," explained Beverly Greer, echoing what almost everyone who knew him said. "He wanted to tell it to you as quickly as possible and he wanted you to understand it and carry it from there. He said that he always let people work out their problems, but whenever they brought a problem to him that they couldn't solve, it wasn't their problem anymore."

John asked Beverly what she thought about their putting out a magazine that contained nothing but editorial comment. "When I travel," he told her, "I always try to get a lot of newspapers from everywhere I hit, and then I try to compare the way that part of the country perceives important issues compared to the way other parts of the country perceives them. That way you really get a full scope of how one issue can affect a lot of people in different ways."

Personally, said Beverly Greer as she thought back, her immediate feeling was that such a magazine would be pretty boring. She told him simply, "Well, I don't know."

"Why don't you put one together for me and let's see how it looks?"

She began to study how she could possibly get all this editorial comment for a magazine. It would be called *National Comment*. She contacted all the syndicates that handled the major columnists in the country and also contacted newspapers throughout the country, explaining the kind of magazine they had in mind.

"We put together a very good magazine. I took up the first sixteen-page section to show him. We were just going to print a few pages and put them together so he could see what it would look like. He said, 'God, this is wonderful,' and he called Kay, his secretary, and said, 'Kay, get me the pilot. I'm flying to New York.'"

He told Beverly Greer he was going to the Hearst syndicate to see if they would distribute it nationwide. He folded the sheets—they weren't even cut or bound in any way—and crammed them into his briefcase, then left for his plane.

When he came back from New York, he had a contract with the Hearst syndicate.

National Comment, which Beverly Greer edited, offered a cross section of comment from the nation's press. A monthly, it published every major columnist, such as Art Buchwald, Pete Hamill, William F. Buckley, Jr., Tom Wicker, and Gary Wills.

But the magazine lasted only about six months. John had known when he went into it that a magazine generally does not turn a profit for three years. He was prepared to go the course, but expenses got so high that the board of directors, he told Beverly Greer, voted him down.

This still didn't mean, however, that John Amos was out of the communications business.

He was a figure to be reckoned with in the television industry.

22

IDEAS AND IDENTITY

For years, John was concerned about the fact that American Family had only one product: cancer insurance. He felt, particularly when the company was undergoing attack from many quarters, that they should also be in some other line of business to fall back on. Leroy Paul, a former executive with RC Cola® who also had an extensive background in radio and television, was hired as vice president of corporate development to help find and establish new businesses.

"We looked at any number of things," recalled Paul, "including a Japanese restaurant, a wood preserving company, mail order companies, five and dime stores."

They finally purchased a local television station in 1977. It appealed to them for several reasons. For one thing, they felt comfortable with it in the sense that the broadcasting industry was somewhat similar to the insurance industry, in that it is very highly regulated. For another thing, the station was in Columbus. It was right *there*, and wasn't too expensive as far as television stations went. And, of course, Paul was experienced in television.

They eventually sold the station because it was the smallest one in town and was destined to remain small. "I went to the Board," explained Paul, "and I said, 'I can't make any money with that station unless I run it like a shlock shop. There's nothing wrong with that. There's a market for used cars. But since this is our home town and our corporation is here, I'm a little concerned about doing that. If you can't make money by producing good quality, sell it.' And we did. That kind of atmosphere was always there."

They eventually bought other stations—as of 1991, they had seven, including the *largest* one in Columbus. Leroy Paul, in addition to being vice president of corporate development, was made president of American Family Broadcast Group, a subsidiary—as is the insurance company, of course—of American Family Corporation.

The stations are located in medium and smaller-sized towns, with a total revenue—again, as of 1991—of about $70 million dollars. Each of them, under American Family, became the number one station in its town.

"As a group," said Paul, "we are a good middle-sized player. That was John's idea, and he was a great supporter. I've often told the story that he was the easiest guy in the world to get to say yes. As a matter of fact, we had to be very careful about going to him with things because he was an easy sell." For example, Paul went to him to tell him that a station was available in Savannah, how much it was, and that they would like to buy it. "We sat on a couch for less than five minutes, and between there and the elevator he said, 'Okay, go ahead.' And that was the total amount of discussion that took place between us."

What they look for in buying stations is that they have a good audience base, not have any technical deficiencies, and have a decent track record. "We don't try to take bad stations and make them into a winner," said Paul. "We try to take modestly successful stations and make them into a giant killer."

A major part of their philosophy is that the more local news the better, and to concentrate on the quality of staff rather than ultra-sophisticated equipment far beyond their range of needs. "We don't like to get behind," said Paul, "but I can take that same money and pay my people more than anybody else in town, and we do. We have never, ever lost a manager to another station in town, or an anchor person, or a weather person, or a sports person, or any department head. Never. Now, they leave to go to other markets, but we never lose our people to the guy across the street. It simply doesn't happen. If you can't work for an American Family station in your town, you've got a problem or you're good enough to go to a bigger market."

John never interfered in the running of a station. "He was a wonderful guy to work for in regard to giving you your head. He did expect results, but not in a demanding way."

One time John came to Leroy Paul and said to him that he thought they should have a Washington news bureau. "We had thought about that, too," said Paul. "So at his urging we established a Washington bureau, but it didn't just work out. We couldn't get stations to use the stories. We staffed it poorly, and it just piddled

163

along. I came to him and I said, 'John, this thing's costing us a lot of money and it just isn't working out.' He said, 'Well, you do whatever's right.' And so I closed it up. He would never say, 'No, by golly, I want you to keep that.' He believed in letting managers manage."

From time to time John would give them mild requests. "He might let us know for instance, that such-and-such a congressman was going to be in the area. But we would already know about it. You don't have to encourage TV stations to go out and cover politicians. But never, never did it get to content. And that's an important distinction. It's one thing to say, 'Leroy, Ted Kennedy's coming to town. I don't want you to cover him.' That would be a problem for us. He never did that. It's another to say, 'Alan Cranston is coming to town and I want you to have somebody there.' But never, ever what questions to ask, what stories to write, how to position the facts."

There was only one time Paul could remember John ever rebuking him. "When we first started, we weren't making any profit. And I said, 'We're going to make a profit this year,' and we didn't. He said, 'Don't ever raise expectations that you can't deliver.' The year after that, we made a million dollars profit, and I tried to tell him. He said, 'You ain't made a million.' I said, 'We sure as hell did. We've made a million dollars.' And I had to work on him a little while before I could convince him that we made a million dollars and here are the numbers on this piece of paper and it's going to be in your statement this year.'"

Paul recalled that when he first came to the company, John would pass him in the hall and say, "You know, I wish you would..." and give him something to look into. Paul would work on it only to learn when he came back to John that John may have forgotten about it or perhaps had given it to someone else to work on also. "The good point was he was never sensitive about that. We used to kid him about it. We used to just openly say that John was the kind of guy who would mail a letter and by the time he got back to the office he'd say, 'How come I don't have an answer yet?' Patience was not a long suit with John. But all during this time he was truly an easy guy to get along with."

When Paul first came to American Family, John had been named chairman of the sesquicentennial celebration the city was planning to put on. Paul's first assignment was to work on it.

"It was a modest success," he said, "but it lost money. We sold tickets, there were sponsorships and so on, but we came up about $25,000 short. Now, this was before John started making big money." John sold some of his personal stock and gave him $25,000 to make up the shortage, and he never said a word to anybody about it. "I said, 'John, I'm terribly sorry about this. I just apologize.' He said, 'If you couldn't do it, it couldn't have been done. You did the best you could.'

"I'd been prepared for him to say, 'Well, you know, you should have controlled the expenses a little better,' or whatever. But there were never any recriminations whatsoever. And I never had any feeling that I ought to be embarrassed when I was around him because of that, because he never, ever held it against me."

John did not get into television so that he would be involved in the glitter of that world. In fact, he only went to one network convention—and didn't go again because he didn't like it.

But he loved the business.

One of the honors that came to him that he esteemed the most was when he was selected in 1986, Georgian of the Year—by the Georgia Association of Broadcasters.

23

MORE INNOVATION

John was a powerful influence on a lot of people's lives, but probably none more so than Sal Diaz-Verson's.

John married Elena before her half-brother was born on December 31, 1951. The first time Sal could remember seeing John was when he was about four or five and John and Elena came for a visit to Cuba. Sal, his mother and Elena's two half-sisters, Silvia and Louly, moved to Miami in June or July, 1959. Their father had preceded them by about six months.

Diaz-Verson senior had barely escaped a firing squad during widespread executions in Cuba.

In his fight against repression and corruption, he had made enemies of both the right and the left—Batista and Castro. He had had to go into exile several times during Batista's regime, and now had to flee Castro for his life.

According to an account in the *Columbus Ledger* at the time, he had been harassed and literally attacked after Castro came into power. His office and home had been looted, and he had barely escaped machinegun fire from a passing car. Then on March 19, 1959, a police captain came to his suburban home in Havana to arrest. Somehow Diaz-Verson was able to talk the officer into letting him spend one more night in his home on the promise that he would show up at police headquarters the next morning.

But that night, he managed to hide on a ferry in Havana Harbor, and he escaped to Key West.

Young Sal, raised in Miami, used to spend a month or two in Columbus almost every summer.

"When I was very young," said Sal, "John just took me basically under his wing and spent a lot of time with me. He loved my father very much, admired and respected him very much. They spent a lot of time together. Anything that happened politically in the world, John would call my father, no matter what time it was, and talk to him about it. What was amazing was that my father spoke very little English and John spoke very little Spanish, yet they communicated perfectly. They'd be sitting in a room and I'd come in and John would say, 'Sal, your dad and I were talking about so and so.' And he would go through the whole thing."

As a child, his first impression of John was that he was strict—he would set down a lot of rules—but he was always very open.

"You could communicate with him," he recalled. "He was a person who always paid attention, no matter what age you were. He was always interested in what your impressions were. I remember when I was about fourteen or fifteen, sitting down with him and discussing politics and what was happening in the world. He'd get your perspective and then he'd give you *his* perspective. He'd tell you what he thought."

John would also regale him with stories he had learned about Sal's father's exploits, about Sal's family background—told him more than Sal had ever heard from his own father. And John would also tell him about his own background, about his mother and father and grandparents.

"If I went to bed before two in the morning," Sal remembered, "that was early."

When Sal was about fourteen, he joined Shelby—they were about a year apart—working summers at the company. But all was not work. John and Elena often took the boys on business trips with them. One time, related Shelby, they were staying at the St. Moritz in New York when John and Elena had to go to a party. They left instructions that the boys were to stay in the room, enjoy television, and order room service. When the boys finally read the menu and saw Maine lobster and prime rib, "We just went wild," said Shelby, "and ordered just about one of everything." But when John learned about it, he didn't reprimand them, even though he must have been upset, because he hadn't given them any limits. But he had figured on them ordering something like hamburgers and french fries.

John enjoyed taking them hunting and fishing. "When we were teenagers," Sal said, "we had to do everything when we went fishing. John was a get-everything-ready-and-I'll-throw-it-in fisherman. We would bait his hook, take the fish off the line."

John was always keenly interested in his education, in his plans for the future. "Originally I told John that I wanted to stay in Miami because my father wanted me to stay home and go to the University of Miami or one of the other universities in south Florida."

John encouraged him, however, to consider going out of town in order to broaden his vision. He especially wanted him to go to an Ivy League school and got him an appointment to the Wharton School of Business.

"I was going to go, but when I went up there," said Sal, "I decided it wasn't for me. I had come from south Florida, and it was quite different. I was used to driving, for instance. There you had to use subways and everything else. I said, 'I'm going back.'"

Prior to this, he had enrolled in the pre-law program at Miami-Dade Junior College, and was also taking some courses in economics at the University of Miami. One day, during a trip John and Elena took to Miami, he informed John for the first time that he was enrolled in pre-law and doing well, that he was thinking of transferring to either the University of Florida or Florida State Law School.

"John said to me, 'To become a lawyer?' I said, 'Yes, that's what I think I want to do.' I was really proud that I was doing well in it. He said, 'No, Sal, we've got enough lawyers in the family. The last thing we need is another lawyer. This family needs somebody who knows how to run the money. Nobody in the family knows how to run money.'"

Sal thought about it, then said to him, "You mean a degree in business?"

"No. I want you to get a degree in finance."

Sal realized that this meant going to a large university that had a good school of finance. The University of Miami, at the time, did not have one. But paying for it would be a problem. He had always worked and was basically putting himself through school. Though his father helped, it wasn't enough to pay the tuition, let alone maintain a car and have a social life.

"I had to supplement what my father gave me," said Sal. "I used to work in the evenings and on weekends. I did a lot of odd jobs—worked in a tobacco store for a while. I was a produce manager at the A&P. So I told John that I wanted to go, but that it would be pretty hard since it would cost a lot of money. And I never forgot what he said. He said, 'Sal, I want you to quit your job.' I said, 'You *do*?' He goes, 'Yep, I want you to concentrate on school. I want you to get a degree in finance, and whatever you need just call me.'"

His secretary then was Linda Bowick. John's specific instructions to him were, 'You call Linda Bowick and tell her what you need and I'll never ask any questions.'"

Sal transferred to Florida State. "For four years," said Sal, "all I had to do was pick up the phone when I got my bill from school. I'd call Linda Bowick and tell her this is how much I need. And he'd send it to me." John paid everything, from tuition to the dorms to an efficiency apartment. "He never once asked me, 'How are you doing in school. Are you flunking? Are you making A's? Are you making B's?' He never did."

In the meantime, Sal was working summers at the company and would accompany John on many business trips. And he had long realized that John had pointed him in the right direction by advising him to major in finance. He felt comfortable with it and was good at it. In articles in the company newspaper and in newsletters, John always wrote about him, always said that Sal could run any bank better than anyone else.

After graduation, with a degree in finance, Sal told John that he had applied for jobs in certain companies, primarily in Florida. But John, with his tremendous prescience, with his eye on Sal's future, said, "Nope, I think what you need to do next is go to Wall Street."

Recalled Sal. "I said, 'Wall Street?' He said, 'Yes, don't worry about it. I'll make a few phone calls. I'll get you an interview. If you major in finance, you've got to spend some time on Wall Street.' I said, 'Okay.' It made no difference because I was single. To me, wherever I went, it didn't matter, because it was just me and some bags, and so I said, "Okay, Wall Street.'"

Linda Bowick sent him money for fare to New York. Sal was interviewed by Abraham & Company, a medium-sized investment house, and they offered him a position. But John still had additional plans for him. He told him, "If you're going to work on Wall Street, you're going to have to meet the right people. I want you to understand the business community, understand New York, understand Wall Street."

John's friend Mark McKee was a member of the Metropolitan Club of New York, a very prestigious private club in Manhattan, founded by J.P. Morgan. It was a huge, luxurious place; women were allowed only in the main entertainment area and the main dining room; the bar, billiards room, card room, and its guest rooms were "gentlemen only." John subsequently became a member. This club would be Sal's home for over a year, enabling him to make many contacts.

A lot of times, John gave him special projects to work on for the company, and Sal would often take business trips with him. But it wasn't until about a year after Sal had come to New York that John mentioned something about Sal working for the company. Said Sal, "He said, 'I'd like you at some point to come to the company.' I said, 'Fine, when?' He said, 'Well, I don't know. I will have to let you know. I don't think they're ready for you yet.'"

It was about a year later that John told him that the person who had been "running the money" for the company had become ill and would be leaving, that Sal should come to Columbus to go through a training program. This was in 1974. From the luxury of the Metropolitan Club, he started off as a trainee at American Family at a salary of $11,000 a year. But it was a road that would lead to his becoming president of American Family Life Corporation, first executive vice president of the insurance company, and chief investment officer. Recalled Sal of the initial salary, "John said to me, 'It's not going to be that expensive living in Columbus, Sal.' I said, 'Okay, yeah, I can get an apartment.'"

When Sal told his father that he was going to work for John, his father not only was delighted, but he loved John so much that he said, "I want you to take care of John."

Sal went through extensive training that included accounting, statutory accounting, insurance accounting. And it was during this time that he met his future wife, Pat, who was working as assistant to the general office manager, Reese Ellison. "All the general operations of the company, except for the financial, came under Reese Ellison—he's since retired," explained Sal. "He didn't know what to do with me, so he basically said to Pat, 'You just make sure Sal is where he's supposed to be.' She would say, 'Okay, you're going to be in claims for two days and I'll check your work and make sure it's okay,' and so forth."

It would be eight or nine months afterwards that they had their first date.

John made it Sal's first priority, upon the joining the company, to learn the Japan market. And for about a year and a half, Sal basically immersed himself in it, making frequent trips there. He also used to travel extensively with John.

"I'd usually be in the office early—about eight o'clock—and John would call me and say, 'Sal, I want you to go with me to Minneapolis. We're leaving in an hour.' I would have to cancel everything. One thing I told Pat when we got married was that she had to remember that John would call all hours of the night. He would call you at one in the morning and you'd go over and he'd say, 'Tomorrow morning this is what I want you to do. I want you to get on a plane, do this, do that. I think it would be a great idea to do it.' That's the way he really liked to work."

Like most people who spent a lot of time with John, Sal spoke of often sitting up with him until almost dawn. "He would often say, 'By the way, there's a breakfast at eight in the morning. I want you to be there. Go for me.' I'd say, 'John, it's three in the morning. *Now* you tell me.' Then when John got up he'd call and say, 'Bring them back to the room after you finish breakfast.' And I'd bring the people back."

The thing he mostly enjoyed about working with John was that there was never a dull day. Generally John would come in every morning between ten-thirty and eleven, but you often started getting phone calls from him by nine or ten.

"He'd normally come to my office first and he'd sit on the couch or one of the chairs, and he usually had a new idea or a new thought. You never knew what he was going to come up with. A lot of times when John would tell you something you never knew whether he was kidding or not. So you didn't know exactly how to answer. He'd say, 'What do you think?' And I'd say, 'Well, John, that sounds pretty good,' because you didn't know exactly. And you didn't want him to make a fool out of you."

One of John's ideas was to build a large paddle-wheeler modeled after ones he had seen in Europe and on the Mississippi. He was sure, he said, that people would charter it, that it would do great business.

Recalling the scenario, Sal said, "'John,' I told him, 'that could be very costly.' And John said, 'Well, just think about it.' Whenever you gave him negatives, he'd say just think about it, and he'd leave the room. And you'd sit there. And you'd get a call probably that afternoon and his secretary would say can you come up, he wants to see you.'" The call did come through. "You'd go upstairs," continued Sal, "and he'd say, 'Did you think any more about what I told you this morning?' You'd say, 'John, I haven't thought about it that much.' He'd say, 'I've been thinking about it,' and he'd have all the numbers. He'd usually have a yellow pad he'd work from. He'd say, 'Well, I did some calculations."

In the case of the paddle-wheeler, John felt that they could get it built for $350,000. And he had calculated how many days they could rent it out, and at what charge, in order to make a profit.

Recalled Sal, "I said, 'That sounds reasonable. I have to check these figures out.' The next morning I said, 'John, I don't think so, but do you think you can?' 'Yep. Do I have the money?' I said, 'John, I don't know, it's going to be pretty tough. This is going to be a tight year for your income.' He said, "Well, okay, just think about it.'"

John went back upstairs, only to come back about two hours later. "Sal," he said, "the only thing about this is, you know—I've been thinking about it—at my age, I don't know how much longer I'm going to be around. I really want it. I think I really would enjoy one. I was thinking, if there's any way to do it, I really would like to do it. Do you think you can find the money?"

And Sal's answer was, "John, I'll find the money. Don't worry about it. Go build your boat. I'll find it."

The paddle-wheeler, which was built in 1980, actually cost $1.1 million. And it will have a further place in John Amos's story.

The story of paddle-wheeler is just an example, said Sal, of how convincing John could be.

"You could tell him no and he'd come back a second time. A lot of times he would play on your emotions. Like about the boat, he would go through about how he was aging. You might think you could say, 'John, all of that is a bunch of crap,' but you couldn't do it. You just said, 'Okay, I give in. I'll find you a boat if you want a boat.'"

John would not tell you how to solve a problem. He would say, "Tell me when you've made a decision on it. Don't worry, you've got to go to the right or go to the left, but whatever you do, don't stand still. Make a decision and go on."

Said Sal, "The biggest frustration he had with me was when I would take some time to think something out. I would say, 'How about giving me until tomorrow to think about that? It's pretty major, John.' John would say, 'No, you've got until this afternoon,' or 'I'll call you in an hour.' Or he'd drop a problem on you and he'd get in the elevator and go upstairs and call and say, 'Okay, what did you decide?' I'd say, 'You just left my office, John. I haven't called the bank yet or I haven't called so and so yet. Can I do a bit more research on this?' He'd say, 'Okay, call me when you got it.'"

Sal doubted very much if John knew until the day he died how much money he had in his bank account. He would call Sal maybe once a week or once a month and say that he was planning on buying this or that, and ask if he had the money. Sal would say yes or no, and that would be it.

"If somebody needed something," said Sal, "he'd say, 'Sal, write a check out to so and so. They have a problem. Loan them the money.' I'd say, 'John, you're probably not going to get paid back.' John would say, 'Pay it. Make him a loan. I'll write it off.'"

Sal had reason to remember one incident in particular. An elderly man, a good friend of John's, came in to ask for a $175,000 loan. The federal government had taken just about everything he had. John, after talking with him, discussed it in private with Sal, asked him what he thought. Sal told him that he had looked at the man's financial statement and was sure that he would never be able to pay back the money.

"I just can't recommend it, John."

"Well, you're my financial advisor. Go tell him you can't recommend it."

Recounting the incident, Sal said, "I went down and told the man, 'I'm sorry but we can't make the loan. John can't afford to lose $175,000 right now. It's real hard but I just can't recommend it.' And the guy just broke down and cried. He said,'Can I see John one more time?'"

Sal called John, and John said okay, fine. "But you already told him?"

"I told him."

Sal took him up to his office. John told his friend the story again, and the friend said he understood, but then added, "I really wish you could help me."

John looked down at the floor. After a few moments he said, "Sal, write him a check."

"Write him a check?" Sal repeated.

"Yep." Then he put his hand out to the man.

But that was not the end of the story.

"A year later," Sal related, "the guy came in and repaid the loan. I had been wrong."

John would lend money to friends, and when they would ask Sal what the interest was, John would tell him he wasn't going to charge them any interest. "One time I asked him how come we weren't charging interest on the money, and he said, 'Sal, I'm just hoping I get my money back.' Those are the kinds of things John would do. He would do something on a handshake—nobody had to walk in with a contract—and if he told you something, he lived up to it."

John, he said, also taught him a lot about politics: how to get things done; how to stay behind the scenes; what buttons to push at what times; not to overplay your hand. "And not," Sal added, "to get carried away with yourself. Though he was very powerful, he was very humble. John never played up his power."

John went through a period where he considered running for the Senate. Sal's reaction when John told him this was, "You're *what*?"

"Running for the Senate."

They discussed it for a few hours, and then John asked him to go to Washington with him, where he wanted to talk it over with some political friends.

"He was really heartbroken after he met with them. They told him, 'John, if you want the Senate, you have to give up American Family. You can't have both. You've got to make a decision.'"

He had hoped he could have both. And there was no way he could give up the company he had founded and to which he had given so much of himself.

Contrary to what a lot of people must have thought, said Sal, it wasn't until 1978 that John made his first large income from the company. Until 1967, for instance, he was paid in the $25,000 to $30,000 range. "One of the reasons John built up quite a bit of debt was that everything the company needed, he did personally. John made all the financial contributions we made to help the company. There were no PACS like there are now. When he worked on the Humphrey campaign, everything was personal. When he worked with Lyndon Johnson's campaign, everything there was personal. If the company couldn't afford to pay for a trip or for someone to go somewhere, if John felt it was an investment for the company he would pick it up personally. He would borrow the money. He bore a lot of the debt. He'd put his stock up. He'd put up everything he had.

And always there was that humility—and that sense of humor, both of which blended together in another incident Sal recalled.

John, Elena, Sal, and his wife, Pat, returning from Japan via Europe, landed at LaGuardia Field in a raging snowstorm. They had about twenty pieces of luggage. Nobody could get any porters—except John. He had them literally lined up.

"Once in a while," Sal recalled, "one of them would say to me, 'I never drink Pepsi. I love to drink Coca Cola.' I'd say great, but I didn't know what the hell they were talking about. Finally I said, 'John, how did you get all these guys to do all this and leave everybody else? And John said, 'Well, I told them I was chairman of Coca Cola.' I said, 'What?' He said, 'Yes, I told them I was chairman of Coca Cola.' I said, 'What did you do that for?'

"He said, 'If I told them American Family, they wouldn't know me. But I figured they would know Coca Cola.'"

24

FAMILY CONNECTIONS

"Uncle John," said Daniel Amos, "was the greatest uncle anyone could have and a wonderful man. I loved him. I really did."

Dan Amos, Paul Amos's son, joined the company field sales force after graduating in 1973 from the University of Georgia, where he majored in risk management and insurance. He worked in sales for about ten years, becoming a state manager and then taking on an executive position in the home office. John, thinking ahead to his succession, would one day name him as future Chief Executive Officer of the corporation and insurance company, and name Paul—who had rejoined the home office in 1974, a year after Dan joined the field force (Bill Amos retired in 1978)—as future Chairman of the Board.

"I was born in Florida," said Dan, "and it was always fun knowing we were coming up and were going to be at his house. He would always have something kind of wild and different, such as fireworks. There was always a kind of mystique about him."

And you never knew what he was going to do next. About 1966 he even built an amusement park for little children, which he had someone operate for him for a while.

Said Dan, "He was always fun to be with. I love to fish and so did he. But the thing that was always hilarious to me about his fishing trips was that if he didn't start catching them immediately, he didn't have any use for it. I mean, fishing is generally considered a sport of patience, and it didn't match his personality at all."

"John," Dan once told Beverly Greer, "would always 'egg' my father on to let me do things. 'Aw, go on and let him do it.'" Dan recalled the time when he was debating whether to go to Columbus College or the University of Georgia. His mother "kind of" wanted him to stay home, since he was an only child, and his father said that if he did want to stay home he would buy him any kind of car he wanted. So Dan did get the car, but John, he said, kidded his father so much about his staying home that his father turned around and told him he could go off if he wanted to. And he went to the University in that new car.

"Growing up," he told Beverly Greer, "I've always been a little close to him and I've always considered him a second dad. I've always loved him."

Dan recalled an incident that took place when he was eighteen and a senior in high school. John gave Shelby and him a trip to the Bahamas as a gift. He also gave Dan $50 and told him to let it ride four times on the blackjack table. Dan won three times in a row and had $400 on the table. He wanted to pull it off, but then said to himself, "My uncle told me to let it ride four times. He would give me more hell if I brought home $400 than if I lost it." So he left it on a fourth time and lost it.

"The thing I liked about my uncle in terms of business," he told another interviewer, "was that he was never scared to take a chance. He would never risk everything, but he was never scared to take a chance. He always felt like he had to be trying new things and looking forward. And of course that's what got us into Japan."

He was also always open to other people's ideas. For instance, John came up with the idea of selling an intensive care policy, which sold well, but then when Dan suggested selling two policies instead of one to meet the rising costs of hospitalization, he approved it quickly. Said Dan, "We started selling them everywhere. The point is, you could always go talk to him and say, 'I've got this idea and I'd like to try.' And he would do it."

Some businesses make it a policy not to employ more than one member of a family. John went in the exact opposite direction. He not only believed in bringing his own family into the business, but bringing in employees' families as well. It was a way of making the whole company a family.

"He believed in knowing their first names, knowing their spouses' names, and having company parties at his house instead of at a country club or hotel. All of that played an important part in the feeling of a family atmosphere."

Something that always amazed him about John was the same thing that others mentioned who knew John—how he would get a gut feeling about something and react accordingly.

"He would have this feeling that this was right. He used to say sometimes that you've got to go with your gut. He would say, 'I can't tell you why. I can just tell you you've got to begin to get a feeling for something and just go with it. And if you're wrong, then adjust.'

"He always used to say to me, 'Cut your losses. It's okay to do something, and it's okay to go wrong. Where the problem is is where you keep trying to correct it when you can't make it work. Go ahead, try what you want to try. Give it your best shot. And then if it fails, take it as a loss and be over with it. So many times in life,' he'd say, 'people want to continue something to try to make it work—when it never will.' And that was something about John. He would cut his losses when he had something that wouldn't work. And if he ever hit something big, it was a winner!"

John never wanted to be predictable. "He *loved* being unpredictable because he felt that it kept everyone on their toes. But I always felt like I could predict him pretty close. I'd miss it sometimes, but I kind of knew the way he thought. I could predict that he was going to be unpredictable, that if things were calm for a certain amount of time he was going to do something screwy just to keep things lively."

His unpredictability came out in so many different ways. One incident Dan enjoyed relating happened when Dan was just out of high school and was in college, and John told him he would like to take him fishing. Dan drove over to his house about six in the morning, which was when they were to leave. John said he would like to go in his own car.

"So I got in his car and we started to go. And he put the car in reverse and he hit my car. Backed up into it. And then he took off. He did not say one word to me about it. He did not get out of the car. He never said, 'Oh, I'm sorry I hit your car. You'll go get it fixed.' He just went right on. And I didn't say a word either. The next day when I came back and got my car, I took it over to the body shop. It was a hundred dollars. I got it fixed and sent the bill to his secretary. And he paid it and he still never said a word to me."

The thing about his uncle, Dan went on, is that he truly enjoyed life. "He maybe died young, but I don't know if anybody ever enjoyed life more than he did. He enjoyed it to the fullest."

Dan told of the time he was working as a salesman in Alabama, when he stopped at a little grocery store filling station to buy something and saw a fish mounted on the wall which he knew would fit in with his uncle's wild sense of humor.

"It was the biggest bass I ever saw in my life. And I knew enough about bass fishing to know that either that was a world record or something was wrong with that fish. No, that it was impossible for a bass to be that big."

He said to the man behind the counter, "Tell me about that fish. Did you catch that fish?"

The man hemmed and hawed, but didn't tell him.

Dan asked again. "Did you catch that fish?"

"No," he finally said, "I did not."

"Will you sell it to me?"

Suspiciously, "What do you want that fish for?"

"I got an uncle," Dan said, "who could tell more stories about that fish. I'll give you a hundred dollars for it."

The man practically jumped up the wall to grab the fish and sell it to him. The story, it turned out, was that the man was a taxidermist, and the fish was a grouper. He had painted the grouper to look like a bass; the only difference was in the teeth.

"Well, I took that fish," related Dan, "and got a rubber worm and hung it down from its mouth. And I gave it to John."

He probably couldn't have gotten him a better gift.

"He put it up in his reception room," said Dan, "and he kept it there for years. When his friends would come in, you could hear him say, 'Man, let me tell you about bringing that fish in.'"

25

AND OTHER AMOSES

Glancing surreptitiously at the old man sitting outside Paul's office, Paul Amos's secretary couldn't help wonder what he wanted of her boss. He was a strange looking old man, with a beard and a long coat, and leaning heavily on a cane propped between his legs. He looked as if he might fall forward if that cane slipped.

All she knew was that he must have a legitimate reason to be here, since he had been cleared by the security officer in the lobby to come up. She busied herself with her work, then looked up at the sound of laughter.

Paul's.

And John's.

John now without the beard and wig.

Oh, that Mr. John, she thought laughing, *you just never know*...

This was certainly nothing new to Paul Amos.

"John had a facade of toughness," he said, "but he had a heart of tremendous size. He liked to shock people."

Paul recalled the time when John and Elena were still living at Fort Walton Beach, and a physician friend of John's, Dr. White, invited him to go with him to a medical association meeting in Pensacola.

"He became separated from Dr. White," said Paul, "and he began mixing and mingling with the crowed. He would introduce himself as a guest of Dr. White—and that he was the Fort Walton chiropractor."

With all of John's practical jokes, did Paul ever play any on him? "No, he never liked to have practical jokes played on him. I threatened to a lot of times, but I just didn't want to get involved where there would be no end. I knew," he added, laughing, "I wouldn't have the last word."

John, he continued, was not only always very family oriented, but very emotional when it came to family situations.

"We were on the elevator one day together and he looked up at me and he said, 'Brother, I love you.' Or I'd come into his office—I might have been away or something—and he'd hug my neck and kiss me. Lots of times he liked to do it when there were people around, to embarrasss me, but he did in private many times. He was a very affectionate person. I'm just not that affectionate."

And John not only cried easily at sad events and was particularly affected when their mother and father died, but a lot of times he also cried out of happiness.

"But people who didn't know him didn't know this side of him. They saw the gruffness and the shortness. He was not one to carry on cocktail conversation, so I'm sure that he appeared gruff to many people. But I think that one of his main characteristics was his sincerity. He was what he was, and you knew what he thought. Regardless of what he said or did, people knew he was sincere."

So many people also knew something else about him—how big and how open his heart was.

Said Frances King Lolley, in what was echoed by every secretary John ever had, "He was a big contributor to any cause in Columbus. You just can't name all the things he contributed to. Anybody who was down and out, if they could find John Amos's office they never left empty-handed. They always seemed to find his office and his home. I've seen him give to people and I'd say to myself, 'How can he give to that sorry man? He won't even work. He just comes here for money all the time.'"

When she would mention it to John, he would say, "Well, he's had a hard time, bad luck, and he's hungry."

"We would try to shield him from them," said Francis King Lolley. "But he might say, 'What's that man doing in the lobby?' I'd say, 'Well, it's somebody wanting some money. He says he doesn't have a job and he doesn't have anything to eat.'" John would always have her tell the person to go to the comptroller's office. In the early days of the company, it might be for twenty-five dollars—a lot of money then. "He'd say, 'Have them take it out of my check. Sometimes I'd think, well you're not going to have enough money to feed your own family if you keep that up. But he never turned anyone away."

She remembered one of the early Christmas parties, which was held at a hotel in town. She noticed a couple of party crashers, who had come in for the meal. When she told John, he said he had already talked to the person in charge of security. He told him, "Just let them eat and then just usher them out, and don't do anything about it."

This happened at other company banquets he gave, and his instructions always were, "Just let them eat and escort them out."

And his secretary Carol Royer recalled incidents when people came in who needed, say, $2000 and John had $1000. "He'd go to the bank and write a note. He'd tell them to come back the next day and he'd go get the money and bring it back to them. He was that way. I always felt like if he had every penny that he ever gave to someone else, he could own Columbus. Very, very giving. Very giving."

And his door was open to just about everyone who wanted to see him, whether with a problem or just to say hello. You didn't have to go through a chain of command.

Robyn Smith, his last secretary, said he used to feel bad if he shut the door between his office and hers, as if he were shutting her off or putting her down. And from his desk he could see whoever walked into her office. "Half the time," she said, "he'd holler 'Hey, come on in.'" It could be anyone, such as the person delivering mail.

And there seemed to be no end to his practical jokes.

One day he came in carrying a grocery bag, walked by her desk quickly, and sat down at his desk, letting out a word that sounded like "whoa." He kept making these sounds, and when she walked into his office she saw him bent over, reaching around inside the bag.

"I want you to see what I brought home," he said.

She walked over, and when she got close to him, only a few inches away, his hand came out. And on his finger—

It was the first time she had ever seen that rubber mouse.

Only she would remember it as a "rat."

"I just jumped back about three feet, lost my breath, and he just died laughing."

Another time they were giving a party in the board room for a retiring member of the board. John always used to say that the next thing after retirement was death. And just about everyone knew this. Before the party, John gave Robyn Smith an assignment, and a time that she was to do it.

"I want you," he said, "to go into the board room and I want you to holler out that Striffler-Handy wants to talk to the retiree."

Striffler-Handy was a mortician.

"I told him," said Robyn Smith, "I can't do that. No, I can't do that. But I did anyway. I went in there and hollered that out and everybody just sort of died laughing."

And then there was the "turtle."

Only a few people were aware of the "turtle" he once had.

It was a toy. When you wound it up, a bell would ring.

"I have to be careful," John said, "because I don't want to insult people."

So when someone talked to him too long on the phone, he would wind up the toy.

"Oh-oh, the other line's ringing. I'll have to call you back. Thanks for calling."

"What was amazing to me," said John's friend and consulting attorney Dick Schweitzer, "was the depth of John's knowledge, reading, and studying in the field of cancer. There was hardly anything in the field that he didn't know about—the scientific developments, the medical research, statistics. John's grasp of the underlying subject matter of the type of insurance he was offering was amazing. And to know this, in addition to everything else he was doing, was really a rather scary thing."

His knowledge of demographics, of where else to expand, was nothing short of amazing, too.

American Family was licensed in most states and a growing number of countries in addition to Japan, including England and Australia. The company was offering additional forms of supplemental insurance, among them a Medicare supplement policy. The corporation moved into the field of printing and corporate communications as well. And all the while John kept looking for further challenges, at one time even the possibility of taking over a small, bankrupt automobile manufacturing company.

And though John and Elena traveled the world more and more, their home on Steam Mill Road never ceased being the center of their social lives. Where most people have a simple grill for barbecuing, John had a barbecue pit constructed of a long, wide sewer pipe with tracks running through it, capable of barbequing about twenty-five turkeys at a time, or two whole pigs.

And his mind never ceased to work in ways that never ceased to astound.

His secretary Kay Stover would never forget when he first began mentioning building a paddle boat.

"I remember when the boat was just a gleam in his eye. When he started talking about it, I thought, 'Oh, he's really crazy this time. How could he possibly do it?'" He said he was going to call it *Elena, Queen of Hearts*. He loved her so much."

The boat was to be a duplicate of the *Delta Queen* on the Mississippi. John and Elena had taken a trip on it once, as well as on another model of the *Delta Queen*, a paddle-wheeler in Europe that went from Frankfurt to Amsterdam.

"I thought it was a wonderful idea," said Elena. "The only thing I didn't like was that it took a lot more money and a lot more time than we thought it would." John even had to change shipyards because every time he went there, no one was working on it and no progress had been made.

Orestes Martin, who had designed the hunting lodge, was out of town when he received a call one afternoon. John wanted to know if he could come to Columbus that day, but Orestes couldn't make it until the following afternoon.

"He didn't tell me what he wanted me for," said Orestes. "When I got into the airport, he was waiting for me. He never used to go wait for anyone in the airport."

John explained the problem on the flight to Alabama, where the shipyard was located. "He said, 'So far they are screwing me for over a million. I want you to take over and finish it up for me.'"

When they got to the shipyard, Orestes almost groaned when he saw how little they accomplished, and they were charging John $40,000 a day.

"They're screwing me," John kept repeating, "and I don't like to be screwed this way."

Orestes agreed to stay on there, to see to it that the shipyard didn't waste more time and money, and to make a number of changes. He concentrated mostly on the interiors, such as making changes in the galley. Elena put her touches in the design, too.

The boat was a far cry from the old *John B.*, the yellow trailer on pontoons that John had designed.

The *Elena, Queen of Hearts*—over seventy-feet in length, and one of the very few river boats that is truly powered by its paddle-wheels— was first docked in Eufaula, Alabama, on the Chattahoochie. Employees would sign up for a day's roundtrip by bus, to have dinner on the boat. Then John moved it to New Orleans, where he thought he might keep it to charter out. But it seemed too dangerous. There were too many tugboats, too much traffic on the river. And too hot and too many mosquitoes.

They finally docked it in Washington, D.C., on the Potomac, where it would be used for entertainment and for charter, a grand lady, with its several decks and staterooms and rich colors and curlicues and huge, slowly-churning paddle wheels.

Truly a queen.

26

EXPRESSIONS OF LOVE

Awards and honors began to come, such as the honorary degree of Doctor of Laws he received from the University of Miami in 1981 when he also was the commencement speaker, and the Doctor of Humane Letters Degree from Morris Brown College, Atlanta, where he served on the Board of Trustees. But these were like a trickle before a flood.

The full extent of John and Elena's generosity and kindness could never be known; these remained, in large part, a secret between themselves and the recipients. But many of their gifts were so large and of such a nature that they could not be kept private. For instance, they donated a practice courtroom—a mock court—to Mercer University School of Law; donated to the Scholarship Funds of La Grange College, Mercer Law School, and the University of Georgia; created the John B. Amos Endowment for the Chair of Special Education at Morris Brown College; and assisted in the creation of the Insurance Program at Georgia State University's College of Business Administration. Yet this, too, was like a trickle to the full flood of their giving.

They also gave of their time and energy. One of the many causes they gave so much of themselves to was the School of the Americas.

The School of the Americas is a United States Army training school for officers, cadets, and non-commissioned officers from Latin America. Originally based in the Panama Canal Zone, it was relocated to Fort Benning, which in 1986 was designated as its permanent home. John and Elena Amos led the campaign to have it relocated there. And they were in the forefront in establishing the School of Americas Support Group, which was formed to help the the school's staff and visiting military personnel and their families adjust to and enjoy their stay in this country.

In his travels John was always on the alert to what he could learn. One of the things that impressed him about the Japanese, for instance, was the way they found needs in the market, which they then went about filling. He himself had filled such a need, of course, with cancer insurance, and so it was as though he had had a kinship with them long before he had ever visited Japan. And they never failed to keep inspiring. He often cited, as just one example of the way the Japanese filled needs, that the Japanese had developed a watch which let Moslems know five times a day that it was time for them to pray to Mecca.

When he was in Italy, he became more aware than ever of the world's "underground economy"—Mafia money and cash transactions, among others—that costs governments untold millions in taxes. In an effort to solve this in the United States, he started a personal campaign of letter writing and speeches in an attempt to create a new currency, whereby there would be periodical changes in the color of the paper money, which would make non-taxed money worthless.

But though he was internationally known now, though Senators and Congressmen were among his close friends, though he had private jets at his disposal, he was still the small-town John Amos who always loved a parade, whether it was a straggly one with high school bands or the most elaborate one with ornate floats. And just as his children, even when they were very young, knew that they could always come to him with their problems, so now could his grandchildren. One of them, looking back on him in memory, would say, "Grandfather always said, 'Set your goals and go after them, and don't let anybody get in your way.'" Another claimed, "He was a very compassionate human being. He would stop everything when you went to his office to see him." And another stated, "If no one else wanted to go fishing with you, he would." And still another remarked, "He was one to help everyone." And there would be so many memories that would evoke laughter, such as the time he took several of them to a restaurant, then didn't like the food, and showed the cook how to make a good grilled cheese sandwich.

And his sense of humor would never diminish.

Matt Metcalfe would have good reason to remember one party in particular at the Amos home.

"I was over at the piano," he recalled, "and there were some women over there. I was singing and carrying on with the rest of them, having a great time. John had an ex-sheriff who worked for him as a bodyguard. He called him over and said, 'Sam, who is that fellow at the piano?' Sam said, "I don't know. Isn't he a friend of yours?" 'I've never seen him before in my life. Sam, he's being obnoxious. In fact, I've watched him. He's being careless with his hands with my guests. He's crashed this party.' Sam says, 'Mr. John, I'll take him down.' John says, 'You'd better do that, Sam. You'd better arrest him.'

"Here I am," Metcalfe continued, "having a great time in my buddy's house when all of a sudden two strong hands—there were two of them—grab each of my arms and damn near rip me off the ground and take me out across the room in front of everybody. Embarrassed the living hell out of me. I didn't know what was going on. They were pretty rough with me. When I got outside, I asked them what was the problem. They said, 'We're taking you down.' 'Taking me down where?' They said, 'Down to the jail. You crashed Mr. John's party.' I started to get rough back, until I saw a gun. And then I knew what John had done to me. So I relaxed and said, 'Gentlemen, John Amos has put you up to this. I've known him for a hundred years. He is just playing a joke on me.' And I convinced them. John thought that was the funniest thing in the world."

And there was the man who had the ability to look at children through children's eyes. When Brooks Massey, the young man John had taken to Florida to get a summer job, got married and had children of his own, he became a neighbor of John's on Steam Mill Road. One Easter he looked across his yard and saw John coming to his house with gifts for his children. And he had on red pants and a green chartreuse jacket, and his hair was dyed pink. "I just thought," John said, "I'd come here as the Easter bunny."

And there was the man without vanity, whom a portrait painter named Pedro Menocal came to know.

Menocal, who had fled Cuba, had first met John and Elena in 1965 at a wedding of a mutual friend. He lived for a number of years in Mexico and then moved to Miami, where he was contacted by Elena in the mid-1980s. She asked him to come to their home and paint portraits of her and John and their family.

"I stayed several days," Menocal recalled, "and we really became close friends. I tried to capture his sense of humor and his basic kindness. He was a very kind man, a very nice fellow. We would sit chatting after dinner—he was smoking and I was smoking, he liked bourbon and I liked bourbon—we drank a lot of bourbon between us. I liked him a lot. He was a man totally without vanity."

For example, the way Menocal worked was to photograph them all and then bring the photographs back with him to Miami and paint the portraits from the photographs. At the beginning of the sittings, said Menocal, John felt that he had to smile for his portrait. "I told him I didn't want him smiling, that smiling portraits are very boring. And he cooperated fully. He would do anything to make Elena happy. It was a wonderful marriage. You could just see it. They would hug and hold hands. He would tease her, but she loved it and he knew it.'"

The person who knew as well as anyone that John never changed was Matt Metcalfe.

"His fleet of jet airplanes, his staff of housekeepers, gardners, chauffeurs, runners, servants of every nature—all of the great wealth he built never changed him. He could never identify with it, in spite of the fact that he had it, and used it, and enjoyed it."

There was the time, for example, when Metcalfe met him and Elena at the Newark Airport, in New Jersey. Metcalfe and his wife were in Metcalfe's company jet. And John had just flown in from Europe with Elena, and an American Family jet was waiting to take them to Columbus. The jets were standing next to each other on the field.

Elena, said Metcalfe, was wearing a necklace of pearls that were so big he didn't think they were real. He had never seen any that big.

John said, "Did you see what I bought Elena for her birthday?"

"John," Metcalfe said, "those aren't real, are they?"

"They'd better be. They cost me forty thousand dollars. The duty cost me eight thousand dollars."

"I said," Metcalfe related, "'She's wearing them, nobody would have known if she didn't declare them.' He said, 'Listen, do you think I want to get in their computer? If you ever get in their computer, from then on they tear your suitcases down and everything else. Lord knows, if I can pay forty thousand dollars for a set of pearls, I can sure pay the eight thousand dollars duty on them.'

"Then he turned to me," continued Metcalfe, "and said, 'Matt, did you ever think we'd ever be in this position where we would have these jet airplanes?' I said, 'No, I never dreamed of it, John.' And he said, 'I didn't either. I can't even believe it.'"

In 1985 John and Elena's oneness showed itself in still another way. For a while now, John had been expressing some interest in the possibility of converting to Catholicism, but it never went further than that. Then on April 15 of that year, he and Elena had a private audience with the Pope. On the way to Rome, they happened to meet an old friend, Neil Reagan—President Reagan's older brother—in Germany, and he came with them. John was fascinated by the Pope, and meeting him, said Elena, went far to help convince him to become a Catholic. John was received into the church by the Reverend Michael O'Keeffe of Columbus.

Not long afterward, Father O'Keeffe moved from the city. Their new priest was the Reverend Kevin Boland, pastor of St. Anne's Church. But Father Boland became more than their pastor; they became social friends as well. He was a frequent guest at their functions. He got to know them, he explained, in the sense that he could come and go as he wanted as part of their household.

"Elena, in a sense, mesmerizes me sometimes with her sensititivity to people, and I think a lot of that was in John, too," said Father Boland. "Maybe we as people are sometimes so overly impressed with wealth and with people who seem to be in this rarified atmosphere that we can forget that they are human beings just like ourselves." This was especially true of John and Elena, in that in spite of all the trappings which came with their wealth and position, they were "people of utter simplicity."

He found John to be decisive in his decisions, and though John might not necessarily agree with you on something, he was always willing to listen to your point of view.

It was well-known of course, continued Father Boland, that John was a philanthropist, that he helped many, many causes. But you really had to ask him about the different causes he helped. He was not one who flaunted it. And in Father Boland's personal experience, he was different even in the way he offered help.

"One day he just called me up—this happened to me two or three times—and said, 'I want to come by and see you.' He walked in and he said, 'This is my church offering for the year,' and then he'd sit down for about five minutes wanting to know, 'How're you doing?' and then he'd stand up saying, 'You've work to do, I've work to do, but I wanted to personally come by and just bring my gift to the church.'"

Unlike some people who, when they give a gift, say that it must be spent in this way or that—in other words, they never really give you ownership of it—John never put any conditions on his gifts. Said Father Boland, "'Remember,' he would say, 'this is given to the church. I don't want to tell you how to spend it. That's your business. It's not mine.'"

A concept John believed in very strongly was that all people should have the opportunity to develop, to be given the chance at education, and to develop their skills. He felt that the opportunity to pull yourself up by your bootstraps should not be available just to the John Amoses of the world, but ideally should belong to everyone.

"In other words," said Father Boland, "his own success was not a selfish success, which is a great tribute to his own development and character." This certainly showed itself in the case of American Family—or AFLAC as it came to be known. "He wanted to make sure that the employees were well taken care of, that it was a good company to work for, that there was spirit involved in it, and that this provided opportunity for others."

He once reiterated to Father Boland a feeling about the Japanese that he had often expressed to others. "He said there was a lot of complaining on the national level about what the Japanese were doing to the American economy, especially in the automobile industry, things like that. 'Well,' he said, 'I don't know. I went into Japan and I've established the insurance company there. I find them marvelous to work with. I don't buy completely that America is getting the short end of the stick, that we've not gone about in the proper way to show them that this thing works both ways.' In other words, he was kind of saying, 'I proved a point, that I could take an American company over there and establish it as a very substantial company. So if the Japanese come over and establish themselves, they've done something right.'"

When asked if to comment on a description that had been made of John as someone who was religious but not in a "denominational" sense, Father Boland said, "I'd say that's accurate—that he was religious, and in the latter years of his sickness I would say that he became profoundly affected by the fact that life had an end, but that life was something beyond life also. I'd say that the spiritual aspect hit him more profoundly when he became sick than maybe in his other years. This I cannot fully ascertain. But as far as religion, in the generic sense, he would have a profound knowledge of the influence of religion vis-á-vis, say, the economics of life that he was involved in; had a profound knowledge of a wide spectrum of human nature vis-á-vis religion, because of his travels and the different types of people he would meet. He could talk highly and very intelligently about all aspects of religion."

One of the things that always struck him in his years of knowing John and Elena, said Father Boland, was his devotion to Elena.

"It showed itself in very simple ways. They might be showing me to the door when I'm going home and he would just give her a peck on the cheek. He was very affectionate, but not in a 'pious' type of way, so to speak. It would be in a look or his holding her hand or touching her cheek, or he would just give her a little kiss.

"It always impressed me that here was a man who was extremely wealthy, a man of influence and power, who built his own kind of economic empire, but in the final analysis of things probably the most profound thing for him was the love for a woman. He didn't lose the touch that the human spirit was ultimately made for love."

27

RECOGNITION BEGINS

Honors continued to come to John Amos and would for the rest of his life—and even after. These included, among so many others (see Appendix A) the Distinguished Service Award from the Small Business Council of America, Columbus Business Leader of the Year, the Humanitarian Award from the National Association for the Advancement of Colored People, the "I Have A Dream Award" from the Alpha Phi Alpha fraternity at Martin Luther King, Jr. College, and many more honorary degrees. And he continued to give money, time, and energy to many community and civic projects, such as to the development of Boy Scout Camp Cason J. Callaway, Jr., and funding the construction of the camp's administration building in his father's memory.

At the same time, Elena was deeply involved in community activities as well . This included serving as Chairman, March of Dimes Fund Drive; Voice of America Fund Drive; American Cancer Society annual fund-raising benefit; and the annual Symphony Orchestra benefit. Among the many Boards she served on were those of the Columbus Symphony Guild and the Columbus Museum of Arts and Sciences (See Appendix B). A wing of Pacelli High School was built and named the Elena Amos Arts and Science Centre in honor of her efforts on the youngsters' behalf.

Just about the only thing that changed in their lives was that, with publication of John's income, he became somewhat concerned about security. At the Metzenbaum hearings, it had come out that until recently he had had had only a small annual income—about $160,000—for the head of a major insurance company, but that in 1979 his total compensation was $1.1 million. Moreover, one day he would be named the highest paid executive in the country. So where he once used to enjoy "tooling around" the city in his car, he now felt it essential to have security guards at his house and as chauffeurs. But they, too, become as much friends as employees. He enjoyed talking to them until all hours of the morning. And he wouldn't own one of those long, long, dark-windowed limousines. He preferred the smaller Lincoln Town Car.

It was in 1986 that he received word of a high award that absolutely delighted him, for it came from his peers in the world of communications. He was to be honored on November 7 as Georgian of the Year by the Georgia Association of Broadcasters.

But he was to get far different news before that event took place.

In September, John and Elena were at a company convention in San Diego when John became very sick with a fever. They came back to Columbus and he was put in the hospital. He was diagnosed as having pneumonia. It was also suspected that he had cancer.

John and Elena went to the Duke University Cancer Research Center in Durham, North Carolina. The Amoses had long been contributors to Duke and were considered part of the "Duke family." There, eleven different tests and a biopsy revealed that he had a very, very small cancer on his left lung.

He underwent surgery. The day afterward, he was sitting up in bed.

On the night of the Georgian of the Year Award, some five hundreds friends of John Amos gathered in a huge banquet hall in Atlanta. It seemed that just about everyone in his life was there— except for John Amos himself. Among the distinguished guests seated on the dais were Senators Sam Nunn, Strom Thurmond, Orrin Hatch, Herman Talmadge, and Representative Richard Ray.

John had released word of his surgery. Concern for him was almost like a *presence* itself.

The guests had finished their main course, and the waiters were clearing away the dishes, when suddenly there was a stirring that seemed to start first on the dais, and then spread throughout the room. A smiling figure in a white suit was walking onto the dais, shaking hands all around. He was slightly bent at the shoulders, but his eyes and smile flashed and his handshake was hearty.

It was a wonder he was there at all.

He had been released from Duke only the day before!

One by one, speakers paid him tribute.

Kirby Godsey, president of Mercer University, told of a call he received from the Internal Revenue Service; they wanted to confirm if John had contributed $100,000 to the University that year.

"I told the agent, " Godsey said, "not to worry—if he hasn't, he will."

Said Senator Nunn, "John Amos built American Family into a great institution. Emerson once said an institution is the expanded shadow of one man...John Amos's shadow has become a vast institution which stretches around the globe...

"His business success is now legendary. His wisdom and his generosity are less well known. John did not believe in cursing the darkness. He believes and he's dedicated to lighting candles for humanity. John has given literally millions of dollars, but more important he's given his time and his dedicated effort to every worthy endeavor that has ever crossed his path. And he has helped millions and millions of people directly or indirectly. He's dedicated to the free enterprise system. He's dedicated to democratic principals and human rights, not just in this country, but throughout the globe. It has been said that greatness lies not in being strong, but in the right use of that strength. John Amos has shown his strength through his business brilliance. He has shown his greatness, however, through the use of that strength for his fellow man."

"John," said Senator Hatch, "truly understands the truth of the Biblical principal that it is more blessed to give than to receive. Those of us who know him also know that money is the least of what John Amos gives. Far more valuable is what he gives of his time, his talents, his wise counsel, and most precious of all, his unswerving fellowship and friendship and loyalty...."

The Japanese Ambassador, Nubouo Matsunaga, thanked John for his enormous contribution "to the internationalization of the Japanese people. Through his business activities, he gave to the Japanese people the sense of internationalization. I am very grateful to him for that...not only grateful but proud of him...."

Senator Thurmond commented, "He possesses the four 'C's': courage, capacity, compassion, and courtesy. And that says it all. I don't know a man...in my lifetime who more impressed me as being such an honorable man and a fine man—a statesman, so to speak; a generous philanthropist; an able businessman; a true patriot, and a great American."

And President Reagan joined them on video screen. "Of course," he said, "we all know John Amos as a brilliant businessman who just over thirty years ago founded an insurance company that has a net worth today of many millions. And then there's John Amos the philanthropist, the former president of Goodwill Industries, the trustee of Morris Brown College, the member of the National Committee of the National Museum of Jewish History, and the contributor to a cause close to my own heart, Eureka College. Perhaps we know John best for his fervent belief in the fundamental values that made America great—hard work, initiative, love of God and family. John is a builder and believer, a man who has given of himself without reserve to his state and nation."

John rose to thunderous, standing applause and cheers to receive the award, then stood at the podium.

He spoke of his cancer, of the surgery, of his undiminished hope.

"God must have something awful special for me to do," he said then. And out of silence came thunderous applause once more. Then, leaning forward, "And if He will give me the slightest hint of what that is"—his thumb and forefinger made an "O—I'll get about the business of doing it."

And those weren't just words. He was in his office the following day.

28

GREATER RECOGNITION

It took him about three months to regain his full strength and vigor. But it was as though he never lost a day creatively; he was still thinking of projects. One of them concerned his own mortality. He was worried about Elena living in the Steam Mill Road house after he was gone. He wanted her to live someplace that would be more in the center of activity. Part of it was concern for her security. But even more, he was afraid she would be lonely there.

"I wanted Elena to be in a showplace that people would want to visit," he explained. "If anything happened to me, I wanted her to be in the middle of everything, because being lonesome is the worst thing in the world."

Elena didn't want to move at first. This had been their home for thirty-three years, a house that had grown from a two-bedroom cottage to a sprawling complex. Here is where they had held weddings for family members and dear friends; here was where they had entertained so many people, from Senator Humphrey, to the Carters, to just about every Georgia governor, to England's Lord Chancellor, to a former Secretary of State and, most important, to everyone they loved. Here were the gardens she had cultivated so lovingly, here the pool where their children and then their grandchildren cavorted, here the fish pond where guests could catch their own meals. It was a house that had even managed to survive two fires.

But if John wanted to move, she would move.

The house he conceived of was mind-boggling. *No one* would have thought of it but John Amos.

Even the photo-spread that *People* Magazine would publish one day wouldn't do it justice—*couldn't* do it justice.

Ignacio Carrera-Justiz, an architect born in Cuba and living in Coral Gables, Florida, had met John and Elena in the early 1960s in

Columbus, where his parents lived. Carrera-Justiz had attended Auburn University about thirty miles away.

Carrera-Justiz's sister, in fact, had been the victim of one of John's practical jokes. John and Elena were invited to her wedding. And even weddings, it seemed, weren't safe from the prankster in John Amos.

Luis Garcia could have warned her about that.

Before Garcia got married, John had a chat with the priest who was to officiate. "He told the priest," Garcia related, "'You know, I really don't know much about Luis. I think he came to me when he was about fourteen or fifteen and I think he left some wife or somebody pregnant in Puerto Rico, and that's why he had to leave.' It took me one week to convince the priest that John was a practical joker. I had to get my baptismal certificate and all of that from Puerto Rico. Oh, Lord, it turned into a zoo. My wife Kathy was about to kill him."

The wedding of Carrera-Justiz's sister took place in New York. At some point John switched the couple's suitcase with that of the priest. And they didn't realize it until they reached their honeymoon hotel in the Pocono Mountains.

But she had long forgiven him—after all, *that* was John.

There was no other architect John would have called. And as John was talking to him on the phone about a potential location for the house he wanted to build, he suddenly came up with an idea.

"Ignacio," he said, "the company owned a seven-story, 750-car garage facing its headquarters. And he thought the roof would make an excellent site for the house!"

The unusual—to say the least—site presented a number of technical problems. For one thing, it had no approach from the street. An elevator would have to be put in on the opposite side of the garage from where cars entered the building to park. For another, it had to be able to withstand potentially strong winds, and there was the fact that the roof would have to hold the weight of a three-story, 10,000 square foot house, complete with swimming pool and gardens. There was the matter of water drainage. And the whole thing would have to be free of noise from the cars beneath it.

Elena wanted a "mediterranean-style" house—a hacienda, with classical Greek and Roman touches. She visualized a plexiglass tunnel on the roof, leading from the elevator to the house. And from there one would walk through a long gallery filled with objects she and John collected—such as the figures of two fierce-looking samurai warrers—that would run almost the length of the house.

"It was really a challenge," said Carrera-Justiz. "I don't think many people have had the chance to do anything like that, and I loved it."

He designed a Spanish-tile roofed structure that one might think was made of masssive stone covered with stucco. But it was actually quite light—"a steel house," he explained, "covered over with stucco."

Now, one of the problems facing the builder was how to get all the materials onto the roof.

Earle Denson, a general contractor who had done a good deal of work on the Steam Mill Road house, would recall John phoning him one day to say he wanted Denson to give him a price "on building a house on top of his garage."

Denson went to his office, where John showed him a set of drawings and asked him to come up with a price within a couple of weeks.

Recalled Denson, "When I looked at the drawings, I got really excited. It was not only an exciting house, but the other thing that excited me was where it was located."

After Denson turned in his price, John called him and said, "Earle, you weren't low bidder on this house but I want you to build it because I know you'll do what I want done. So you've got the job."

But John put a stipulation on it. He asked Denson how long it would take to build, and Denson said it would take a year. John said, "You've got ten months."

About two days after Denson and his men started working, John had a security guard come up on the roof and put a big bulletin board on one of the walks. Written on it was, "300 Days Left to Completion." Then every day, a guard would come up and take off a day to remind the workers how much time was left.

"It was real funny," said Denson. "Then about two months later, the job kind of just bogged down. It was the stage the job was in. We were waiting on this, we were waiting on that. I called the security guard and said, 'This weekend don't take only one day off the board. Take thirty days off.' Well, you should have seen the job pick up the next week. We built this house and we did about $300,000 worth of extras. And we did it in ten months and seven days."

All of the materials, he explained, were delivered to the parking lot and then lifted to the top on a buck horse—a freight elevator they mounted outside the building; they never used a crane for any lifting.

John came around every day, would walk through the construction over the lumber, everything. One of the changes he made was to put in an elevator within the house itself. If he ever got to the point where he needed a wheelchair, he told Denson, he wanted an elevator.

Recalled Denson, "He would always comment when he came up there. 'I like this or if you want to add something, just tell me, or if Elena wants something, then you do it.' He was pleasant. Nobody was a stranger—he was cordial and friendly with everybody—from the common laborer, to the steel mechanic, to the executive. He was very down to earth. He was on a level with everybody. He loved to talk. He'd call me in his office and he'd say, 'Earle, I want to add a sauna in that space we talked about.' And that would be the end. Then we'd talk about fishing and hunting and everything. He'd tell me jokes and stuff, and that was it. He'd say what he had to say, and that was history."

While the work was going on, John also had his decorator, Orestes Martin, stay on top of it.

"Two months before the house was finished, when we still had a lot to do," said Orestes, "he came to me and said, 'Orestes?' I said, 'Yes, sir?' He said, 'Do me a favor.' And what he said made me cry. He told me, 'I want to sleep in the house at least one night. So finish it up. Push every button you have to push, but I want to sleep there at least one night.'"

John and Elena spent their first night in the house on November 19, 1987. John was to spend three Christmases there.

He could literally wave to Elena from his office balcony.

And whenever anyone asked him why he built his home there, his usual answer was a smile and, "My daddy said if you want to be successful, you ought to live on top of the store."

It is a U-shaped house—barely visible from the ground—that one reaches by a private elevator that is like a foyer to the house itself, is mirrored, has fluted columns, a marble floor and a French provincial bench. The plexiglass tunnel one enters is richly colored with flowers and alive with the sound of multi-colored finches. The marble-floored gallery that stretches ahead is some 60 feet long, with a 27-foot ceiling, and opens to terraces and pool and gardens, and to living room, dining room, kitchen, and family room. Curved marble staircases lead up to the two wings, in one the master suite, complete with library and gym and sauna, in the other bedrooms for grandchildren and guests. Among the rooms on the first level—a staircase down from the foyer— is John's old office, his portrait— Pedro Menocal's—looking down, a kindly, knowing look that Menocal truly captured. Outside, the richness of bright colors, too—the roof covered with curved Spanish tiles, the sharply-white stucco, the white stone tiles of the terraces, the shaded arbors, the white of the lion's head over a fountain, the sun glinting on the swimming pool—and all the shrubs and flowers and trees, set in wooden tubs and in literally hundreds and hundreds of Italian terra-cotta pots.

It took just a little while, but Elena finally came to grow comfortable there and to love it. It was almost as if nothing had missed a beat from the time of their moving from Steam Mill Road. It became filled with friends, became the scene of gatherings and dinners and barbeques of suckling pig. The "Mansion in the Sky," as the *Atlanta Constitution* called it, was not only a home; Elena gave it the feeling and warmth of *homeyness*.

As for their former home, which was valued at several hundred thousand dollars, John donated it to a struggling community center aimed at helping black youngsters.

29

A NEW DREAM

Kay Stover was John's secretary during the planning and building of the house, leaving in 1987 when it was not quite finished. When he would talk to her about why he was building it there, he would give her the story that his daddy said he should live above the store, but there was no smile on his face when he would tell her what was truly in his heart, that when he died he wanted Elena "close by." American Family Life was more than a name to him. It *was* family; he wanted Elena close to family.

Robyn Smith replaced Kay Stover, having worked for her since 1986, so she, too, as could anyone looking down from the tower, witnessed the building of the house, starting with an "outline" of it on the roof. It came to be generally known as the "penthouse." Senator Ernest "Fritz" Hollins of South Carolina remarked that it was "the fanciest garage apartment" he ever saw.

For the first year or two that Robyn Smith worked for him John rarely seemed to have a bad day physically, and when he did he would usually attribute it to the weather. And having a bad day generally showed itself in small ways, such as his not feeling like going out with somebody, or leaving a bit earlier than usual or coming in somewhat later, or simply not seeming as energetic as on his good days.

During the years she worked for him he never raised his voice to her. He would always thank her for bringing him a cup of coffee. "He was so uncharacteristic of someone in his position," she said. "He was not a snob. He was proud of the things he had done, but it was almost as if he thought everybody could do something like this. He didn't just attribute it to himself."

And she was witness to how he dreaded firing anyone. "He got so upset," she said. "There was a fellow who worked in the maintenance department who was great. If we needed something, he was one of the ones Mr. John would prefer to do it."

The man called her to say his boss had fired him, and he said, "If I could just talk to Mr. John, explain to him what happened, he would understand."

Robyn Smith talked to John. His answer was that he didn't want the man to be fired, but that he couldn't get in the middle of it, that all he would do if he saw him was give him his job back, and this would ruin the authority of the man he had placed in charge of the department.

"He had the biggest heart of anybody," said Robyn Smith. "The person who fired him probably never thought about the guy again. And there was Mr. John saying he would probably give him his job back, no matter what the reason was he was fired."

And then there was the matter of one of the secretaries in their office who never came in on time. He knew she had to be fired, but he himself couldn't do it.

"He said that I had to do it, and then I wouldn't do it. And so we made Sal do it. He was so different. I had worked for people who were nothing compared to him. They didn't have the success he attained or anything. And yet they would holler and fire people in the office just like that."

All the while, John was as busy and involved as ever. And so was Elena. That year, 1987, the Concharty Council of Girls Scouts in Columbus was receiving nominations for their annual "Woman of Achievement" award. They wrote to Elena, inviting her to be a nominee. John wrote a letter to them, one that has been called—with every reason—a love letter. The beauty of that letter and the depth of his love for her could not be fully conveyed without the letter being read in its entirety.

On September 11, he wrote:

> Mrs. Amos discussed with me your invitation to be nominated for "Women of Achievement." Mrs. Amos is a very demure and private person. For this reason, it would be impossible for her to complete your biographical profile, and I have taken it upon myself to fulfill your request.
>
> Elena came to the United States from her native Cuba in 1944 as a student at the University of Miami. We were married as students in September of 1945. Her goal in life was

to find happiness for herself, her family, and those around her. In the outset, she wanted twelve children, but settled for two. However, her home has always been open for other children to come or go as the need dictated. She raised two boys in addition to our own two children and had a constant presence of some child temporarily in distress. She has provided college educations for seven children that I know of and I feel assured that you could add to that several more that she did not tell me about.

She has been an active speaker in schools at all grade levels on the differences in culture in Latin American countries and our own. She has been dedicated to the internationalization of Columbus. Her home was the embassy for the Cuban Bay of Pigs soldiers who were captured in Cuba, later freed and sent to Ft. Benning. She assisted in their housing and settlement in the community. She was a founder of the Latin American Studies Group which for many years was a joint effort of our Latin community in Columbus and Ft. Benning and people from all walks of life in Columbus. They studied the cultures and language, and many professional and other people of Columbus actually mastered Spanish conversation. The highlight of the year was the Columbus Day celebration.

She was a founder of St. Thomas Episcopal Church and of St. Mary Magdalene Church, the latter to which she was a major contributor making the church building possible. She contributed to that church its Parrish House as well.

She has been active with the Cancer Society and Girl's Clubs and has a Girl's Club annual award in memory of her mother. She has been active as a grandmother in the St. Anne's School and Pacelli High School and in 1986 personally provided for the renovation and modernization of the Pacelli High School building and facilities.

She has been active in race relations in Columbus. It was in our home that black men and their wives and white men and their wives first broke bread together. For her interest and activities in race relations, she was in 1965 awarded with lifetime national membership in the Alpha Kappa Alpha sorority.

She was the impetus for the foundation of the Columbus Support Group for the School of the Americas at Ft. Benning, and her personal visit with the Secretary of the Army in Washington and her description of Columbus and the welcome mat it has always given to the Latin Americans at Ft. Benning is felt to have had a great effect on the decision to permanently locate the School of the Americas at Ft. Benning.

In addition to this, she has served as First Lady of American Family Life Assurance Company in the 32 years since its beginning in every sense of the term with every duty implied. She has cooked and served at her home more meals for civic and company affairs than can be calculated after these many years. Her present home on Steam Mill Road was built with a commercial kitchen with these responsibilities in mind, and upon the completion of a new home will become the property of and home of the 10th Street Center, an underprivileged children's organization.

She has been the mother confessor and intervenor for hundreds of women working at American Family to whom she is known as 'Elena.' In her role as First Lady, she has been a large factor in the high employee morale that American Family Life has experienced and enjoyed.

She has had the honor and privilege of entertaining in her home or as house-guests Governors, Congressmen, and United States Senators from many states; one Vice-President and one President of the United States as well as foreign diplomats and dignitaries.

The Command at Ft. Benning through these many years has had her on call to arrange for the local entertainment of the wives of military dignitaries visiting Ft. Benning from all parts of the world.

The sun today never sets on the active interests of American Family or Elena Amos. She is welcome and feels at home as a representative of Columbus and her adopted United States in any nation of the free world.

I can't list a lot of Presidencies in organizations because that has not been her inclination or her role as she envisioned it. Her role has been one of active and full support for anything or any cause in which she believed. *Privately*, I can tell you that when everything else has failed, she has been the court of last resort for countless individuals and organizations. But she is quick to deny anything she sees as an imposition.

She's a good wife; a good mother; a good grandmother; a good citizen of Columbus, of the country, and of the free world, and I love her and am very proud of her personal achievements."

Elena Amos was named *Woman of the Year.*

30

AND FOR ELENA

Even in the midst of his concern about his own health, John was always ready to help others. Probably nothing could illustrate this more than his reaction to a call he received one day from Tokyo.

It was from the wife of one of his employees, a Japanese man who not only was John's friend, but was important to him in the business. The woman was calling to ask John if he could possibly help her. Her husband, she said, was severely alcoholic and was abusing her.

John, who was in California at the time, told the woman to come there with her husband. He would pay first-class fare for both of them. But she was not to tell her husband why John wanted to see them.

John's next call was to Matt Metcalfe. He told Metcalfe to contact Dr. Joseph Pursch, a world-acclaimed authority on alcoholism—one of his most famed patients was Betty Ford—and that Metcalfe and Dr. Pursch should meet him at a hotel in Laguna Beach, where the Japanese couple was to join him.

John wanted Metcalfe there for a very good reason. Back in 1981, Metcalfe had gone to Dr. Pursch for treatment, and it had worked. Several years later he had gotten John, who was churchillian in that drink did not disrupt his thinking or affect his humanity, to go for help, too. But, burdened by the tensions of illness, it was a struggle he would continue within himself but never win.

Still, it was important to him that he help his employee, even—almost unbelievably—paying their way over.

The five of them, said Metcalfe, were seated in the hotel suite—the couple, Dr. Pursch, John, and himself. Recalled Metcalfe, "John, in his typical way, said to him, 'You've got a drinking problem.' The man denied it and was indignant—the usual things that happen in denial. And John says, 'Don't tell me that, damn it. I know you drink too much whiskey. I do, too. Now, Dr. Pursch, here is the world's eminent authority on it and he's going to help you. I'm not going to let you go home until you're cured.'

"He hits him like that," continued Metcalfe. "Of course the man continues to deny it and says, 'Oh, John, I take a drink once in a while.' John says, 'No. you don't. You're a drunk.'"

By now the wife was petrified. She began denying everything she had told John. At this, John turned to her. "Now you listen. You're talking about life and death here. You called me and told me how he beat you up."

The result was that the man began crying like a baby and admitted he was an alcoholic.

"John," Dr. Pursch said, "you didn't need me."

John made arrangements for the man to be admitted to Dr. Pursch's clinic at the South Laguna Beach Medical Center—actually *took* him there and then arranged for the wife to stay at a hotel, and paid for that, too.

"That was John," said Metcalfe. "He told him what he was going to do and he wouldn't let him out of the box. The last I heard, the man has been involved in the work himself, helping others in Japan."

Several months after John's surgery, Jan Liberatore, M.D., and her husband Duke moved to Columbus from Philadelphia, Pennsylvania. Dr. Liberatore was a bariatrician, a specialist in preventive medicine with an emphasis on weight control. About eight years before, her husband, an entrepreneur with a good knowledge of business and the stock market, had decided that they should purchase American Family stock. Subsequently, he had been following the stock over the years.

After Dr. Liberatore had received her board certification and they were looking for a good place for her to practice, they decided on Columbus. One of the deciding factors was that this was where American Family was located. Another was that Fort Benning—a stabilizing force in the local economy—was located here.

"Duke felt," said Dr. Liberatore, "that if John can locate his headquarters here as opposed to moving to New York, then we can make a living here too."

"One of the things I remembered in my reading about Family Life," Duke Liberatore said, "was that family members were involved in the company. And there was the name 'Family.' We were looking for a community that had that type of atmosphere. All of that came into play."

One of the first things they did upon their arrival in Columbus was to take a ride by the tower.

They were in Dr. Liberatore's office one day about a month before they were to open—they were cleaning and setting up and hiring people—when the phone rang. Duke Liberatore, who was in charge of the business side of the office, answered.

"His face," recalled Dr. Liberatore, "went pale. And he's going 'yes, sir. Yes, sir. Yes, sir.' And he puts his hand over the receiver and says to me, 'Whatever he wants, give him.' And my husband never talked to me like that. Never!"

She got on the phone. The voice on the other end said, "I'm John Amos."

For a few moments the name didn't mean anything to her. John went on to say that he understood she was one of two bariatricians in the state, and he wanted her to treat his son.

"I said," recalled Dr. Liberatore, "'Well, Mr. Amos, that's fine. And I'd be happy to do that.' And I'm saying, 'However,' and Duke's going—he's writing on a paper—*No howevers. See him now!* And we don't even have the office opened."

She told John that would be fine, that she would see his son whenever he would like. John said he could have him there in two hours. A company plane would pick his son up and bring him to Columbus. What followed was like an old-time comedy.

"We zipped down to K-Mart," said Dr. Liberatore. "I bought a white coat. We bought my mother, who was with us, a white uniform. John bought a scale so we can weigh Shelby. I bought a blood pressure cuff and told my mother, 'Just fake it. Just take his blood pressure. Pretend what you're doing. I'll recheck it to be sure it's right. Don't worry about it.' But I wanted to look like I had a nurse."

Shelby came by himself. The Liberatores were not to meet John for several more months. In the meantime, they kept hearing wonderful things about John from patients who worked for American Family.

"They just loved Mr. John," Dr. Liberatore said. "I always would hear what a good boss he was and how much people loved him. I thought, 'I'm trying to be a good boss, too. Maybe I can meet him and learn from him.' It would be a great opportunity for us to meet someone who started a company himself."

Her husband urged her to call for an appointment, just to say hello and to thank him for sending Shelby.

"We had heard," said Dr. Liberatore, "that John was really, really thrilled with Shelby's progress. So I called and they said fine and gave me an appointment. I mean, it was not a problem getting an appointment with him. It wasn't as if you had to wait six months or you had to go through a hierarchy."

When she went to the receptionist at the tower, the woman called John's office, then said into the phone, "Oh. Oh, really? Well, fine." John wanted to see her in the penthouse.

"I thought," said Dr. Liberatore, "'Oh, geez. Such VIP treatment.' And I was so nervous when they took me up. All those marble halls...."

But John was very unassuming and unpretentious. He thanked her for her help, and they chatted for about twenty minutes. Sometime after that, he came to her to see if she could help him quit smoking. This was part of her practice in preventive medicine. But after several months of his alternately giving up cigarettes and then going back to them, both of them realized that he really didn't want to quit. "He would keep giving me his ashtray and his cigarettes," said Dr. Liberatore. "I must have four hundred ashtrays and cigarettes from John."

One of the things that had happened was that he and Elena went out on their paddle boat, he vowing again that he wouldn't smoke. In fact, none of the crew was allowed to take along a cigarette.

Said Dr. Liberatore, "But damn if John didn't flag down the U.S. Coast Guard and get some cigarettes from them."

Still, John continued to come in, no longer really trying to stop smoking, but to talk. He wanted just to talk. Dr. Liberatore and her husband, meanwhile, became social friends of his and Elena's.

"There will never be another John Amos," said Dr. Liberatore. "Ever. Everybody in this world he dealt with has looked at his power, looked at his money, looked at his ability to solve problems. John did everything for everybody."

But another side of him began coming out when they first started talking about why he smoked.

"He would say smoking shows that people are under a lot of pressure," said Dr. Liberatore. "He would say to me that he had spent the whole day giving advice. It was as though no one ever thought *he* needed advice. He was a superman in everyone's eyes, he'd say. The world thought he was perfect, but 'I have my problems,' he'd say. 'I have my weak spots. I'm not allowed to make mistakes—you know—with my stockholders. The bottom line is that I have to show an increase in my quarterly report. If I want to expand the company or do this or that, it doesn't matter as long as I show an increase in the bottom line.'"

The first time he cried in front of her was when he talked about his father. He missed him tremendously; he would talk a lot about him. "He truly loved his father. He said that one of the hardest things for him was not being able to talk to his father."

John, continued Dr. Liberatore, had an incredible ability to make people he touched in life feel important. So many people of great wealth tend to make others feel insecure and inadequate, whereas John would make you feel special.

"When you meet somebody of John's stature," added Duke Liberatore, "you don't expect that you meet him one time and the next time you see him he'll remember your name. And he'll address you as an equal."

He was never in a hurry, said Dr. Liberatore. "If you stopped John in the hall to ask him a question, he gave you his undivided attention. His body language, his eye contact, let you know he was giving you his undivided attention. He'd listen to what you would say and he was quick to give an answer. He wouldn't say, 'Well, I'll think about it.' It was never, 'Well, ask my secretary. She'll get it for you.' And another thing. You always felt you could trust John. You never felt that he would take advantage of you."

During one of the first visits Dr. Liberatore had with John, she asked him something she asks most of her patients: What were his goals? Where did he see himself in three years? In five years? In ten years?

"I expected him to explain these things, but he said, 'I'll be dead in five years.' I said, 'What makes you say that?' He said, 'I'm telling you. I've lived my life and I've done the things I've wanted to do.

There's nothing left that I want to do. I'm just getting everything in order."

One of the things John would talk to her about was dying with dignity. "He would say, 'I'm getting ready to die just like I got ready to live. I wish people would respect me for that and understand that."

They also spent a lot of time talking about his guilt that his cancer was due to his smoking and helping him try to come to terms with it.

Once he said, "I don't want the headlines of the paper...."

When he didn't finish, Dr. Liberatore said, "John, what do you think the headlines of the newspaper are going to say when you die?"

"'Cancer CEO,'" he said, "'Dies of Lung Cancer.'"

Still, when he, Elena, Dr. Liberatore, and Duke Liberatore went to the American Cancer Society ball held to raise money for the cancer wing, he lit up a cigarette. But nobody looked at him askance; it didn't stop people from wanting to sit at his table.

Several years before, during John's very *first* visit with her, he had asked her, "Is there anything you need? What do you need in Columbus? What can Columbus do for you, because you're an asset to this community, and I want to make sure you're successful here."

"As a matter of fact," Dr. Liberatore answered, "there is something I would like."

"What is it?" He reached into his pocket for money.

"No," she said, "I don't need any money. We're going to get that on our own. But there is something I want, John. I want your picture."

John gave her an 8 x 10 glossy, with her name and the date written on it. She hung it in her office.

"I wanted it because I was proud to know him. And that picture commands such respect. I've had people come in and stand there and cry when they look at it."

31

HEALTH AND HELPING

There seemed to be no end to the awards that would continue to be bestowed on him. For instance, *Forbes* Magazine named him as the Chief Executive Officer of the most innovative insurance company of 1987. The Professional Business Communicators established a perpetual Entrepreneur of the Year Award in his honor. He received the Shingleton Award for Distinguished Service by the Duke Comprehensive Cancer Center. *Financial World* Magazine presented him with the "CEO of the Decade" bronze award for the Insurance Industry Category. He received the Jim W. Woodward Memorial Award from the Columbus Chamber of Commerce for outstanding service to the community. The Columbus Medical Foundation announced that its future comprehensive cancer treatment facility—there had never been one in Columbus—would be called the John B. Amos Cancer Center. John had spearheaded a fundraising drive that raised over $3 million dollars for the Center.

In 1988 he and Elena were honorary co-chairpersons of the American Cancer Society's First Annual Crystal Ball, an event that launched the drive. And in tribute to their work on behalf of the School of the Americas and its Support Group, John and Elena were presented the Department of the Army Decoration for Distinguished Civilian Service, the highest award the United States Army can bestow upon civilians

In the meantime, in October, 1987, a malignant tumor was found in his other lung. He underwent cobalt radiation treatment. "That was very, very hard on him," said Elena. "He lost all his appetite, and his spirit was broken. But he got over that, too."

He continued on with his work and social life and his sense of humor, trying to live as though nothing were wrong. But though he could fool other people, he couldn't fool himself or Elena. He heard that there was a program at Duke on learning how to live with your problems. He and Elena went there and lived in two rooms, a far cry from their penthouse, but, as Elena said, "We had a great time. He was in a support group of about eight people, and he was becoming more open and doing more swimming and walking and other exercises."

Then a doctor called her into his office one day and told her that cancer had reappeared in John's lung. Elena pleaded with him not to tell him.

"John," she said, "had a week more to go in the program, and he was happy. He would take a little lunch box and go to class. I said to the doctor, 'One week won't make any difference. Let him finish. If he lives one week or ten years, he's happy now.'"

The doctor assured her he wouldn't say anything. But the next day when Elena went to meet John after class, she found him lying on a stretcher.

"The doctor had told him he had cancer. I just had enough of doctors! There was no reason for that."

When they returned to Columbus, John was soon making plans once more. He wanted to go to Japan again—he used to go there several times each year—and his love for the country was drawing him back.

About a month before he left, he had a conversation—an amazing conversation, considering how ill he was—with Terry Hurley, owner of a pharmacy across the street from the tower.

Hurley, who had come to Columbus in 1963, had known of John Amos over the years as a "growing legend." But he had not gotten to know him personally until his illness. One time Hurley wanted to purchase a house and a lot next to his store, which he needed to expand his business and parking facilities. Each time he and the owner would come close to an agreement of sale, said Hurley, the owner would have the property reappraised and would raise the price. From what Hurley heard, someone told the owner that John, who was buying up property all around the vicinity of the tower, would pay more than Hurley would. But John, learning that Hurley was interested in the property, refused to buy it.

"American Family," said Hurley, "has probably always had the highest employee loyalty that I have ever seen anywhere, because of Mr. John's serious devotion to them. There were several times that he would call me and say, 'If such and such a patient doesn't have the money to pay for their child's medication, you put it on my bill, but don't you tell them. Don't you tell them.'"

Hurley recalled that during a tremendous heat wave several years ago, John personally put fourteen air conditioning units in older people's homes, doing it under his mother's name.

A pharmacist, explained Hurly, gets early signals of when a customer is seriously ill. It may start off with the person saying, "I've got this little spot, but my doctor isn't worried about it." The next time, the customer might say, "Well, my doctor's not really worried, but he wants me to do this."

Unfortunately, said Hurley, that was what happened with John Amos. "But Elena wouldn't let him die. I have never seen a man so cared for by his family and so supported by his family. I never heard one negative word. If I talked to Elena on one of those days when Mr. John was real bad, she would say, 'John is not feeling good today. He's going to be better tomorrow.' It was not a pie-in-the-sky thing. She kept him going, I know, two years longer than he ordinarily might have. I think it was strictly through her care and her love and her devotion."

Before John went to Japan, he called Hurley to come to the house. "He wanted me to go over his medications," said Hurley. "After we did that, he said, 'You know, I want your help.' And I said, 'I'll be glad to help you, Mr. Amos. What can I do for you?' He said, 'I want you to go to Washington with me.' And I said, 'I beg your pardon?' He said, 'Yes. We are all concerned about the rising cost of health care. This is something I want to devote the rest of my life to. I'm going to do something about it.'"

John went on to say that as a young man he had only gone to a doctor twice. The rest of the times the neighborhood pharmacist had taken care of him.

"He said," related Hurley, "'I want legislation changed to give area pharmacists more lateral access to patient care than they have now, because you're working with your hands tied. It's a great American resource. That would greatly decrease the cost of medical care.' And he said, 'I want your help in that.' I said, 'Mr. Amos, I'm not sure that I'm the man to help you. I'll be glad to do anything I can, but I could put you in touch with some other friends.' And he said, 'No, I want you. I've got the power to do it. I've got friends and we can get something started. That's what I want to do in the latter part of my life.'"

Even at that stage, he was thinking productively, thinking of what he could do to help people.

But he was never able to see this particular dream through.

John and Elena left for Japan in May. They were accompanied by Chiko and Clinton Wardlaw, John's chauffeur, whose mother and grandmother had worked for the Amoses in their Steam Mill Road home, and whose grandfather had helped build the fish pond. Wardlaw, who would always be grateful that John had encouraged him to return to high school after he had dropped out, had gone with him on many a hunting and fishing trip.

They traveled not only to Japan, but to Taiwan and Thailand as well. "He had a schedule of things to do," said Elena, "and he did very well." His itinerary included a visit with the Japanese prime minister.

Said Chiko, "We took turns taking care of Mr. Amos at night because he couldn't sleep. And he needed assistance getting in and out of bed."

Flying back to Columbus, John became ill and was hospitalized in Seattle. He was a dying man, but he managed to maintain his sense of humor. When his brother Paul flew up to see him, John took his hand and smiled. "If you think you're going to a funeral, you son of a bitch, you're wrong."

It was a couple of weeks before he was able to be transferred to Columbus Medical Center. Elena was always by his bedside. Dr. Liberatore came there not as his physician but as his friend, and both helped explain to the family what to expect and served as a medical interpreter to them.

One night, an exhausted Elena called Ira Meyers and asked if he would stay with him that night. John would sleep all day and stay awake at night, and he didn't want the nurses to be with him at night. He wanted someone close. Ira spent the night with him; he had been visiting him frequently, would sit him up in bed—John hated lying down—and would put on his glasses, would often read to him; once, he had to refuse him when he asked for a cigarette. On this night he read the *Wall Street Journal* to him, talked about stocks and politics. When John's brothers came to visit him in the morning, recalled Ira,

John, sitting up, bowed slightly as though to show his strength, his spirit.

The following night, one of his grandchildren, John William Amos, stayed with him. This was the grandfather who used to tell such wild stories to them, such as the time he said, "Don't expect any Christmas presents." He'd "shot Santa Claus to stop him from coming down the chimney," but of course there were probably more gifts that year than ever. And this was the grandfather who, no matter how important a meeting he was in, would stop everything when his grandchildren came up to the nineteenth floor, would come out and introduce them to whomever he was talking to, and would tell them how much he loved them.

It was about two or three in the morning when one of the hospital team told the young man to call his father and grandmother, because they believed he was going to die.

John Amos died at 3:45 P.M. that afternoon, Monday, August 13, 1990.

32

LEAVING

The viewing was held in the bright, floral-massed foyer of the penthouse he loved, the long, grand, marbled gallery stretching ahead through the house. From behind, in the flowered, glass tunnel leading from the elevator to the foyer came the many little sounds of birds. Hundreds of people filed by the casket slowly during the next couple of days. On Thursday, August 16, the funeral mass was held in St. Anne's Catholic Church.

In a deeply-moving homily, one that so many people were to say captured as closely as possible the heart and humanness of that complex, remarkable man, the Reverend Michael O'Keeffe compared John Amos to St. Francis, calling him a man "gifted with encouraging people, with drawing the best out of them."

Pat O'Connor spoke, in his eulogy, of John Amos's love of politics: "He loved his country and he enjoyed being involved in the democratic process.... He considered politics a necessity and basically an honorable profession.... John was a unique and compassionate individual and he did believe that one person could make a difference."

The church was so crowded that many people, both black and white, went to Pacelli High School, where they heard a broadcast of the service. Other people simply stood on the curbs and streets around the church, as though just to be near it. Before the casket was closed, John Amos's grandchildren placed their photographs in it.

Afterwards, hundreds of people followed the procession to Parkhill Cemetery, where he was buried next to his mother and father.

John Amos's pallbearers reflected the wide spectrum— from the left to the right—of close political friends he had made. They were Senators Orrin G. Hatch, Howell Heflin, Strom Thurmond, Jesse Helms, and Representatives Richard Ray and Charles B. Rangel. Among the mourners were former President Carter and his wife Rosalynn, and Senator and Mrs. Ernest Hollings.

The grave site was bright with flowers and wreaths that came from around the world. There were flags from the School of the Americas—a school to which the Amoses had given so much of themselves—representing the many Latin American countries whose armed service people were teaching and studying there. The graveside service was brief—somehow fitting for John Amos, when a church sermon got too long, it was said, would tap at his watch (the few times he would wear one) as though to get it started, and surely to attract the pastor's attention. And the same John Amos who tended to slip out of convention halls away from the brain-drumming sound of *any* long speech.

The service was interspersed with quotes from Shakespeare and the Bible. Then, finally—probably the single most solemn sound there is—a soldier from Fort Benning played Taps.

A couple of weeks later in Japan, over three thousand people attended memorial services for John Amos. The services were held in twenty-six cities, including Tokyo, Kyoto, Kobe, Okayama, Hiroshima, and Sapparo. Elena and Shelby attended the ceremony in Tokyo, where some 1100 people filled the hall. John's photograph was a smiling centerpiece amid thousands of flowers—chrysanthemums, orchids, and white roses. There were brief speeches by executives of the Japanese branch, after which each executive placed white roses beneath John's photo. The president of the branch, Yoshiki Otaka, said in part:

"The great success of the Japan branch—being ranked nineteenth out of thirty companies in terms of premium income—in a very short period of time since the establishment, owes very much to his farseeing intelligence by introducing cancer insurance and to his deep understanding of the Japanese market.

"Mr. Amos was a Japanophile. In the 1980s, when the Japanese market was adversely criticized for its exclusiveness, Mr. Amos enthusiastically supported Japan by testifying before Congress...I now recall that his last trip to Japan in May was his farewell trip to the Japan he loved so much. His great contributions to promotion of the U.S.-Japan amity will be long remembered in many of our hearts."

Afterwards, Elena spoke of John's commitment to Japan. She spoke only briefly; that was always her way.

A lot of people, said Mayor Frank Martin several months after John Amos's death, didn't realize until John became very ill how much of an individual Elena was.

"She was so strong and came to the front on behalf of John during his prolonged illness," he said. "It's only been in recent years that Elena was not just John's wife, but her own individual person. I heard a lot of people comment during his illness that Elena is a very dynamic person in her own way. She is a very unique woman."

The many tributes to John were of tremendous help to her. There was former President Carter, describing John Amos as "one of the most extraordinary entrepreneurs in our nation's history.... A visionary who shared the values inherent in strong family, hard work, and service to his fellow man, John has faced his illness with the same courage and grace that guided his life. He will be missed by all those whose lives he has touched." There was Representative Ray, saying that John Amos's legacy was all the good things he had done for so many people." There was Edna Kendrick, a Columbus City Councilor, saying how much he helped in the betterment of the community "on big projects and projects that are not even known." His "last gesture to the city"—the establishment of the Cancer Center—would be of untold value to the community.

Then on December 14, 1990, came word that the Japanese government was posthumously awarding John the highest decoration the Emperor can bestow upon a non-Japanese: the Order of the Sacred Treasure, Gold and Silver Star. The Sacred Treasurer Award, which the Emperor bestows upon the recommendation of the Japanese cabinet, was previously awarded to such people as Nobel Laureate Professor Milton Friedman, Federal Reserve Bank Chairman Paul Volker, and former World Bank President Alden W. Clausen.

The Japanese government explained that John Amos had been selected based upon four major contributions to Japan: introducing and expanding health insurance products which have contributed to the health and well-being of the Japanese people; creating public awareness of cancer, thus contributing to the prevention and cure of the disease; marketing dementia care protection in Japan, which contributes to a greater awareness of the problems of the aged; and contributing toward easing trade friction between the United States and Japan.

On the night of January 30, 1991, Elena, family members, Bill Amos, Paul Amos, Dan Amos, and members of their families, as well as a number of her and John's friends, gathered in the huge but delicately-decorated Washington residence of the Japanese Ambassador, Mr. Ryohei Murata, for dinner and the presentation of the award. There, too, were several Senators and Representatives, including Senators Nunn, Hollins and Presser, and Congressman Rangel.

Ambassador Murata paid eloquent tribute to John, and Shelby, as Elena wanted, accepted the award. He and then his mother spoke briefly, Elena literally glowing with pride while hiding her struggle against tears.

Then on April 16, 1991, ten Senators gave tributes to John to be included in the Congressional Record. Senator Thurmond spoke, as would all the others, of John Amos's background and his rise in business, and how he broke new ground with Japan. Then he went on to say:

"During their forty-five years of marriage, Elena Amos worked at John's side in every venture. As we take this time today to honor his memory, I know he would want his wife to share in every aspect of this tribute. Their cooperative efforts resulted not only in the fine company which bears their mark of distinction, but in their countless acts of charity and generosity which have touched the lives of thousands.... Those of us in this Chamber who called John Amos a friend deeply feel his loss. Our love and support are with his widow, the lovely Mrs. Elena Diaz-Verson Amos, and the entire Amos family...."

"Our Nation lost a patriot, an entrepreneur, and a wonderful citizen when John Amos died. I lost a dear friend. John Amos has been heralded and will continue to be heralded for his achievements nationally and internationally. I particularly remember his contributions to his chosen State, his city, and his region...

"John loved the democratic process. He loved politics and our political system. And John Amos devoted himself to supporting what he felt were the most capable people for offices at all levels, from local to national...John Amos's friends will remember not just the things he did that earned him plaques and plaudits, but the fact that whenever anything was important to the State of Georgia, or to Columbus, or to our Nation, when anything was good for its citizens, he would be behind it with his influence and also his financial resources.

"John was very proud of Elena, who supported his dream from the beginning. During their forty-five years of marriage, she was truly a partner in every aspect of his life. Our sympathy goes out to her and to their children, Shelby Amos and Maria Teresa Amos Land, and his grandchildren, John Beverly, Elena Maria Teresa, and W. Donald Land, Jr., and John W., Chana Gail, and Jacob O. Amos, and other members of their families...John Amos was a close personal friend, and I relied many times on his comments, his keen insight, wisdom, and experience. He will be greatly missed by all of those whose lives he touched."

"I rise today," said Senator Heflin, "to pay tribute to and celebrate the life of one of my dear friends, Mr. John Beverly Amos. His death this past August left me with a void which will not soon be filled, a sadness which will not soon be lessened...

"Many Senators knew John in one capacity or another for he was the kind of man who easily traveled among influential circles. Perhaps one of the characteristics which made John such a great man was his desire to help make life a little easier for those who were not so influential. He dedicated the better part of his life to establishing an insurance company and developing insurance products to ease the burden of illness or death on working families...

"John Amos is one of the few people in this world who dreamed grand dreams and then had the fortitude to work and toil to realize those dreams...As all of my colleagues can imagine, John Amos was an extremely busy man. It says something about John's character that he was able to make time for numerous philanthropic and civic activities...I feel fortunate to have known John Amos and I know how proud of him they [his wife, children and grandchildren] are. He provides us all with an example of how to fulfill our dreams while making others' lives easier."

Said Senator Helms, "There was nothing holier-than-thou about him. He was simply a man who understood the miracle of America, the free enterprise system. And, as I was to learn later—from others, not from John Amos—John had an abiding love for his fellow man. During his lifetime, he did so much for so many, but he never said anything about it. He did his good works privately and quietly.

"He was a loving, caring husband, father, and grandfather. Later on...I came to know John's dear wife, whom he loved. He unfailingly credited Elena Diaz-Verson Amos with, as he put it, 'what little success' he had enjoyed. 'I'm a lucky man,' he often said.

"John's word was his bond, and he was trusted as well as admired. Then...he became terminally ill, but he never complained, nor did he ever feel sorry for himself. I remember sitting with John and Elena at a breakfast in New York a couple of years ago. Never once did he mention his ill health. Instead, he talked of his wife and family and the wonderful people who worked with him at the American Family Corporation. 'I am a blessed man,' he said quietly.

"Finally the news came that John was gone. He had fought valiantly against the dreaded malignancy that eventually claimed his life, just as he had fought for, all his life, a set of principles that deserve to survive.

"Several of us in the Senate who had known and loved John Amos were honored to be asked to serve as pallbearers at John's funeral...It was a sad yet uplifting occasion. The clergymen who conducted the services were magnificent in their personal memories of John and the way that John Amos so quietly but sacrificially helped others less fortunate than he. It dawned on me during the services that those of us who were mourning the passing of John Amos were, in fact, sorry for ourselves. We had lost a friend. The Nation had lost an example of its greatness. But for John Amos, it was graduation day. He had been lifted into the arms of his Heavenly Father whom John had served so long, so faithfully, and so well. Of some men it can be said, 'He was one of nature's noblemen.' John Amos was one of nature's noblemen."

Said Senator Pressler, "I rise today to join in paying tribute to a man of outstanding business accomplishments who improved the lives of countless people at home and abroad. John Beverly Amos...was an ingenious businessman and someone who devoted himself to the welfare of people everywhere. I was privileged to know him and count him as a good friend...

"At the close of World War II, John entered the University of Miami, where he met his wife-to-be, Elena Diaz-Verson, the daughter of a noted Cuban journalist and author. He practiced law until 1955, when he and his family moved to Columbus, Georgia. There, with less than $40,000 of capital, he founded American Family Life Assurance Company. At the close of 1990, the assets of American Family exceeded $8 billion. Much of this growth resulted from the exceptional business success John Amos achieved for the company in Japan. American Family continues to dominate the Japanese market for cancer insurance. More than 90 percent of the companies trading on the Tokyo Stock Exchange offer American Family's products to their employees. Its assets in Japan are now valued at more than $6 billion.

"Despite the demands of business, John Amos devoted much of his effort to furthering the welfare of others, including the improvement of racial relationships in Columbus and elsewhere. Throughout his life, John Amos was a consummate family person. He was devoted to his wife Elena, their children, and grandchildren. We honor here today a truly great person."

Senator Grassley said, "I rise today to commemorate the outstanding accomplishments and contributions of John Beverly Amos, who was not only a legendary success in the international insurance industry but also a delightfully warm and generous human being. Those of us who called John Amos a friend deeply feel his loss, and our love and support are with his wife, Elena Diaz-Verson Amos, his children and his grandchildren. Mr. Amos was more than just a businessman; he was a man of vision.

"John Amos's life was full of many honors, each of which was well-deserved. One of the greatest honors he received, the Order of the Sacred Treasure, Gold and Silver Star, was presented to John posthumously by the Emperor of Japan. This honor is the highest award a non-Japanese can be given and it is only given upon the recommendation of the Japanese Cabinet on the basis of distinguished service and contribution to Japan.

"It was not just his business accomplishments which endeared Mr. Amos to the Japanese people. He earned the trust and respect of the Japanese people and at his death, thousands of mourners honored him by attending memorial services held in 26 Japanese cities.

"But he was not alone in his work. During their 45 years of marriage, Elena Amos worked at John's side in every venture. If John Amos could be with us today, I know he would want his wife to share our praise for his accomplishments. But I cannot match John's own words in a tribute to his wife. He said, 'She is a good wife, mother, grandmother, and a good citizen, and I love her and am very proud of her personal achievements.'

"John and Elena's cooperative efforts not only resulted in an outstanding company which bears their mark of distinction, but in countless acts of generosity which have enriched the lives of thousands of people. I believe it is fitting that their children, their grandchildren, the members of their families, their friends, and the countless others enhanced by the quality of the life John built with his wife, Elena, may look with pride as we celebrate their lives. I commend them both for the incredible contributions they have made to their family, their community, this Nation, and the world."

Said Senator Hatch, "I come here and rise to pay tribute to two of my best friends, John and Elena Diaz-Verson Amos. They have been two of my best friends since I have come to Washington. They have always gone out of their way for me and have always tried to help us with the work we do in the U.S. Senate.

"I want to pay tribute especially to the late John Amos. John was a man who was not only a successful businessman and entrepreneur, but he was a true friend to many of us in this Chamber. He was a loving father and he was a wonderful husband to Elena, as she was a wonderful wife to him....

"He is one of the greatest Horatio Alger stories in the history of this country. I wish those who are currently managing those businesses have great success as they...continue the legacy of John Amos.

"Mr. Amos supported a number of charities and helped numerous people who desperately needed his assistance. As I knew him, he was always willing to lend a helping hand to the less fortunate. He went out of his way all the time for people. I will never forget the friendship, the advice, the counsel, and the downright love and kindness that he gave to me over the years, and I miss him very much...

"I want [Elena and their children] to know that he is not forgotten here and elsewhere throughout the world. This man is going to live in the memories of a lot of us for all of our lives...

"He never complained. I saw him suffer tremendously in his lifetime. He never once complained. He would sit down and give me the most practical homespun, commonsense advice of anybody I have known in my political life. I personally am not a bit reticent to tell everybody who watches this or reads the RECORD or hears what I have to say that I truly love John Amos and I love his wife Elena and I consider them two of the best friends I have ever had on the face of this Earth.

"I wish Elena and her family the very, very best. I wish the business to continue and set the stage, and the example, and the trends in this very important phase of insurance. They have done an awful lot of good for people all over this country...

"I do not want to prolong this, but I do want to express my love and affection and appreciation for the friendship that I have had and for the friendship that has been shown to me by these good people and thank all of the Senators who have shown the kindness and courtesy and love for them this day...I do not have anything more to say other than I love Elena and her family very much and wish them the very best and hope everything goes well for them in the future."

Said Senator Shelby, "...John was the son of John Shelby and Helen Mullins Amos. Some of you may have noted that I share a name in common with the Amos family. I am sorry to note, however, that we are not kin. I would like nothing better than to claim a man of such integrity, foresight, skill, and kindness as a relative...

"John did more than build a successful business. He built a life—a life that was completed by his family and his work to better his community, this country, and our world...John Amos wrote how proud he was of his wife, Elena, and of her many accomplishments. She has come from their home in Columbus, Georgia, to express her pride in John's achievements. It is important to note just how instrumental she was in the attainment of all John's goals...

"Today, we salute John Amos. His legacy is one that will live on through his wife, his children and grandchildren, and in the many employees and beneficiaries of the American Family Life Assurance Company."

From Senator Fowler, "I rise today to honor the memory of John Beverly Amos, a great Georgian and a personal friend of mine. His death...left a void in our community that can't be filled. We lost a fine man who believed in our Nation and our political system, a man who did all he could to improve both and to encourage others to exercise their civic duties as well...He did more than establish a business, he created livelihoods for more than 3,500 men and women who serve the company's claimants, policyholders, and stockholders, 11,000 independent licensed sales associates in the United States, and more than 14,500 In Japan. He created an insurance organization that, with assets of more than $8 billion, protects more than 38 million people worldwide...

"For all of his success, accomplishment and recognition, John Amos will be remembered for much more than his astute business judgment. He will be remembered for his generous philanthropy, his strong sense of family, his loyal friendship, his belief in the democratic way, and his warm sense of humor. These are the qualities that make all those who knew John Amos miss him sorely.

"Mr. Amos's life stands as an example for those who dream of better lives for themselves, their families, and those in their communities...John Amos lived his life in a manner that set a standard of excellence that serves as an example to any American longing to live a life that will uplift his community, that will positively affect his neighbor, and that will make his family proud, because this is how John Amos lived. I am honored to have been fortunate enough to have called him a friend."

And, lastly, Senator Hollins remarked, "When John Beverly Amos died last summer, the United States lost a truly remarkable and innovative business genius. Those of us who had the honor of his friendship and counsel will remember, above all, his fine personal qualities—his loyalty, his generosity, his warmth and wit. Those who did not have the pleasure of knowing John personally are more likely to remember him as a business titan, as a spirited champion of the free enterprise system, and as an entrepreneur who wrote the book on how Americans can successfully penetrate the Japanese market...

"In part, John Amos's special status in Japanese eyes was a by-product of the stunning success of AFLAC in the Japanese market. In part, it was John's dedicated efforts in Japan to create public awareness of cancer and—at the request of the Japanese Government—to design and deliver dementia care protection for the Japanese people. Yet the biggest reason for his special status in Japan was simply his unique and sterling character as a human being.

"We mourn the passing of John Beverly Amos. However, our fond memories of this exceptional man remain vividly with us. Two nations—his native America and his adopted Japan—are better today because of John's life work."

33

IN RETROSPECT

The headquarters of AFLAC stands towering over that remarkable penthouse that John built for Elena's security, for her to be "in the middle of everything." Life, as the saying goes, goes on. Employees are going in and out of headquarters. The inner machinery is at work. Elena, however, is not home on this particular day; she is in Miami on a special mission.

She has just turned over many of her father's papers to the University of Miami, and will be turning over the rest. They are important in the recent history of Cuba, and they are important to the University's archives.

It is a warm, bright day, the sky a clear, clear blue. Elena has come to a park in Miami, bringing with her a few good friends. The year before, a bronze bust of her father was erected here in tribute to his struggle against the dictators—both Batista and Castro.

Salvador Diaz-Verson, 1905-1982.

The inscription reads: *A tireless writer who fought strongly since 1925 to frustrate a sinister plot of international communism over the island of Cuba. And who also foretold the disappearance of a criminal Marx-Leninism from the face of the earth.*

She looks at it for several long moments, then puts her arm around it.

She says something very quietly, but at least one person overhears. "Daddy. Daddy, tell Johnny I love him."